Overlanding the Americas

La Lucha!

by

Graeme Robert Bell

OVERLANDING THE AMERICAS
LA LUCHA

Disclaimer: Please be warned, this book may contain traces of strong language, humour and satire.

MORE TITLES BY GRAEME BELL

We Will Be Free
Travel The Planet Overland
Europe Overland - Seeking the Unique

www.a2aexpedition.com

For Luisa, Keelan and Jessica AKA Ginger Ninger, Schmidt and the Jellybean. I love you

Introduction

We Will Be Free was a Declaration of Independence. La Lucha! The Fight is the liberation movement, the guerrilla war we fought, to be free. Independence never came without a fight!

Our Land Rover Defender has, at the time of writing, taken us to forty-one countries over six years. Not once have we been arrested, none of us (a family of four) has contracted malaria, we have not been robbed, shot at, beaten or deported. How utterly depressing.

I want to write the story about how, that one time in Tanzania, I had an argument with a soldier and was thrown into a dark, dank cell which I shared with 57 large, aggressive men, men who I dominated through intelligence and blinding violence, ensuring that I would be unmolested and would get my share of the fat rats. I want to regale you all with tales of how I managed to challenge the system from within, unite and organise my fellow captives to overthrow the corrupt prison management and start a revolution with the political prisoners my leadership freed; all while suffering from cerebral malaria and Ebola. But, this is not Shantaram (for those of you who have suffered through that fiction dressed as fact, you understand) and we are committed to telling the truth, the whole truth and nothing but. We have worked too hard to compromise our reputation with click-bait titles. We overland tenaciously, country by country obeying most of the important laws, never overstaying our visa periods, never working illegally (though trimming Marijuana for $300 a day in California was tempting), politely and diligently dealing with the bureaucracy which, other than finances, usually presents the largest, most stubborn obstacles.

Ok, there was that time Jessica contracted bilharzia in Malawi, and there was that virus which ravaged me in Mozambique, and the night-time fever which plagued Keelan for months and the gastroenteritis which almost tore Luisa apart, from the inside. But, do you think anyone would be thoughtful enough to throw us in a cell while we suffered, granting us a truly magnificent story of adventure, perseverance and courage? No! Instead, they give us antibiotics and blood tests and hydration. What is this world coming to?

At this rate we will never have that explosive story to tell which will sell thirty-three million books, enrich us and catapult us to international fame. George Clooney will play me; Julianne Moore will portray Luisa (both will need many hours with us to perfect our South African accents), and the kid's roles will be decided by the fat cats when the screenplay is sold. You know, even the FARC in Colombia didn't want to kidnap us. Pathetic. Ok, I was almost viciously beaten by Chavistas in Venezuela because of my public criticism of the Maduro government, but I managed to talk my way out of the confrontation. Dammit. That was my chance. I should have slapped the snot out of that kid leaning on my Land Rover, talking to me with contempt, I should have fought bravely against his friends lurking in the shadows, I should have created an international incident and been thrown in a cell with Leopold Lopez. That was my chance to be part of a revolution! But, no. I controlled my ego and did not take the bait, I stayed calm, considering my family waiting in the grungy motel room and walked away from my provocateurs, angry, insulted, but calm and free. I am a disgrace. Great men are forged in the fire of combat, not peeking through the blinds every half an hour, checking that the Land Rover has been left unmolested by communist thugs.

The Defender itself doesn't help our helpless cause at all. People are always staring at her, no matter where we go. If people are always staring at her when are thieves supposed to try and break into her? She is incredibly capable off-road and hardly ever gets bogged down or stuck despite the dunes, mountains, jungles, and beaches we subject her to. She does not break down (touch wood) as often as she might, instead reliably and predictably housing and ferrying us across continents and she is always showing off, playing the good Samaritan, winching trucks out of holes and lesser vehicles out of mud and sand.

Perhaps Asia will be more exciting, maybe the Middle East will live up to its reputation for war and mayhem. India or Pakistan will surely provide the chaos we need to elevate this story to dizzying, improbable, new heights. It is more likely though that we will just cruise along, explore wondrous places and make many new friends with exotic names and welcoming homes.

Dammit.

To recap, We Will Be Free ended...

Is This The End?

West of Arequipa lies the ocean and the endless expanses of sand which blow up against the Andes. The ocean attracts us like moths to a warm glowing light, the mountains have unparalleled beauty and majesty, but we are not mountain folk. We are feet in the sand, camping on the beach, cold beer and baggy shorts, suntan and sunset people. Peru's coast, however, is not that kind of chilled, hammock and volleyball experience. If you hate palm trees and the colour green, want to surf massive Pacific Ocean waves, then sit on grey sand next to a fire in jeans and a hoody, surrounded by prehistoric rock structures, being sandblasted by a constant wind then this is your stretch of coast. A well-paved and sand assaulted road runs within view of the sea along almost the entire length of the country and is a much faster, safer and infinitely more boring border to border route than the constantly weaving, climbing and dipping mountain road. In the future, once a new civilisation has grown from the ashes of our current suicidal, consumption-driven insanity, archaeologists will find the remnants of that paved road, chicken bones and tuk-tuks, a VW van with a Subaru motor and six-foot fishtail still strapped to the roof, preserved beneath the dunes.

At the Nazca lines, Keelan and Luisa bought more jewellery carved from bone before we continued towards Lima and that God-awful traffic, asking a Range Rover Classic, with diplomatic plates and a gum-chewing blonde teen in the passenger seat, for directions to Mira Flores. Perhaps one day we will replace the GPS, I don't know if I want to though, we get around ok. We did not hang out in Lima too long, the hostel usually had a vibe and some hardcore Overlanders to drink and braai with, but we were surrounded by a German clique in soft-core campers. We ran screaming for the desert and the road north, leaving on a Sunday when the city traffic is less constipated.

The Landy carried us up along through the coast and back into Ecuador where Luisa had found a cottage in the mountains for us to take a break from the road. It is in this little cottage that I sit today writing these words, putting the finishing touches to a body of work which has taken over a year to write and edit, consuming my thoughts and dominating my days. Luisa has planned our route north to Alaska and the kids have worked to get up to date with their homeschooling.

Looking back over the last two and a half years, I have to ask myself if leaving our safe home and prosperous life was the correct choice. Has the experience been worth our life savings, an uncertain future and the many mountains we will have to climb as a result? Have we helped or hindered our children, and have we compromised their futures by being reckless, spontaneous, impetuous and rebellious? What have we learned, and what have we taught?

I awoke the other morning to a tent full of laughter. The kids and Luisa playing together, engaging in wordplay, teasing each other ruthlessly with love and compassion. Well, most of the time, anyway. Keelan and Jessica are on the road to self-determination and a love for lifelong learning. Yes, they do not have the benefit of a structured school education and associated discipline, but we do not see that as a disadvantage. They do not have childhood friends with whom they share every day and dream, but they do have friends from many countries and cultures. The one lesson, the core of their home-based education, is that what we are doing is impossible, we were told we would fail, that the danger was not worth the risk, but if we can achieve the impossible as a family what will be impossible to them as individuals? With a knowledge of the world, very few people have they will have the keys to success in whatever they choose to do with their lives. Imagine their CV's one day, sitting in front of a suit in an interview. "So, you have travelled the world by land and sea can speak five languages, have a distance high school diploma from the United Kingdom and a university degree from Norway. Your interests are sustainable architecture, trafficked rainforest animal rescue, classical guitar recital and Land Rover maintenance. We would like you to be our CEO".

And what of Luisa and I, has our quality of life improved? Are we hairy hippies hoping for a handout, begging our families for money and praying for a miracle? Are we two steps from disaster and a ten-step program? The opposite, except for the hair. I truly believe that we are becoming the best people we can be, confident, hardworking, generous and relaxed. Most of the time. We were born and raised separately as the two halves of one person, what I lack she has, and what she needs I provide. Despite our terrible sex life, we have never been closer and work together to achieve our goals. I have her, and she has me, and we believe in each other and love and music. We still have a lot to learn but have decided to keep on travelling, to see the world, learn and grow, teach and love.

Our journey is not yet over.

South America

1

A Swift Exit

Leaving our little cottage in the mountains south of Cuenca, Ecuador was accompanied by the now-ubiquitous mixed emotions. After being on the road for so long, living in a tent and braving the elements daily, a comfortable home and fully equipped kitchen are truly appreciated, but the call of the open road is irresistible, and we had a date with Alaska. After almost two and a half years in South America, including almost two circumnavigations and the depletion of virtually all our resources, we were looking forward to a change of scenery and culture. But first, we had to drive through Colombia and reach Cartagena in time to catch the ferry around the Darien Gap.

Ecuador is a tiny country where the currency is the US Dollar, and you can choose either to chill on the beach, explore the Andes or experience the far western reaches of the Amazon jungle. That jungle is almost entirely avoided by most Pan Am overland travellers and we never regretted our decision to complete the first circumnavigation of that intoxicating continent, the opportunity to drive through the upper reaches of the world's greatest jungle and to spend three days on a ferry joining two of her cities is an opportunity very few have experienced. The only problem with trying to get anywhere in a hurry in South America is that, unless travelling by air, it is almost impossible to get anywhere swiftly. The most direct route between Cuenca and the capital city, Quito is only 458 kilometres long, but

LA LUCHA

the road runs along the spine of the Andes. A single lane road of congested traffic, slow-moving trucks and endless mountain switchbacks, reduces travelling speed to an agonising crawl, as vehicles manoeuvre around each other, the faster overtaking, the slower, often on blind rises and corners. Vehicles will ignore your flashing indicator and rush up to overtake both you and the truck in front of you, a game of shared direction chicken, he blaring his horn, claiming the right of way by virtue of his greater speed and threatening you with metallic violence if you do not allow him to pass. Our passage was further hindered by the early onset of darkness and the descent of curtains of rain swept up to the peaks from the moist jungle to the east. Overlanding at a slow, comfortable pace, over undiscovered roads and through virgin territory is the dream, rushing to a deadline over roads you had travelled before and disliked immensely is a nightmare. It took two days to reach Colombia, the last stretch from Otavalo to the border, a dusty hell of road construction, delays and endless climbs, falls and switchbacks.

At the border, one we were comfortable with because we had navigated it before, we struggled to have the officials allow me to enter Colombia with my British passport as I had exited Ecuador on my South African passport. Luisa, being the bureaucrats worst enemy, had confirmed by email and telephone before we had left the cottage that the passport switch was permissible. She had all the correspondence printed, in hand, with full particulars of the contact official in Bogota. It was important that I entered Colombia on the British passport as my South African passport was full, and it takes a year for the South African bureaucracy to print a new passport. The obstinate border official was no match for Luisa, and eventually, a supervisor produced a large book where the transfer was noted, and, after the customs procedures, we were free to enter Colombia as the sunset. The number one rule of overland travel is Do Not Drive at Night. We were breaking this rule every day in our determination not to miss that Darien ferry.

Despite the obvious and desperate need for a permanent ferry around or road through, the Darien Gap there has never been a long-term, professional ferry service or any successful attempts to build a road. Depending on who you speak to, there are various reasons for this lack of basic infrastructure. Some say the Americans do not want a ferry to operate, that the failed but persistent war on drugs dictates transportation policy in the Caribbean. The infamous failed war had often backfired spectacularly in Latin America. In the '90s, the US administration had pressured the Bolivian government to illegalise the cultivation of coca, believing that that would kill the production of the famous Bolivian marching powder. However, the consumption of the coca leaf in a country up in the clouds is a tradition going back to before the Inca. Chewing the coca leaf gives the chewer the ability to work hard and walk very long distances while combating the draining effects of altitude. It is a sacred plant used in traditional ceremonies. It is as Bolivian as the altiplano. The Bolivians simply did not have the resources or the will to eradicate coca and, having used coca to combat the altitude, I understand their reluctance. There is no "high" achieved by shoving a handful of leaves into your cheek and spending the day swallowing the bitter green saliva tea, but you can breathe a little easier and think a little clearer. The Americans were not happy with the Bolivian refusal and responded by flooding the worlds copper market, a market the Bolivian economy desperately relied on. Copper prices crashed, and most Bolivian copper mines went out of business, rendering many thousands of miners unemployed. With no options for employment, the majority of these unemployed miners became farmers, working under the sun and in the fresh, thin air growing the only crop which would bring them a decent income. That crop? Coca.

The Darien remains a natural paradise and a drug smugglers heaven. The region belongs to the cartels, and the reputation of that small green strip of land is so foreboding that very few are brave enough to access even the accessible areas. A road through the Darien, which is only 100 km long, would allow effective policing and control of the area but there are those who do not want South, and Central America connected geographically, particularly the DEA and CIA. The cartels would also, no doubt, prefer to be left alone to their illicit business.

In 2015, an Italian company, Ferry Xpress, sent a large, modern ferry across the Atlantic to establish themselves in the Caribbean, hoping to turn a decent profit in a largely uncontested market. They faced a few obstacles from the outset. Firstly, for years there have been various shady companies selling tickets for fictional ferries, operating for a few months, taking large cash deposits from anxious travellers then disappearing with the money as the sail dates approached. More than a few overlanders have been duped by these con artists. Secondly, in recent history a German expat had set up a ferry service which ran into trouble on its maiden voyage when they were not granted permission to dock in Cartagena, the travellers onboard, including motorbikes and vehicles, found themselves unable to leave the boat which was very low on supplies of food and water, the German subsequently went out of business. Thirdly, Panama does not have the facilities to accommodate large ferries in the Colon harbour and is reluctant to upgrade those facilities given the sketchy history of the various ferry operations. In sharp contrast, Cartagena has excellent facilities to cater for cruise ships, including professional immigration facilities, snack and curio shops and a zoo to entertain travellers. Confidence in a reliable ferry service was understandably low, and the Italians took a significant gamble sending their ship and staff to establish the venture in the Caribbean.

The Ferry Xpress began running in 2015, while we were in Argentina making arrangements to ship our Land Rover from Zarate to Panama. Reports from overlanders who took the first few journeys with the Italian company were good. The company had a physical office, professionally staffed in Cartagena, the ferry was well equipped, and her staff as professional and courteous as Italians can be. We did the calculations and determined that it would be far cheaper for us to drive from Argentina to Colombia and take the ferry than it would be to ship the Land Rover by a container to Panama and fly the family over. We did not anticipate breaking down for a month in Northern Argentina or letting ourselves be seduced by a little cottage in the mountains of Ecuador. We had self-published our first book, We Will Be Free, just before leaving that little warm Ecuadorian cottage and I had promised Luisa that this book would generate the finances we needed to pay our daily expenses. It was a massive gamble, but I had faith in the story, and in writing and in the audience, I hoped to reach. Our finances were not great. The South African tax authorities had still not refunded the bulk of our resources which they had wrongfully appropriated and promised to return; and our currency, the Rand, was in free fall against the Dollar. We had liquidated what was left of our assets in order to complete our goal to drive from Argentina to Alaska. You may ask why. Well, at some point during our travels we had discovered that travelling had become almost the most important thing in our lives, more valuable than money or comfort, but much less important than our children who were enjoying a unique experience of the world they live in.

We had less than two months to make the journey from Ecuador, around the Darien Gap, through the many tiny Central American nations and gigantic Mexico to the Land of the Free, Home of the Brave. We had done this to ourselves, we had set a date for the Overland Expo to be held in Flagstaff, Arizona in May. There I would sell a thousand books and establish ourselves within the American overland community, the book would go viral, television chat shows would invite us to talk to them about our courageous exploits and our financial woes would surely become a thing of the past. If you have ever accused me of being naive, you may well have a valid point.

LA LUCHA

There were only two scheduled ferry journeys remaining in the season and no response from the Italians whether the service would resume. We were determined not to be on the last gasp ferry and bought tickets for the second last trip, the total cost was $750.00 for a cabin for four and the transportation of and the Landy Rover. Not a bad rate considering the alternative.

But first we had to drive up to Cartagena and having just left the border with Ecuador, we headed for Pasto, the far southern Colombian city where we would spend a few hours trying to find a safe place to sleep. The soldiers at a military base on the outskirts of the city turned us away, the national park on the other side of the city was closed, and we could not find any service stations which would allow us to open the roof tent and get a few hours' sleep. We also had some business to attend to in Pasto. A year earlier we had been in Cartagena planning for the last leg of our circumnavigation. The Colombian Land Rover club (Legion) had proven to be wonderful, trustworthy people and we had mistakenly bought a set of widened Land Rover rims from a legion member called Carlos (the reason we were heading to Pasto at night was that we had agreed to meet with Carlos at 7 pm, we arrived at 7.30 at the agreed address, and Carlos was nowhere to be seen) who lived in Pasto, we then had the wheels shipped up to Cartagena at our expense only to find that the wheels were un-balanceable and leaked air, resulting in a squat Land Rover after only one night. We had decided to put a set of large mud tyres on the Land Rover in anticipation of the muddy Amazon and, as Land Rover wheels and parts are very scarce in South America, we thought we had stumbled upon a great bargain. An email battle ensued, and eventually, Carlos agreed to refund the money when we returned the wheels, at our expense. Through Legion friends and a courier company, the wheels were returned to Pasto.

After a year of countless emails and empty promises of payment, Carlos the Bastard, never expected that we would ever darken his door and demand the return of our money, face to face. Eventually, we found a gas station on the outskirts of the city after Carlos stood us up and at 6 am we were parked outside his business waiting for him to show up and hand over the 500 000 pesos. I was prepared to remove any article from his business which had equal or greater value and sell it to recoup our losses if he tried to evade us again. Our anger was tangible, rarely do I allow myself to give in to anger, but I was prepared to be significantly unpleasant. Carlos the Bastard did not show up until then, I suspect his workers had called him to tell him that a very large, red-faced man was standing in the doorway, scaring away clients and refusing to move. A Toyota Land Cruiser pulled up in front of the business, and a fat, smiling man wobbled and bounced his way out of the driver's seat. He approached us with a warm smile and held out his hand, "Hello, I am Carlos, let's go have some breakfast". "No, thank you. We do not have time if you could pay us we will leave". It took a while, ten patient minutes while Carlos tried to save face until eventually we were invited up to his office where he opened the safe and took a pile of cash and handed it to us. We counted the money, he tried to make small talk, we left, headed for the long road to Popayan.

The road to Popayan is long and winding, the first section a hot, dry mountain pass of tall bridges, long tunnels and very little humanity. The area is unstable and a hotbed of FARC guerrilla activity, not the kind of place where you want to have a breakdown or travel at night. The second part of the journey is through a cool valley where poor villages crowd the verges of tree-lined roads, the majority of the population are the descendants of slaves, and the area has a reputation for bandits and criminals, and military checkpoints and toll booths announce the entrance to each small town. A winding jungle road climbs up from the valley, old trucks filled with workers that produce fouling the air, as they grind progress to a slow, dangerous game of cat and mouse, identical to the scenario played out daily on the terrible single lane roads carved into the rock of the Andes across the various nations which try to prosper on those cold, hard, infertile banks. Colombia has the worst roads in all of South America and the highest tolls to use them, an ultimately unsatisfying combination particularly when you are driving long days trying to cross the country. It always amazes me that a country can survive without a decent highway system to connect north to south, east to west. It costs more in tolls than it does in fuel to cross Colombia, we can only imagine where all that money goes, it is certainly not being spent on the roads. What Colombia lacks in road infrastructure it compensates with the most wonderful people, almost all the Colombians we have ever met have been wonderfully kind and hospitable. We made it to Cali under a thundercloud. The camp we found was shared by soggy lawn and an unlikely French couple; an old, mousey lady and a good-looking, rugged younger man. We made a fire and relaxed after that long hard week on the road. We sucked on some cold, delicious beer and went to sleep in a storm.

A decision had to be made. We had wonderful friends in Bogota who had made a significant impact on our lives. The Botero family had welcomed us into their homes warmly in 2014, and we had left as family, promising to return. We will return one day, only the hounds of hell will be able to keep us from South America, and even they may fail. Our schedule did not allow the 2000 km round trip and an inevitable week of merriment a detour to Bogota would entail. Instead, we decided to head for Medellin, a city we had not yet visited. If you look at a map of Colombia, you may be amazed that there are only two large towns on the Pacific coast, called Buenaventura and Tumaco and one road leading from the interior to either. Almost the entire Pacific coast of Colombia is uninhabited, a coast where the jungle meets the sea and black sand beaches wait to liquefy at the command of massive earthquakes. Hardly anyone ventures out there except for the Narcos, it is relatively untouched by humanity, the ideal destination for any brave or foolish traveller seeking solitude and unique experience. The FARC and

ELN "freedom fighters" hide behind communist ideology and the green expanse of the coastal jungle while producing thousands of tons of cocaine every year. In the absence of the traditional drug cartels, the guerrillas have taken over the drug trade and enrich their leadership while squabbling with each other over trafficking routes and routinely blowing up and murdering Colombian civilians in the name of Revolution, for the sake of protecting their drug empires. That does not mean that you cannot drive to either Tumaco or Buenaventura, the government tries to control the roads and those towns, and we witnessed a holiday season migration of thousands of vehicles heading to Buenaventura from Cali, a migratory herd determined to drink Poker beer and aguardiente, eat corn arepa and chicharron, prawns and rice, listening to extremely loud music while dancing under straw hats.

Outside Medellin, we encountered a strange and unfortunately common Latin American cultural anomaly. The closing of the road. If you and your colleagues are unhappy about your pay or working conditions, go out, burn some tyres and close the road. If your government is terrible, go out, burn some tyres and close the road. If you want to bury a deceased relative, take the funeral procession for a march down the main road. If it is the day of Saint Whatshisname, throw a robe and massive crucifix at the lightest skinned child, you can find and take the faithful to the road. Blocking the main road in any Latin American country is entirely acceptable as a form of protest, mourning or celebration. This man lived a good life. It is right that you should sit in the sun for an hour or three overheating and breathing fumes, share our pain. The bus drivers keep the city moving, they want ten more pesos an hour, they will shut down the city and not allow you to leave even though you have absolutely bugger all to do with either their city, their grievance or their services. Inconveniencing hundreds or thousands of people lends credence to your activity. We saw it in Venezuela when we had to take a three-hour detour on a dusty shithole island because five students blocked the road (I do sympathise with the Venezuelans). In Mexico, when the taxis blocked the entrance and exit to the region's largest town, in Argentina when the miners wanted a pay rise, in Peru when the police were on strike and in Bolivia shutting down the entire country is not uncommon. Outside Medellin, it was the light-skinned kid, the robe, the crucifix and all the old ladies of the community walking three kilometres from one small village to another, at the slow, dignified and reverential pace of one kilometre an hour.

Motorbikes would wiz past the growing traffic jam to block the road at the front of the overheating vehicles which either climbed one of the endless hills or slowly rolled down the other side. If the vehicles started moving and you were too slow to start up the engine and roll forward, the cars behind would gun their engines and speed into the little space between you and the vehicle in front of you. For three hours this slow, painfully torturous dance continued, tempers flaring in the hot, humid still of the day, strangers becoming accustomed to the faces that surround them, fellow sufferers and competitors for slivers of paved real estate. Eventually, the pale substitute angel led his pious procession off the road into the town plaza. This was the cue for the hundreds of vehicles locked in metallic tangles on either side of the town to race towards each other, jostling to pass the truck which had overheated in the centre of town, blocking the road and allowing space for only one vehicle to pass at a time. The police stood around idly, joking and doing nothing to alleviate the congestion. The cherry on top of this steaming shit cake was the toll booth at the edge of town, which charged us the equivalent of $7.00 for the privilege of suffering a slow death. We refused to pay, they refused to let us pass, we harassed the toll booth girl, not something we would ever normally do - she does not make the rules, but we felt incensed that as tourists we had to suffer the insufferable and then have to pay for the displeasure. A chorus of loud, continuous honking erupted behind us, of all the obstruction these people had to suffer on what should have been a short commute they now had a big white Land Rover full of purple-faced gringos having a shouting match with the flustered, pert-breasted toll booth girl, blocking the single toll lane with their huge gringo holiday machine. The irony that we were now a part of the problem was not lost on me. Regrettable behaviour, we know better. The real fun now started as the hundreds of pissed off motorists jostled for position on the thin strip of mountain pass which led to Medellin, one of Colombia's largest cities.

Hungry, thirsty and thoroughly pissed off we drove into Pablo Escobar's hometown and searched for a burger joint. We drove under a massive highway overpass, shocked to see a village of homeless people living under the bridge, hundreds of eyes stopped to stare as we drove past on the now deserted roads. Two things impressed me. First, it seemed like every homeless person in the city lived under that bridge, a seething mass of dejected humanity which had apparently been gifted this one small piece of unusable real estate where they could prey on each other, unmolested. No doubt they had earned the land by blocking the highway. Second, the highway served only the city's residents and terminated at either end of the city in unloved potholed single lane roads where six lanes of traffic would suddenly bottleneck into one. To be a long-distance truck driver in Colombia is to live in purgatory, if not Hades itself.

With bellies full of very good fast food, we headed towards our date with the bottleneck which thankfully was not corked. Luisa had me turn left, then right and up we went. I refused to believe that this terrible little mountain pass was the main route to Cartagena, but Luisa insisted that this was the correct road. We prayed to a little angel that the communities on this side of the city were not blocking the road in the name of the day's saint. Up we climbed into beautiful green, moist farmland and pasture, passing herds of cattle contently grazing the lush lawn and passed green mould houses. As the sun began to set, we crested a rise and were greeted, in the distance, by a town built into the side of a massive hill, each home has a view over the house or building in front of them. The golden reflection of the sun off the village glass contrasted beautifully with the ripe green of the surrounding land. A roadside gas station was our camp that night, we awoke to find a village less beautiful in the clarity of morning light than it was in the yellows of dusk. Thankfully the days driving was less eventful, but hard work nonetheless. Driving in a straight line for more than a few hundred meters was rare and welcomed, we drove until and beyond the sunset, struggling to find a decent place to either free or wild camp. The road began to descend at first gradually and then drastically. The vegetation changed from grassland and meadows to thick-leaved trees, from cool crisp air to the muggy, moist air of the jungle. Communities lined the road and children played on the verges, like trucks and buses and normal passenger vehicles, either struggled to retard the grip of gravity or motivate overworked engines to force the tyres to grip and climb. These homes were built mere meters from the road, headlights illuminating the faces of people who sat in garden chairs squinting, watching the silhouettes of vehicles pass in the night. Young people buzzed about on motorbikes, beautiful girls with long black hair and tight jeans sat side-saddle on the back of the bikes, staring at their smartphones, barely holding on to the boys with white vest and midnight black Justin Bieber haircuts, who piloted the fast, modern donkeys from one huddle of social interaction to another. Our descent seemed never-ending, the GPS told Luisa that soon we would reach a bridge and that bridge would lead over a river to a town with a few gas stations to choose from.

The gas station is the long-term overlanders best friend, particularly in areas where there are no options for conventional camping. Approaching the bridge, a very large unsmiling soldier blocked the road. He and another soldier had a good look at us with suspicious eyes. We might have been in for some contracted questioning had we not had the children in the back seat. Another soldier sat behind a wall of sandbags his hand resting lazily on the barrel of a 50mm machine gun which was pointed in our general direction. We made small talk with the soldiers while they had a look at our passports. "Is there any camping around here, is it safe, where can we get a cold beer and a drink for the kids?". We always find that asking soldiers tourist questions motivates them to be good, helpful soldiers. Asking directions will change the tone of the conversation if you suspect the soldier or policeman who has pulled you over may be looking for trouble.

Luckily the big guy was quick to smile, amused by the distraction we provided. "No camping, but you can get beer anywhere". A spike strip was removed from the road, and we drove across the bumpy steel bridge onto the flattest, straightest road we had driven for a very long time. At the edge of town, on the banks of the raging river a Texaco service station, the first we had seen, lit the night. We asked the petrol attendant if we could open the Land Rovers roof tent in the corner of the forecourt, he told me to ask the boss. A man wearing a sombrero and surrounded by chickens was the man in charge, and he agreed to my request with a smile. The sombrero was also the first we had seen, and the combination of that large hat, the random chickens and the Texaco sign was probably the most Latin American generalisation I had ever seen which was peculiar because I had never seen a scene like this in all our time in South America.

The underground youth network spread the news of the strange gringo's and the tent on top of the cool truck-like scurvy on a pirate ship fresh out of lemonade. Too cool to crowd; three or four motorbikes would pull up to pump and each put in ten pesos while pretending not to stare at us. Only the ugliest boys did not have a jet black-maned beauty sitting side-saddle behind him staring at her phone. Right now, as you read, those boys and girls are riding around on their noisy little bikes, desperately searching for relief from the boredom of a dull jungle.

LA LUCHA

The Texaco had a clean toilet, and a shower fed directly from the rain-swollen river. In the morning, we each had a shower, washing away the dust, sweat and memories of the last few difficult days. A shower can completely revitalise a weary traveller, we were a day's drive from Cartagena, a Friday and a weekend away from our date with the ferry. The road we were driving followed the river for a while, the surrounding vegetation green and well-nourished by the abundant supply of water but as we continued north, the road broke away from the path of the river and almost immediately the vegetation suffered from the divorce. Leafy palm and banana trees gave way to thin branched, grey scrub, the soil lost its dark rich wealth and became grey and sandy. Every 50 kilometres a town crowded the road, the inhabitants selling the same food, fruit and novelties as the towns before it and all the towns to come. Every town had a police or military checkpoint, a toll booth and horrible, unmarked speed bumps. Cheap sweet coffee was poured hot and free at every gas station, and a crowd of police cadets gathered around the Land Rover when we stopped outside a police training school to make some sandwiches on the 130's tailgate. By late afternoon we were at the outskirts of Cartagena, and by evening we were parked in the parking lot camping area of the Hotel Bella Vista, where the tall walls and black gate protected us from the wind howling off the Caribbean. We had made it to Cartagena after 6 days of hard driving 2400 kilometres. The Landy had done an excellent job, despite the terrible roads and we had spent the 500 000 pesos on food, fuel and tolls.

Our first job was to get refunded the cash owed to us by Cartagena Carlos who had bought our old wheels and tyres a year before, promising to pay within three months. He had been a great guy when we first met, he showed us around the city and helped us import new wheels from the UK when the wheels from Carlos the Bastard turned out to be unusable. Cartagena Carlos was passionate about Land Rovers and had his own beaten and horribly scarred Td5 which he was forever repairing. We had been asking him for months to pay the money owed and every time he promised and every time he let us down, then, when he heard we were headed to Cartagena, he stopped responding to our emails. Luisa did some research and found his address out near the harbour (he never told us where he worked and only sent personal emails), so we drove out to surprise him. As you can imagine, he was surprised. We never managed to get any money from him, but he did help us find a workshop to replace our windscreen which had poorly been cracked by a rock on a dirt road in Ecuador back in 2013. I later publicly shamed him on the Land Rover Colombia Legion Facebook page and the other members hurled abuse at him incessantly until he paid two-thirds of what he owed. More school fees. As long-term travellers, we cannot afford to be anything less than serious about the money we have or is owed to us.

I burned my right arm quite badly the next day replacing the rubber stopper on the fuel cooler, which sits directly under the exhaust manifold, in the middle of Cartagena while Luisa and Keelan went into the FerryXpress office to confirm our booking, collect our tickets and discuss the loading and immigration procedure. The rubber stopper was Land Rover's solution to the redesign of the TD5 cooling system, instead of sealing the second coolant outlet on the oil cooler, they just stuck a rubber stopper on there, to degrade over time and vomit coolant as you sit in traffic in some foreign country. We like Cartagena, particularly the old city and the wealthier suburbs along the coast. In 2014 we had rented a beautiful apartment over the holiday season and had grown very fond of the salty city.

We arrived at the designated customs and immigration building the next morning after jumping over some final bureaucratic hurdles. The customs official sent three Britons and us on BMW GS1200's to the car wash across the road because our vehicle was too dirty to be allowed on the ferry. Luisa and I paid for the car wash then washed the Land Rover ourselves after it became clear that one car wash guy was going to spend the rest of the day making love to the BMW's. The Beemer boys watched with delight as Luisa scrubbed the Land Rover if there is anything that woman loves it is to make the dirty clean and organise the chaos of the universe. We rushed back to the customs parking area just in time to wait for four hours, sitting in the sun, eating almost all our pre-prepared ferry food. Our fellow travellers were an interesting assortment of overland travellers. Aside from the Beemer boys, who called themselves The Long Way Up, ahem, there was the golf playing Canadian and his wife who had driven down from Canada to stay in hotels and play golf every day; the tall, American, ex-football player professional fisherman, a hippy family from Costa Rica and a Mexican couple in a heavily branded company car.

Eventually, we were allowed to enter the customs area after paying a stupid amount of money for a man to spray pesticide on our vehicle, the sun cooked hot, the ground melted the rubber soles of our shoes. Luisa discovered the zoo and kept the kids entertained while I kept an eye on the Land Rover. Trust no-one.

South America has, without a doubt, the largest concentration of infinitely lovable stray dogs and cats we have ever encountered. Almost every camp we had made or paid for had its own resident stray who we would feed scraps and water, entering wordlessly into a reciprocal arrangement; we would provide food, water and tummy rubs and our new friend would provide security and a food disposal service. Jessica loved taking care of the abandoned animals and, unlike Africa where strays tend to be quite hostile, we never feared that the animals would become aggressive. Each animal we encountered was desperate for adoption, and they knew how to work each one of us according to our personalities. Often, we had been tempted to liberate an animal, but we had to be realistic, we already had two children to take care of as well as limited space and resources. How expensive can a free dog be you ask? The following story is a perfect example.

The Costa Rican hippy family waiting for the ferry had two small children, and they had all fallen in love with and adopted a large, grey Ecuadorian dog. They confided in us that they were going to try and sneak the dog onto the ferry to Panama. Apparently, the company operating the ferry had a no pet policy and the alternative to the $750-dollar ferry fee for the family and the vehicle to sail around the Darien was a $2000 container shipping fee, $1000 for flights (plus a full ticket for the pooch) and another $500 for pet friendly accommodation while waiting for the container ship in Panama or a $700 three-day sailing trip around the Darien via the San Blas islands. Our new friends were obviously optimists who believed that they could smuggle a large dog out of the country Pablo Escobar had called home, to a country which shared terra firma with the USA.

Late in the afternoon, we were instructed to head to immigration while the drivers were instructed to drive the vehicles to the agricultural and narcotics inspection area where heavily armed soldiers, sniffer dogs and women in tight uniforms waited to discover whatever we might intend to hide.

The drivers were instructed to open and empty their vehicles then stand against a wall. I was reluctant to unpack the entire Land Rover and removed only our clothing crates and the kid's backpacks. Miguel, the hippy, parked in front of me, was looking very pale for someone who spent most of his time on the beach. The customs officials and heavily armed counter-narcotics police moved slowly from vehicle to vehicle questioning the driver and guiding a couple of highly motivated sniffer dogs in repetitive circles around each vehicle. Miguel's vehicle was third in the queue, and he visibly began to sweat as the procession approached his colourful camper. Miguel, being an expert smuggler, had come up with a fiendish plan to conceal the animal – he had covered it with a folded blanket, surely that would be enough to deceive the highly trained inspectors. Discreetly I watched as a large, muscular sergeant dressed in black combat gear and a beret opened the rear door of the hippy bus and pulled back the blanket. The large, grey Ecuadorian dog sat up and licked the sergeant's forearm.

I thought Miguel might faint. He, the dog and the camper were immediately and quietly whisked away to another location. Later we would learn that the vehicle was stripped down and searched and, after questioning, Miguel was sent to the ferry office to explain. Miguel, being fiendish, was ready for this scenario, and he explained that his children had learning disabilities and the dog was a service animal, highly trained and absolutely essential to his children's emotional well-being. It only took seven hundred US dollars to convince the ferry management to agree with him.

After the vehicle inspection, I re-joined my family to wait for immigration procedures. Four queues snaked towards the immigration counters. Almost everyone shuffled forwards patiently except for one sizeable Arabic family. Four men, six women wearing burkas and about ten fat and loud children pushed their way towards the front of the queue, creating a commotion as they clambered under and over ribbon barriers, their large and heavily laden luggage trollies employed as battering rams. Eventually, their obnoxious progress came to a halt when a very large and grumpy man told them to go to the back of the queue. A shouting match ensued, and after much spittle and emotional blackmail, the family accepted partial defeat and set up camp where they stood. All that drama just to save a few minutes simply does not compute. When the family eventually reached immigration, the Colombians, who have an acute sense of justice and irony, carefully searched through every one of the mountains of suitcases. They were the last group to board the ferry and, true to form, they immediately began pushing their way to the reception desk only to be met by a wall of humanity who had clearly had enough of their antics.

Driving the Defender onto the ferry was an emotional moment for me, we were leaving behind the continent and the people we had grown to love so dearly. Travelling South America had been life-changing for my little family, we had grown tremendously over the almost three years we had spent exploring. Brazil had stolen our hearts, Argentina and Colombia had embraced us warmly, Bolivia and Chile had challenged us but had also granted us great rewards. Guyana, Suriname and French Guyana had shown us that we had the ability to travel where few others do. Venezuela had broken our hearts, a cold slap in the face.

Without a doubt, we could one day settle down in South America. Yes, Spanish is difficult to learn, as is Portuguese but, they are only languages, and we already speak English and Afrikaans, immersion and a good teacher would be shortcuts to fluency. Northern Argentina or Southern Brazil are strong contenders for our future home/ overlander camp/ dog sanctuary. Many thousands of Europeans have, over the centuries, chosen this region to be their home, and this immigration has had a profound and positive influence on architecture, culture and industry. Northern Argentina is particularly attractive with its natural beauty, excellent food, beautiful people and great weather. Starting a new life in Brazil would be more challenging, but the country has a relatively stable economy, and we are confident that we would make a good life for ourselves there. My dream would be to live in a rural community where we could open an English school and a small restaurant in the village. We would invest in a small farm where we would run a rescue and adoption sanctuary for the many stray and neglected animals we encountered in that part of the world. Jessica would be in heaven taking care of the animals, and we would invite volunteers from across the globe to help with the care and rehabilitation of the animals. Visitors would be welcome to join the daily walk of a hundred dogs and, if they are worthy, one of the dogs will adopt them. We will create everything with our own hands, grow the food to be served in our restaurant and our students from the English school would be welcome to hang out with our international volunteers and practice their new English language skills. A portion of the farm, preferably the grassy, shaded patch on the banks of a river, would be developed as an overlander camp where our friends, old and new, will be welcome to camp for as long as they like in exchange for a donation of either cash, labour or expertise. There will be solar-powered campsites, a communal fire pit and a bar adorned with overlander art.

Overlanders looking to make a bit of money will be able to use the kitchen and sell plates of food, work in the bar, teach overlander kids, do mechanical repairs, etc. We will dig a pit in the workshop and, for a small fee, will allow overlanders to use our extensive tools to do their oil changes, services and repairs. There will be a swimming hole and hiking trails and small cottages to rent, there will be free Wi-Fi and a small business centre, a library full of travel books and guides, we will run Spanish classes for travellers new to South America. Every second night we will make a bonfire and grill large chunks of excellent beef, lamb and pork. Wine and beer will flow, guitars will be strummed, and we will solve the world's problems, again and again. Perhaps we will set up one of these camps on each of the six hospitable continents, and we will call them Sanctuary 1-6. Trusted overlander friends would run each camp on a timeshare basis and would be able to earn enough income to be able to continue their travels.

This is the dream which I will return to once we have achieved the dream of travelling the world.

Returning to South Africa is still an option, but the more I see of the world, the more I see the faults of my motherland. I despise what the ANC has become, I loathe what the fat cats have done to the country in pursuit of their own enrichment. Nelson Mandela was a leader who inspired the best in men, regardless of race or creed. He led with dignity and honour and was content with the sufficient wealth he had accumulated, honestly. He was a man who treated all with respect and led the nation through the darkest post-Apartheid days. Jacob Zuma, President from 2009 to 2019, is not fit to share a continent with Mandela, let alone have his portrait hanging on the same wall. Under Zuma's atrocious leadership, South Africa has plunged into debt, suffered xenophobic riots and escalated crime. It used to be that if you wanted to emigrate, other South Africans would call you a coward and a traitor, now they too are desperately looking for a way out. The writing is on the wall, it is not too late for the country to turn around, but that will take a quantum shift in culture and a leader who can unify the country. I have written about this all before but, where previously I was eager to return to South Africa to rebuild our lives, I now wonder if that remains an option. A farmer in Argentina does not have to surround himself with razor wire and guard dogs while living in constant fear that his family might be brutally raped, tortured and murdered and if he did, the government would surely allow him to possess weapons for self-protection. A citizen of the USA or England would expect that the police force would be there to protect his family and property.

I think I left my heart in South America.

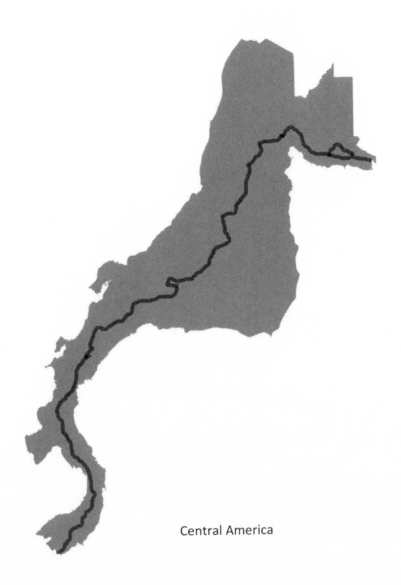

Central America

2

Central America

The Fast Ferry was staffed by well-dressed and beautifully scented Italians, most of whom would instead have been anywhere on the planet than on that boat. I drove the Land Rover up and into the bowels of the beast, a suave deck hand instructing me to park close to the wall. I made sure to introduce myself to the most senior crewman in the load area, memorising his name and pleading with him to take very good care of my Landy, explaining to him that she is our home. He told me, "not to worry, of course, she will be ok, we are Italians here". Those who know me know that I hate ferries simply because all my eggs are in one basket and that is hardly ever a good idea.

Luisa and the children joined me to triple check that we had everything we needed from the Landy and that she was locked and secure, before making our way up to the reception where a bored crew waited to serve with minimum effort. A wall of perfume greeted us as we shuffled towards the reception desk. Eyes weighed down by eyeshadow and eyeliner and thick, incredibly long eyelashes, avoided contact. Cheeks, heavily blushed and powdery, hardly moved as robotic words forced from plastic lips informed us in a Mediterranean accent that we should feel welcome and the staff of Ferry Xpress is here to serve. We had been assessed immediately as we approached the desk. Our blonde hair and blue eyes did not compensate for our old clothing, not terribly stylish, and obviously, hand washed. We did not smell of an expensive scent, and we did not have the decency to carry designer luggage. We spoke with a weird accent and were definitely not going to be getting the cabin upgrade we jokingly asked for. I left the desk with the profound impression that this woman had been ripped from her career as the newest, hottest, freshest fashion designer and thrust into servitude upon this well-lit but badly vacuumed Caribbean slave galleon.

The cabin was surprisingly comfortable and clean. We took turns freshening up in the compact bathroom and set out to explore the ferry. We explored our deck for emergency exits and lifeboats before visiting the barren customs-free shop. The moon rose above Cartagena as a powerful wind blew us out of port. Slowly the ferry began to gain speed and the lights of the continent we had grown to love so much faded from view.

To kill time, we wandered the huge vessel. The food on offer in the dining room was very expensive and hardly fresh. As no actual ferry service had survived more than a season, local confidence was low. The ferry we were on was running at about 30% capacity, and it was obvious that she would soon be sailed back across the Atlantic to resume her normal duties in the Mediterranean. Which all explains the terrible food available in the dining car. Limp fruit dishes sat dejectedly in slightly chilled display cases, a few hot dishes and sandwiches pretended to be appetising but failed on closer inspection. We settled on a pizza which was the one thing made to order, what else do you order from an Italian? The pizza was tiny. A couple sitting behind us ate half their salad and left. Keelan and I eyed the salad. I actually considered eating it and might have had Luisa not drawn a line in the sand. We had changed so much over the years on the road, what seemed impossible had become common, and we had done many things in the name of penny-pinching but, apparently, eating from a stranger's plate was a bridge too far. "But, honey, they seemed like a nice couple, clearly quite hygienic". "If you touch that food, you will never touch me again!". I am grateful to Luisa for maintaining her standards. We were not starving, merely hungry. We returned to our cabin as a middle-class family on a wonderful voyage, not as the savages one bite of that salad would have reduced us to.

Through the night, the ferry rumbled, buzzed and gently swayed. Occasionally the lights of a distant ship, boat or island would appear on the horizon, then disappear as we dozed. We awoke in the morning as the ferry approached the dreary port city of Colon. I was expecting palm trees and jungle but what greeted us was a flat dry outcrop of land with a few cranes and container ships scattered about the harbour. In contrast to the modern Colombian port infrastructure, we were greeted by a disused pier supporting a large, neglected warehouse. Vehicles had to disembark the ferry on to a small square of concrete then drive up wooden planks on the pier. This was another nail in the coffin of the Colombia Panama ferry as the Panamanians refused to build adequate landings for an unreliable ferry service. The egg and chicken dilemma. Luisa and the children had to disembark on foot as I drove the Landy off the ferry after a thorough inspection revealed that the truck had survived the journey unmolested. Carefully I drove the vehicle up the wooden planks and headed towards the large "immigration" warehouse where large black men angrily herded the passengers into one of two queues – Resident / Non-Resident. The immigration official who eventually attended to us did not believe that we were from South Africa (and the UK) but was convinced after some friendly banter.

That noisy Arabic family again began an assault on the immigration queues, they had been one of the last groups to leave the ferry, probably due to the sheer quantity of their luggage but hopefully because someone had locked them in their cabins. The children wailed and complained, the men harassed each other and whoever was unlucky enough to be in their vicinity and the women clucked and shot lasers from their exposed, heavily painted eyes. I wondered if they wore lipstick beneath their burkas. As someone who has zero tolerance for religious zealotry. I am nervous of travelling particularly the Middle East where I will no doubt have to at least pretend to be Christian to avoid a sound stoning.

Again, the horrible family was stopped in their tracks, and again they were thoroughly searched, and only the Overlanders and vehicle owners took longer to clear the port. Perhaps if they had treated others with some respect...

The various vehicles which had disembarked the ferry were parked in a row outside the warehouse, and the owners instructed to stand in the sunshine. Each vehicle was scanned by an excited brown sniffer dog and picked through by the customs official, after which the vehicle had to be driven to a parking lot near the port gate where an impromptu customs office had been established inside a few, predictably, dilapidated white buildings. One by one, the vehicle owners were called into an office where a large black woman sat behind a computer, surrounded by officials who did little other than joke and argue and try to look important. The adjacent office held an old copy machine and the customs officials had come up with a sly plan to extract some cash from us detained travellers; the large lady behind the computer would inspect the vehicle papers then request four copies of each page as well as four copies of the passport bio page, four copies of the Panamanian entry stamp, four copies of the Colombian exit stamp and four copies of each page of the relevant insurance document and finally four copies of the driver's license. The lady manning the copy machine charged $1.00 US per copy. The customs lady would then single finger tap the vehicle information into a temperamental and unreliable computer program. There were ten vehicles in total, including three BMW motorcycles and, at full speed, the customs lady managed to input one vehicle every hour. Our group became increasingly irritated as the day drew on, and the sun beat down. Tempers were flaring, and the customs lady reacted to any criticism by working slower and demanding more information. Eventually, it was our turn to be put through the wringer, but

Luisa and I have a secret power, we were immigration specialists in our previous life and dealing with third world bureaucracy is our cup of cold, tepid tea. We greeted the big lady with smiles and sat down on either side of her. Luisa complimented her on her awful jewellery and the photo of her family on the desk. On-demand I ran off to make extra copies of our documentation while Luisa helped our captor make sense of the customs program, South Africa did not appear on the drop-down menu. Eventually, Luisa takes over the keyboard and types in our vehicle information while I keep the customs lady laughing with stories from our travels. Within twenty minutes we were finished and hugged our new friend goodbye, ten minutes later we are liberated, driving on the streets of Colon.

If there is one thing in particular that we are learning as we travel the planet, it is that generalisations are almost always redundant. What comes to your mind when you think of Panama? In my mind's eye, I pictured a typical tropical, 3rd World paradise, populated by Latinos with enormous moustaches and unbuttoned shirts, heavy gold chains being polished by a thick mat of black chest hair. We drove through the port gates into a city which reminded me more of my mind's eye image of New Orleans. Old, colonial-style buildings shadowed treeless avenues, the entire population seemed to be black, and most spoke Caribbean English. Little girls with long blue skirts and perfect white shirts carried green school satchels. A bus bullied its way through the traffic, men stood on streets corners, joking and eyeballing the women making their way home after another day in an air-conditioned office. The Land Rover was attracting a lot of attention, as always, but not all the eyes were friendly. Luisa hung out of her window and struck up a conversation with the passenger of a taxi, killing time. I asked her to ask them where we could find a gas station. A couple curious pedestrians joined the conversation, and we soon had a little group slowly walking and talking as we inched forward. "Where you be from?". "South Africa". "Really? I don tink I belief you". Any hostility we had felt or imagined disappeared. We were now in the care of our new friends, and almost all the people of this world want you to enjoy their country, particularly if you treat them with respect.

We reached the other side of whatever bottleneck was holding up traffic and immediately found a gas station. We did not have any Panamanian currency, and there were no card facilities, we could not top up the tank and instead headed out of Colon, onto the highway and joined the stream of vehicles heading towards and past Panama City, sure that we would find a roadside gas station. We had no desire to visit the capital city, though we had considered a visit to the Panama Canal. Tourism was not our priority. Unfortunately, we had a date in the USA, which meant we were, essentially, in transit. Besides, I am a terrible tourist, being far more interested in the everyday life of a country. I want to live like a local, eat their food and live their lives. To me, that is the best experience one can have in a foreign land. Night fell as we circled Panama City. Luisa had found a campsite along the Pan American road, and we suddenly had the urge to tan some meat and throw back a few beers. We were running out of fuel and found a town next to the highway where we stopped to put in fuel and stock up on braai essentials.

Unfortunately, none of debit or credit cards was accepted at the gas station, we were running low on funds and were regularly going through the embarrassing process of trying every card until one magically produced some cash. Also, we often had the problem that the card which did have a positive balance was rejected as it was either not Visa or not Mastercard. Keelan and Luisa went searching for a cash machine while Jessica and I waited with the Land Rover. The oil cooler had begun leaking coolant in Cartagena, and I took this opportunity to check the temporary repair and fluid levels. It took almost an hour for a flustered Luisa and the man-child to return with a handful of green notes. We backtracked towards the highway and a supermarket we had spotted on the side of the road. Again,

Luisa and Keelan disappeared for an hour while Jess and I parked outside a store selling smoothies and waited.

I have a rule. It is not wise for us to be separated while travelling, therefore we always pair up. If Luisa and I feel safe in an area, we will leave both kids in the Landy while we pop into the shops. If Luisa must go anywhere without me, she must be accompanied by Keelan, who is now larger than most men and who I know will defend his mother and keep her from making silly purchases.

When Luisa and Keelan did eventually return, they were carrying only a small bag of groceries and a 12 pack of beer. I put the beers in the fridge, and we resumed the drive to our designated campsite, which was located, as it turns out, less than one hundred meters from the Pan American highway. A wiry, moody and ancient little American woman greeted us with a snarl. "I ain't got time for shit sunny", was the message her body language conveyed. The camp area was a large dry lawn which supported a large, low hanging palm frond gazebo, a small swimming pool and two other campers. Our neighbours were a German couple in a Toyota Land Cruiser and a semi-deserted camp with no campers in sight. The Germans poked their heads out of their camper once and left early the next morning. The other, semi-deserted, camp was interesting, to say the least. A typical roof tent stood atop a frame which had shade cloth draped around the sides, a small table stood in the middle of the floor, surrounded by camping chairs and large, transparent boxes of children's toys. Clothing hung, dry as a bone, on a washing line strung between two trees. This was no Gypsy camp and if anything looked like the temporary home of a middle-class family who had perhaps fallen on hard times or had given up on normal life to roam neighbourhoods at night, knocking on unsuspecting doors before thrusting Jesus inside.

LA LUCHA

After inspecting our surroundings and negotiating a reduced rate from Velma, we gathered together some firewood, took out our small stainless-steel BBQ and made a braai. By now, we were so practised in setting up camp that we were settled in our chairs within five minutes, discussing the road ahead. It was good to be on the road, with the ferry crossing we had started a new chapter in our journey, and we were now on the same landmass as the USA, the lighthouse which beckoned in the distance.

3

Central America. Unite!

There is no good reason why there should be seven, mostly impoverished, countries lying between Mexico and Colombia. If anything, all seven should make up one country (conveniently called The United States of Central America), or they should all be part of Mexico. A Supreme Court would oversee a federal government with limited power, and each region would have a significant degree of autonomy. Actually, the Government of Norway should govern the entire planet, and we will all just get along and do what we do. It is a waste of time and resources to play catch up with politics. Look at Venezuela, FFS, thieves masquerading as democratically elected officials rape the nation and steal her natural resources. The Norwegians would not do that. In South Africa, the ruling elite steal and plunder, divide and intentionally render the population ignorant. The Norwegians would not do that. In the industrialised world, people are regarded as consumers, first and foremost, and very little stands between a man, his hard-earned cash and the corporation which hires a team of psychologists to manipulate society into a consumer society while lawyers print the cash to regurgitate and write the laws to protect themselves. Norway does not do that. We should just give up on this silly idea of sovereignty and nationality and hand the essential jobs to those who do it the best with a few quid pro quos, i.e., corporations may not make donations of any kind to any political organization whatsoever, education and the advancement of the population is to be the number 1 priority of government, voting is compulsory, and war is banned. Simple.

Central America was split and forever disabled by politicians and lawyers who looked to consolidate their own power and carve out their own slice of the pie. Instead, of one vast country, sandwiched between North and South America and in physical possession of the only maritime trade route between the left and right of the Americas, with fertile soil and rich culture and history, you now have Banana republics desperate for McDonald's. I swear, the more I travel, the more I realise that this planet is governed by a large and loosely related clan of angry Muppets who play chess with flesh and bone and who are, essentially, terrible at the one thing they pretend to do – govern. Incompetent, corrupt, elitist nincompoops (enjoy that word, savour it) grow fat at the teat of the man chained by his own mind. And no, I am not advocating Communism, neither am I a fan of unregulated Capitalism. I am merely impatient, waiting for humanity to wake up and move on, into the utopian future where people have fewer babies, can care for and properly educate those they do have and live productive, calm lives with dignity and purpose. The Norwegians are the future, elect them now and let them lead the way.

We woke late and decided to stay in the camp for a few more days. We had some work to do, promoting the recently self-published We Will Be Free, preparing the route ahead and the kids had to catch up on their home-schooling. Luisa and I packed the roof tent and, leaving Keelan in charge, drove out onto the dry, grey freeway to search for a decent supermarket. To the immediate north lay only a small complex where a farmer's market refused to stay open after lunch, and we backtracked 20 kilometres to a town where two supermarkets competed for regional dominance, though I suspect they were owned by the same person or corporation and were supplied by the same suppliers, the difference in name creating the illusion of choice and competition. While I waited, Luisa ran between the two supermarkets, price checking and inspecting the range. A portly man in his late sixties approached me and began chatting. He was an Israeli who had had a house in New York, but he chose to move to Panama where his dollar could be stretched and where he married a local woman and started a family. He liked to talk and knew a bit about South Africa and was impressed that I had lived in Israel for a year. Luisa returned having chosen to shop at the Big Buck Food Market, I excused myself and drove the Land Rover around the block to find safe parking close to the entrance of the large and surprisingly modern shopping complex. Within a minute of entering Big Buck's, the Israeli man located us and designated himself our local guide. Man, did he love to talk! He took our trolley and began shopping for us, telling us, "yes, this brand is very good, it is local and a good price, you could maybe get it cheaper across the road, but this is a good price, and it is very delicious. Have you tried this before? No? That's ok, you will try this then, and it is a good price. Come this way, I will show you the butchery, the meat is OK here, but it is not so good as in the USA, I know the butcher, you want a good steak, I am sure of it. Oh, no, my butcher friend is not here today, I am sure I saw him earlier, just now, in fact, never mind you can choose from any of the cuts here, do you want chicken, pork or beef? I would not recommend the chicken, and I don't know anything about pork, but they do sometimes have a good steak. Oh, you only want to look around for a while, no problem, I will help you, what are you looking for? Prices? Good, that is good, I suppose you have been all around the world it is always a good idea to look at prices. My wife likes to do the shopping, but she does not look at the prices. She used to look at the prices and only bought local food and did all the cooking and cleaning but after she had the first boy four years ago, she became exhausted and did not to do the housework anymore and since the second baby she never cooks. She likes to shop though, she buys only the best but never looks at the prices. She is bigger now as well, I think it was the extra weight from the babies, I thought it would go away but, there is more now than ever. She also wants a new house, but I told her she must be crazy! I bought the apartment building we live in, and we live at the top, and I can do all my work and collect the rent and keep an eye on the place from up there. If we move, who will take care of the place? She is crazy, she told me to break a hole through the wall and make two apartments into one large apartment, but we do not need six rooms and two kitchens and four bathrooms. She has a big family, and they always come to visit and never pay for anything. If I had such a big apartment, they would visit and never leave, and none of them will speak English. Now I have the keys to the apartments, and I won't let any of them into the other apartments but if there is a hole in the wall they will never leave, and I won't be able to keep them out, I can't tell them there is no space for them if the space is empty and they can walk through the hole in the wall, and they can see the empty rooms and the extra kitchen and the two bathrooms. And I will lose money, I could sell the apartment for good money, the Americans are expanding the Canal, and we are only half an hour's drive. No, a hole in the wall does not need keys, and I like doors almost as much as I like keys. What? No. Wait I will show you this, have you tried this? It might be cheaper across the road, but I don't think so. And the price is OK. It is very good that you keep an eye on the prices, no, what? Oh. OK then, here is my card, that is my number, if you need anything let me know, I can tell you where you can get anything, and we have very reasonable apartments, American standard, the rent is very good, I am sure you will like it, let me know. Oh, before I forget. What! Oh, OK, yes, it was nice to meet you too. Yes, I also must go, goodbye".

Luisa lacks the ability to stop a talker. I have a horrible uncle who would trap the poor woman in a corner then spend the next few hours having a conversation with her chest. She could never break away. The talker just wants to talk, what would they do if you just excused yourself and carried on with your life? Never speak to you again? Preposterous, that would-be self-flagellation, no you never have to worry about a talker giving you the silent treatment; besides, they don't give a crap about what you have to say, you are only valuable as you have ears. You will never catch a talker trying to communicate with a deaf person because their goal is not communication, they are seeking an audience, they want to tell you what they know because you clearly do not know what they know. Wankers. Oh, my apologies, was I monologuing?

We emptied the trolley of the stuff our freshly departed friend had kindly recommended and resumed our walk through the aisles. We found a surprisingly good variety of food and condiments and had a good look at the local populace which seemed to include a good percentage of greying American expats. All that talking had delayed us by an hour, and it was dark by the time we returned to the camp, worried about the kids and feeling guilty and irresponsible for leaving them with only a packet of food and a few litres water. We need not have worried. We found them holding court with a group of young backpackers who had taken up residence in the pool. I did not know that the house had dorms or even a bar, but apparently, the young, tanned bodies had found both. Enthusiastic water sports and poolside joking filled the night air with a chatter we soon ignored. Our kids had been telling the group where we had been, and Keelan gave the men a tour of the Landy. The large gazebo stood between us and the pool, and I was happy to not engage any of the group in conversation. Telling our story in a one on one conversation is usually quite enjoyable but talking to a group informally has its own set of dynamics, particularly when alcohol and young men are involved. At first, the group is in awe and full of questions, expecting us to be some kind of trap, skin and devour, bush family. When the group eventually relaxes the competition for the class clown, and alpha male begins. I have no interest in these social shenanigans, we have nothing to prove and are not a reality TV show.

The next day we woke early and packed, ready for a slow drive to the Costa Rican border. To label the network of roads which lead from Alaska to

LA LUCHA

Argentina the Pan American "highway" is at the very least presumptuous, only in North America will you drive on any decent length of the actual highway. The Panamanian stretch was, mostly, single-lane tarmac with short sections of double lanes. We were nervous as we approached the border have heard countless stories of corruption and ineptitude. Leaving Panama was relatively easy but entering Costa Rica was not to be as uneventful.

Swatting "fixers", we parked the Land Rover in what seemed to be the designated parking area, amongst numerous trucks, and made our way towards the immigration and customs offices. A large white tent staffed with people disguised as medical personnel stood in our way. A nurse asked us to approach a long table where we had to produce our passports. I was travelling on my British passport since Colombia and was asked to wait while the Africans, whose green passports had caused a stir, were instructed to approach the table. There they were questioned about where we had been and how long we had been there. Ebola was ravaging pockets of West Africa at the time, and the medical tent became quite excited at the prospects of having real, but very pale, Africans to assess. A laser gun was produced and aimed at three foreheads, one at a time. Bear in mind that Guinea, Liberia and Sierra Leone are about as far from South Africa as they are from London. With temperature readings within the normal ranges, all passports were returned, and we were allowed to proceed to the immigration counter where we were charged $1.00 (US dollar) each for the immigration forms. We were then charged $5.00 each for the privilege of a queue number and then asked for another $12.00 each for the visa. With the immigration process out of the way, we had to take care of the customs. Again, we were charged $5.00 for the application form, and a fat and desperately unhappy woman then gave us vague instructions to the Aduana (customs) office. After a long search and a short wait, a voice behind smoky glass asked for our papers and a $20.00 processing fee. A long wait and a short conversation later our registration papers were returned, and we were instructed to return to the fat, unhappy woman who took our papers and instructed us to buy insurance at one of three counters staffed by two equally miserable but thankfully better-looking protagonists. $50.00 changed hands before fat and unhappy charges us $5.00 to return our papers and allow us to leave. We had never paid for applications to be processed in South America and had only once had to pay for a visa to enter Bolivia. The border process itself had not been that difficult but had been infuriating solely because of the never-ending demands for our precious dollars.

Away from the border, Costa Rica surprised us by being beautiful, green and relatively well organised. We stopped at a small restaurant to buy a couple fruit batidas (smoothies) to share and enjoyed an afternoon driving twisting roads through the pristine jungle. An American overland vehicle sped past us shortly before we rounded a corner and witnessed the carnage of a truck accident which had only just recently occurred. A small crowd gathered around the injured driver while others collected the fallen beast's cargo. A truck accident in a third world country is an opportunity for wealth distribution, and locals will arrive from nowhere, as if by a miracle, and load vehicles with as much as they can carry. The scene reminded me of a dozen similar accidents we had witnessed in Africa and across the Americas, and we felt sympathy for the driver who would most likely be held solely responsible for the loss and damage, despite the roadworthiness of the vehicle or vehicle worthiness of the road.

Storm clouds gathered on the horizon as the afternoon drew to a close, Luisa searching our broken old mobile device for a campsite using a free navigation tool we had been told about by a kind man in a defiantly modern Venezuelan town. The navigator took us to a well-loved and beautifully maintained neighbourhood devoid of any campsites.

A family in a vegetable van stopped next to as we parked off the road, at an intersection; with heavy rain battering down, searching our maps and GPS for a place to camp. The border had taken longer than expected, and we had to decide whether to continue to find the camp we had planned to stay at which would mean running the risk of driving after dark. The man opened his window and rested a large, bare and hairy arm on the door frame of his Kia truck. Two small children sat between him and his wife, craning their necks to get a look at us. After a short, damp chat, the man suggested that we drive down to the nearest bay where he was sure we would find a place to camp. We thanked the man for his help and turned left at the intersection, waving happy goodbyes to our new friends. The road to the town Golfito was bordered by quaint and well-kept homes, green lawns and no camps. Arriving in town, we withdrew some cash from the ATM and began our search for camping but found nothing but little hotels and large resorts. After an hour of searching, we were about to give up and head back to the main road when the small Kia truck pulled up next to us again. The bare and hairy arm was not happy that we had not found a place to sleep, it picked up a phone and called a friend who had a place where we might be able to park up for the night. The arm belonged to an equally hairy but thankfully less bare man called Carlos whose friend said that we could park outside his home on the water's edge, wedged between two large hedges and close to a covered parking area where we could cook out of the rain. Throughout the evening, various members of the surrounding homes came to welcome us, and we eventually managed to prepare a quick meal before falling asleep to the patter of rain on the tent. In the morning the world was wet, green and clear blue skies. Keelan and I scavenged a few mangoes from the massive mango trees which dotted the lawns that surrounded us. We were tempted to go for a swim before the heat of the day set in and worked up a clammy sweat closing our huge rooftop tent which continued to amaze us with its sturdy construction and durability. That tent had housed us for almost four years of continuous camping and, incredibly, the tent looked like it could handle at least four more years. We had done our best to maintain it and, apart from the weak link rain cover, the regular treatment and care of the tent had paid off.

At a yacht club, frequented mostly by American anglers and yachtsmen, we used the bathroom and baulked at the price of coffee while taking advantage of the free WIFI. That bay was beautiful, worthy of a few days of exploration, if only we had time. And money. Already I began to feel that we were wasting an opportunity to explore a beautiful country by rushing towards the USA. Luisa reminded me often that our financial situation was not ideal, and we essentially had very little left, perhaps not even enough to make it up to the Texan border. Every night I went to sleep with a heavy head. We could have driven around the world with the resources we had left home with; instead, we had fallen deeply in love with South America and had travelled nearly 100 000 kilometres on her soil alone. Had we been foolish? Perhaps. But there was no way we could have predicted that our South African currency, the Rand (which in 1990 had been equal to the dollar), would lose 50% of its value since 2012, slashing our savings and income in half. We also could not have predicted the South African tax authorities emptying our bank accounts due to a clerical error (well, if we had received the numerous threatening letters, we might have had an inkling). We had published our first book, We Will Be Free, shortly before leaving Ecuador and royalties would begin to trickle in after Amazon raked in 75% of the profits and gave itself 60 days to pay the difference.

I found myself reassuring Luisa of the plan. We would promote the book as well as we could and hopefully, my writing would be decent enough to accurately convey the immensity and pure adventure of our journey. We would print a few hundred books (cutting Amazon out of the equation) in the week before the Overland Expo in Flagstaff, Arizona and we would sell all those books, even if we had to beg people to buy them. We would then use the proceeds from the sales of those books to print more, and we would approach Rotary Clubs and Land Rover dealerships and bookstores to allow us to give presentations about our journey and sell our books. Somehow, somewhere the media would cotton on to our story and we would do TV and radio interviews. Interest in our journey would explode, and we would sell thousands of books. Trust me, honey, I have a plan. How could we have predicted how low we would have to fall before we could begin to climb? Within two days we were crossing into Nicaragua, being fleeced again.

The Nicaraguan border crossing was again, the now-familiar process. Swat away the helpers and touts, hand over piles of cash for each step in the procedure, hand over another wad of money for insurance, have the vehicle fumigated and eventually enter another country, similar to the last despite the line in the sand. Except Nicaragua is not like Costa Rica at all.

Luisa had done her research and suggested that we drive to San Juan del Sur, a popular holiday town on the Pacific coast where we were sure to find camping. We followed the No 2 road towards the beach and drove the last ten kilometres to the town along a sandy coastal road. Beautiful villas hugged the coastline, and we caught glimpses through large wooden gates of how the other "half" lived. Glistening pools and palm trees offered refreshment and shade, which we could not dream of enjoying. Young sexy creatures drove Jeeps and quad bikes and waved at us, assuming we were one of them. Luisa said nothing, but I knew that she was deeply concerned and more than a little disappointed. We had left behind a very comfortable life in South Africa and soon we might be juggling spanners at traffic lights to earn fuel and food money. Descending into San Juan del Sur, we were amazed at the sheer quantity of tanned gringos flitting between restaurants and surf shops. Some were just so cool, skinny, bronzed, tattooed and embedded. We searched for an ATM and managed to retrieve some Nicaraguan Cordoba's (the currency) and made our way past the boobs and scooters and taxis and touts back out of town. We followed a corrugated road up a hill, past more villas and the contrasting homes of locals, each who had set up a pub along the road where they would eat dust each time a big, shiny jeep came bouncing by.

"$25 US for camping. You can use the toilet but not the shower. No, we do not have WIFI. No, we do not have electricity. No. Try there". "There" was less than desirable and only allowed ground tents. The only greenery in sight was that of the tall, depressed palm trees who lazily pretended to be exotic. By now, we were the type of overlanders who would pay for camping if we needed security or WIFI and laundry facilities. To pay a quarter of our daily budget for a parking space and a bad attitude was beneath us and we set off, back towards the town to find a free camping opportunity. On the beach, we found two bars where locals dressed in the confidence of belonging and happily went about the business of marking products up 300% and reluctantly trudging through the sand to deliver those products in either a chilled or cooked state to people who sat in limbless plastic chairs under burnt brown palm-frond umbrellas. My lack of currency had made me critical of anyone who could afford a few cold beers and a fish lunch without compromise. I admit it. Bear with me.

We decided to park in the bar parking lot and wait until dark before opening the tent and enjoying a night of cool coastal breeze. While Luisa and the kids went for a walk on the beach and a swim in the sea, I prepared lunch on the tailgate. People came and went, asking questions about the Land Rover and quizzing me about our journey. I had never been exposed to so many Americans in my entire life, and I noticed that everyone was friendly, polite and genuinely interested in our journey. This bode well for our plans to travel in the USA.

So far, we had come across a few religious, missionary families, overlanders and party kids backpacking in small groups or travelling in the safety of a large group. The missionaries were always, without fail, simply weird. Either curious and naïve or evasive and neurotic, perhaps the former eventually becomes the latter.

The American overlanders we met tended to be well balanced, well-educated and prone to travel in groups. Almost all drove Toyotas and gave themselves names like Team America! which we adapted to Team Japan because they drove Toyotas, not Jeeps! Overlanding is trendy, and in the past, you would expect to meet overlanders in 4x4 vehicles equipped with mud terrain tyres, winches, jerry cans and axes but, that day on the Nicaraguan coast, we met the antithesis of the khaki-clad, dirty nails, burnt skin and drinking problem overlander. They called themselves The Juicing Nomads, a couple of estate agents from New York. Juicing was their Thing, they were not selling Juicing machines or even Juice, they were selling the idea of Juicing as a way of life. Much like surfers and climbers dedicate themselves to attaining the ultimate peak, but not quite. Apparently, they had fallen under the spell of an Australian who was once Fat, Lazy and Reeked of Death. I struggled to compute the lifestyle. How did they make Juice over a fire? Did they ever make a fire? How does one Juice a steak or a rack of ribs or cornbread or peri-peri chicken with a side of crispy fries and a Portuguese bun? Apparently, you can't Juice those things, and smoothies are simply inferior to a good Juice, much like rollerblading sucks compared to skateboarding and Nascar (turn left for four hours) does not come close to the intricacy and sheer spectacle of Formula One. Smoothies suck, they are full of crap, you see, flesh and pips and fibres. Juicing extracts the essence of the plant, the really good stuff which the Good Lord in all his wisdom chose to hide deep down inside the organism, a soul of sorts, waiting until his creation had evolved to the point that they could construct a shiny, $400.00 for an entry-level machine, which could extract that soul and nourish their bodies, correctly.

My new friends listened patiently to my misgivings and answered, by rote, the questions they had heard so many times before. They lived in the clear light of Juicing, their bowels clean and minty, their BMI's a trophy on the mantelpiece of their Toyota Tacoma. They endured the mocking tone in my voice, the endless questions which their less evolved cousins, the vegetarian and vegan, always had to endure when meeting someone like me – a meat-eating, beer-bellied, 4x4 driving, gun-loving, opinionated reprobate. Ean, the male of the pair, had been pussy whipped so hard by his lovely Natasha that I was determined to convince him to abandon this foolishness. It is a super healthy, sometimes tasty drink, not a way of life! You are driving to Argentina, the meat capital of the Universe, abandon this green and unsatisfying foolishness!

Our lifestyles were poles apart, but they were friendly people, I enjoyed their company and secretly wished that I had a super cool Juicing machine, so I could torture the fuck out of wheatgrass instead of bending over the tailgate trying to keep the flies off the roasted chicken mayo sandwiches, fresh garden salad and French onion chips I was preparing. We have stayed in touch since then, and I did not feel even the slightest hint of jealousy or outrage when, on December 2016, Buzzfeed chose to highlight them as overlanders and broadcast a slick video to 12 billion people. None at all. Not even a little bit. They did drive the Toyota from New York to Argentina, and anyone who can achieve that deserves respect.

A jeep pulled up, and six tanned supermodels extracted their long, cramped limbs and short surfboards from the vehicle. They all paid attention to me, standing alone next to the expensive-looking Land Rover. Had I been a single man I could have joined them for a surf, a drink or two and a game of pool. I would have regaled with tales of the adventures I had in Africa and circumnavigating South America, almost twice. They would have been quietly intrigued and would coolly begin competing for my attention. I would ignore them all while subtly continuing to flirt with each. The competition for my attention would become fierce, each beautiful woman needing to confirm that she was the most beautiful and desirable of the group. I needed to do and say very little. I would be invited back to their small villa where we would swim in the pool, and I would cook a spicy dish of shellfish and yellow rice, served with a large salad and a bottle of rum. After dancing and a late-night swim, I would open my tent on top of the Land Rover and go to bed. Someone would have joined me.

But. I was not a single man, I was a family man. I smiled at the large, mostly blue eyes, dismissively and continued to prepare the family lunch. My Luisa had stuck with me through all the ups and downs in my life, from a failed business and massive debt to my financial recovery and success in Cape Town. She had stood by me always and was dedicated to me, she would kill for me and had I chatted to the supermodels, she would have killed me. I am not afraid of much, but I am wary of my wife, I sleep deep.

Keelan and I body surfed that afternoon, then we joined my girls for a walk down the littered beach. In Ecuador, we had stayed at a campsite/hostel on the beach in a little town called Canoa. There the owners of the hostel had offered a large, free cocktail to anyone who collected a large bag of trash from the beach. It was a great idea which benefitted all concerned, and Luisa cleaned the beach with great enthusiasm. A short while before we left an asterisk and cocktail limit disclaimer magically appeared on the cocktails for litter sign.

That evening, after the bars closed at 7 pm (it was a Sunday, the best day for border crossings in our experience), we collected dried coconut husks and driftwood, moved the Landy to a level patch and made a fire over which we grilled chicken. We had no cold beer, but Luisa found an old bottle of rum at the bottom of the kitchen area of the Land Rovers load area, which we sipped, enjoying the warm evening and discussing the past few days and the days to come. Luisa planned to spend a few weeks in Mexico exploring the Caribbean coast before we crossed into the USA. Central America was not going anywhere, we would hopefully return one day and explore her better. The cool ocean breeze wafted through the roof tent as we joined the kids to sleep. Both Keelan and Jessica had had a good day on the beach, the salt and sand had matted their hair. They had always been beautiful children, and they trust us faultlessly, they know that they will be safe and secure and that we will always protect and care for them, no matter where we are in the world.

The next morning, we awoke to a quiet beach. A couple of French guys had arrived in a van, long after dark, and parked close to our vehicle. We made small talk with them while packing the tent away then set off back onto the No 2 road to the city of Leon which was in parts modern and beautiful, and others neglected and crowded with people aggressively begging for dollars. At every traffic light, an army of window washers would descend on the trapped cars, smearing muddy water with oily cloths across the windscreens of the nicer cars. We stood out like a gold-plated silver thumb in our exotic Defender, and two washers/beggars would assault us simultaneously. "No, gracias, no, el parabrisas está limpio". "No, ¡basta!". (No, thank you, the windscreen is clean. No! That is enough!). We had just had a new windscreen installed in Cartagena after years of staring through cracked, scratched and pitted glass, the last thing we wanted was someone gouging the new windshield with an oily, gritty rag. The street soldier, wearing gaudy sports clothing and gold earrings, would look at us with a sullen, disgusted face. "Malo gringo". (Bad American / whitey). We would then have to endure the gang and the street vendors talking crap about us until the traffic light eventually changed and we were able to move on to the next traffic light where the process would be repeated. Malo gringo. Basta, pendejo! We managed to get lost finding a way through the city and found ourselves in a mixed industrial and residential area. A billboard of two very well-fed men wearing pastel golf shirts and holding hands advised us to always wear a condom. The navigation tool failed completely, and we wound our way through the city by asking directions and edging our way through the traffic. By now we had become very good at getting lost, one day we will invest in a GPS, but we seem to be having a great time without it. Sometimes getting lost makes the journey that much more adventurous, this was not one of those times, unfortunately. We made it through the city early enough to reach the border and cross into Honduras.

Once again, the border crossing was far easier than we expected. My theory is that many overlanders begin their journey in the Americas heading North to South. The Canadian, USA and Mexican borders are relatively easy to cross, and the Central American border crossings are without a doubt a pure Third World (or the more politically correct term, Developing Nation) affair. It is the ease of the North American border crossings which make the Central American crossings seem tedious and difficult. I also suspect that as these countries modernise and crackdown on corruption, increase computerisation and streamline processes, the border crossings are not as awful as they have been over the last few decades. We had experienced a similar situation in Africa. I suppose the keyword here is, experience. Once you have been through enough borders overland, you begin to realise that patience and preparation wins the day and he who has the most paper wins. A calm and friendly yet professional attitude, with a good understanding of your rights and what you represent as a tourist, will lead to success every time. Well, almost every time. Because we were moving across the isthmus (a land bridge between North and South America) so quickly, we were struggling to come to terms with the exchange rates and values of currency from country to country. The friendly and chatty Honduran immigration officials added a zero to the visa fee, and we handed over a pile of cash (luckily there was a cash machine nearby where I could withdraw Honduran Lempira). After immigration, we entered a large room full of officials who seemed somehow better dressed and educated than the immigration officials, a few spoke English. We asked why the visas were so expensive, having had a bit of time to work out the exchange rates, we smelled a rat. The Aduana officials were surprised by the question and confirmed that we had paid ten times as much as we should have, Keelan and I marched back to the Immigration desk and asked simply for our cambio (change). Incredibly our money was handed back to us with only a bit of nervous laughter and mumbling.

Honduras seemed far greener and more relaxed than Nicaragua, and we made good progress until the sun began to set. We had not had much time to research camping areas along our route and were lucky to come across a gas station which stood alone next to a green grass field. We asked the man behind the desk if we could park for the night and, after a phone call to his boss, we were told that we could. At first, I planned to park just off the forecourt, but the attendant told me that I could drive onto the lawn and between the palm trees where a well-manicured garden waited for us. Score! We had paid good money to camp in places much worse than this. There was even a clean toilet and a cold shower for us to enjoy. Luisa and I made a pasta dinner while the kids explored the field. A crazy chicken adopted us and pecked around the Land Rover, chased Jessica and spent the night sleeping under the vehicle before waking up at dawn to crow at the setting moon. I made breakfast while Luisa planned the route to Guatemala. At less than 600 Kilometres between borders, we were in for a relatively short drive. We were going to be in Honduras for only two days, and I had a feeling that we would have enjoyed at least a month travelling that beautiful country.

Another day, another border crossing, this was becoming ridiculous. Luisa warned me that we would be doing a bunch of tourist crap in Guatemala. Apparently, there had once been a great indigenous civilisation here, and it would be prudent for us to explore the skeleton of that empire. Well, ok then, if we must.

Guatemala is very similar to Costa Rica in that it is relatively well-governed and popular with expats who buy land and invest in the tourism sector, mostly. We drove up to Lago Petén Etzá to search for camping and plan a trip to visit Tikal, the world-famous Mayan ruin. We found a hundred hotels but no camping except at one hotel close to the edge of a town called El Remate. The lake reflected stark sunlight as did the white stone of the hotel parking lot. Inside an open restaurant area, a group of blonde tourists ate lunch. The Land Rover likes to show off in these types of situations, and she growled at the tourists, announcing our arrival. Grr. Luisa asked a confused waiter how much they charged for camping and the eventual answer was a disappointing $40.00. That was just too dear for us poor overlanders, we essentially needed WIFI, as we needed to check our finances, promote We Will Be Free, take care of all the typical day to day crap and plan the route forward. One of the blondes gave Keelan the WIFI code, and we tried our best to connect to the internet. A trickle of the omnipotent world wide web made its way through the ether into Luisa's shattered tablet, she managed to download our emails and a map of the area.

Tikal was the main tourist trap ruin in the area, and everyone insisted that we simply had to go there. The entrance fee was ridiculous $22.00 per person plus another $13.00. We drove around the lake for a while looking for wild camping but found nothing suitable or not signposted. We then decided to drive to Tikal to see if we could find a better rate and, perhaps, permission to open the roof tent outside the park. Fat chance of that. The Tikal National Park staff had obviously received their customer relations training from the Machu Picchu (Peru) staff. They were aloof, unfriendly, disinterested and unprofessional. "No, you must pay what it says on the board. No, you cannot pay here. If you enter now, you must leave in an hour. No, you cannot use today's ticket tomorrow. Yes, it is late, but it is your fault for being late, not mine. Yes, the little one does not pay. No, you cannot open a tent here, this is not a camping site. No, it does make a difference that the tent is ariba. No, I cannot tell you where you can camp". A German tourist who had been standing nearby came to us as we sat in the Landy discussing our options. "Try Yaxha, it is not far and much cheaper". He then left, and we decided to heed his advice. We drove out of the Tikal and back onto the No3 road and drove about 30 kilometres southeast, then turned left and drove a long grey corrugated road until we arrived at the entrance to the Yaxha-Nakum-Naranjo National Park. A friendly ranger approached us, and we soon learned that not only were the entrance fees a third of those at Tikal, the fee also included free camping along the banks of Lake Yaxha. Sold.

We found the campsite set on the side of a green hill and a camp spot near the lake. Keelan and I played Rugby while Luisa and Jessica had their first shower in four days and then it was our turn to hit the shower. Howler monkeys barked at the moon rising over the lake, and we made a fire. We only had a few neighbours, including a Canadian with a broken motorbike which we offered tools and assistance to. He was a very quiet man and did not seem to like the idea of company at all, even if he needed help, he would rather do what he needs to alone. I can respect that.

The atmosphere was spectacular, and we felt the presence of the ancient Mayans. The lake shimmered in the moonlight, the fire crackled, the Howlers howled, and the rum tasted sweet, hot and spicy. We awoke that morning to fresh, crisp air, a blue sky and green jungle. We were expecting the ruins to be overrun by tour buses and noisy, bustling tourists. What we found was the complete opposite. Apart from a few disinterested groundsmen and a lone French tourist, we were completely alone. While others were scrambling for photo opportunities and getting under each other's feet as they clambered over the ruins of Tikal, we strolled from pyramid to pyramid to games area to public baths to temple. The lone French girl crossed our paths once and looked at us longingly as if she missed her own family or at least someone she could share her experience with. I suggested we should ask her to join us, but Luisa has grown weary of younger women becoming friendly with us – they either fall in love with Keelan or me, and that always ends in tears. Yes, we are that irresistible, and apparently, even though I am an African man, I do not qualify for a junior wife.

All morning we explored the beautiful site, imagining that we were walking the city when it was at its zenith. The labour expended to build that civilisation is simply mind-boggling, and the Mayans had mastered organised agriculture, mathematics, politics, astronomy and war. I often wonder if their religion made them, destroyed them or both. It is also incredible that their descendants populate the Americas to this day and that this miracle of humanity began with an overland journey across the frozen Bering Strait to Alaska and then down the North American coast all the way to South America, 20 000 years ago. We had been travelling in the opposite direction of that migration and hoped to one day make it to the Bering Straits and gaze upon the land we now call Russia.

The crossing from Guatemala into Belize was frustrating. The Guatemalans had us jump through a few hoops before allowing us to stamp out of the peaceful, beautiful little nation. A pretty girl employed by the tourist board gave us a gift of braided cotton bangles and encouraged us to return soon, an offer I would gladly accept. Interestingly, we have found that of all the countries we had travelled, those with a British colonial past tend to have the most pedantic, passive-aggressive border officials. Belize did not disappoint. A huge black lady greeted us in English, initially a welcome relief, and began to interrogate us. Perhaps the white faces and South African passports riled her. Apartheid was dead before we entered adulthood, but we must accept that, even though we do not believe that Apartheid benefited our generation directly, we did have the advantage over our black neighbours. We had the privilege of a decent education and a powerful economy in which our parents and grandparents had been permitted to participate and, possibly, thrive. Though Luisa and I had received almost no significant financial assistance from our parents, we had the tools needed to prosper through our own hard work and sacrifice. True democracy came to our homeland in 1994 and the responsibility for the relative poverty the country suffers today, can only be shouldered by the ANC government who inherited one of the largest economies and civil infrastructures in the developing world. They, the ANC, chose to enrich the elite at the expense of the entire nation. Luisa and I have always worked hard, and in the era of Affirmative Action and Black Economic Empowerment, it was that hard work which allowed us to be able to set off to achieve our dreams. We have a story to tell, but it is not easy to explain. Prejudice is based on assumption and generalisations, which are, more often than not, not based on experience.

The Belizean immigration lady, dressed in an ill-fitting and faded uniform, pre-judged us and it was crystal clear that, given the opportunity, we might be in for a bit of a ride. For twenty minutes our captor flipped through each passport asking us specifics like "when did you enter Venezuela" and "why were you there for three months", "why did you return to Brazil so often", "how did you get from Colombia to Panama" etc. She asked for my South African passport, once she heard that I had dual nationality, for which I had to walk back to the Land Rover and search.

Luisa and I had a quick word in Afrikaans and switched into happy, friendly, "you are the boss!" mode. Jessica and Keelan were gently nudged between the official and us, and they began answering questions, and one look into those big blue eyes soothed the savage passport stamper. She asked for the vehicle papers and for an explanation of how we managed to tour for so long, we answered that I am an author and Luisa is a photographer. Having just recently self-published my first book. I was not convinced that I could claim to be an author, but I relished claiming that as my profession.

The immigration office was a large, white and tropically airy building. I was instructed to bring the Land Rover up to the side of the building for inspection, and a young, smiling man had a quick look around and inside the vehicle before waving us through. We were free to drive on Belizean soil, it was the end of the month, a royalty cheque had been deposited in our bank account, and we had heard of a camp not too far from the border. Although we had had a fire the night before we had not had any meat to grill and Luisa was suffering from her bi-weekly braai withdrawals. A quick drive around the treeless town revealed very little in the way of grocery stores. One large Chinese store offered dusty tins of food, heavily iced, dirty and almost empty freezers and a huge array of plastic containers. We asked where we could find a butchery and the lady behind the counter, who had been very friendly when we entered, semi sneered an answer. "Down there around the corner". What she really meant to say was, "Whydafuk you not buying the chickens and fishers in a freezer, uh? Very good, no problem, is coz you no likea Chinese? No, we don have a nee coke cola in two litres, one litre is good, fat pig, fukoff". Welcome to Belize, enjoy your stay.

The butchery down the road had only frozen chicken, and we were told that there was another butchery up the road. A large, friendly man opened the door to the butchery/hut and showed us what he had available. He had slaughtered a cow recently, but most of the good cuts were gone. We settled on chicken breasts, and I offered to cook a curry. We bought a six-pack of local beer and a couple of one-litre fizzy drinks, a treat. Just outside of the town, Benque Viejo del Carmen there was supposed to be a camp called the Trek Stop. The owner was once mildly famous and had built the lodge with his own hands. He has since retired, and his awful children have taken over the running of the camp. There was a temperamental restaurant which only served food and drink when it felt like it, the WIFI dribbled bytes of information sporadically, and the gardens were maintained by footstep. A few cabins were scattered about the property, and in the centre, next to the patch of grass we camped on, was a filthy little kitchen which was cleaned regularly with a metal mop and a bucket of the clingy mud. The pots and pans under the crusty sink had been left unwashed, to preserve them of course, and the local rats ate any leftovers and left their droppings to prove that they were diligently doing their job. We were so enamoured with the place that we decided to stay for two nights. It had been a while since we had washed laundry, the Landy needed some TLC and Luisa needed to catch up on the administrative crap which keeps our wheels turning.

On the second night, the blondes from the Guatemalan hotel on the lake booked into the Trek Stop. There were a couple of skittish males in the group, but the majority were Scandinavian girls seeking adventure. Two of them had a shower then sat on their cabin balcony in just their bath towels, others took to walking up and down, past the glorious kitchen where we had set up a base. Again, if I was a single man... We chatted to the eldest, bravest blonde for a short while. She looked Danish but came from New York and worked in the banking sector.

Before sunset, on the second day, we took a walk down to the river. Rivers are instinctive meeting places for people, and all across the Americas, we had seen how the river would serve as a meeting place, particularly in small, poor towns which did not have public recreation facilities. Men would drive their cars down to the water for a wash, children would play in the water and chase each other on small sandy beaches, groups of women would gather to chat about the men washing their cars and families or groups of friends would make cooking fires and drink beer and local spirits. A couple of teenagers would ride a motorbike with half an exhaust system, blasting up and down the road which ran parallel to the river. Sometimes the river was merely a stream, periodic and prone to disappearing underground while others would be fast flowing permanent rivers. The locals would tailor their activities to whichever type of river they were blessed or cursed with. Usually, the banks of the river were strewn with litter, but sometimes the river would be pristine, and a general rule of thumb is the cleaner the river, the more educated the local populace.

The Mopan river was emerald green and flowed steadily, tranquil pools dotting the banks. The litter was moderate, possibly because the population density was low but hopefully because they knew better. The river sucked us in and carried us, the children laughing, Jessica clinging to me as she always does when we go swimming in any body of water larger than a bathtub. The river forked, and we chose to swim towards the banks where we found a small, still bight to relax in. A local family cruised past, waving and laughing. It was a Tuesday afternoon but had the slow, quiet buzz of a Sunday. I had the feeling that every day was Sunday here. I could picture the ancient Mayans relaxing in these waters, bringing their slaves down for a drink and wash, children playing in the water and chasing each other on small sandy beaches, gangs of girls and women giggling and chatting about the men washing the donkeys, families and groups of friends would make fires to cook the fish they had caught, drinking Xtabentún liqueur and Balche. We swam for a couple hours then returned to the messy camp for an early dinner and bed.

Belize is quite lovely. Large wooden houses sit on large, grassy plots of land. Traffic is minimal, and the roads are straight and well maintained. We had a short drive to Chetumal, Mexico, and we made the most of the beautiful weather, driving slowly and stopping often. Mennonites sold watermelons while their horses grazed, people worked in their gardens and laundry floated in the breeze. We did not have any plans to head to the coast, which is unfortunate; apparently, the reefs are incredible and the diving spectacular. Another reason to return to Central America one day.

After a 255 kilometre drive, we arrived at the Mexican Border. Three years earlier, when I had phoned the Mexican consulate in South Africa to inquire about visa requirements, I had been told that we did not need a visa for Mexico if we had one for the USA. We were hoping that the border official would be aware of this and not deny us entry into the country. Driving towards the Mexican border, after stamping out of Belize, we were met by concrete and razor wire. It was by far the most sophisticated and modern border we had ever seen. A border guard instructed us to park the Landy and directed us towards the large, air-conditioned immigration and customs building. We waited patiently while a Mennonite family endured the passport procedure and then had a conversation with the very witty and intelligent Mexican immigration official who spoke excellent English with an American accent. When asked where he learned to speak English, he told us that he had a year off after high school, when he did not much more than sitting on the couch watching the American sitcom, Friends. By reading the subtitles and matching the words he learned to speak English! That was his story, and he is sticking with it. After each passport was scanned and stamped, we said goodbye to our new friend and started the customs procedure for the Landy. A friendly lady helped us through the process and took a large deposit from us, a standard procedure, for the entrance of a foreign vehicle. We were impressed by both the character of the officials and their efficiency, we had grown weary of border officials and had in the last 10 days done 13 crossings (in and out of 7 countries). To be treated like a human was wonderful and if these two Mexicans were an attestation of the general Mexican population, we would surely be happy in the land of tortilla, tequila, Corona and La Cucaracha.

Eventually, we were able to squeeze the $300 vehicle deposit out of our bank cards and were given a very impressive temporary import sticker to be placed inside the windscreen. We climbed back in the Landy and headed towards the narcotics inspection area where looking severe guys and gals looked ready for a fight. As vehicles drove through, they were selected randomly for inspection, a loud alarm would sound, and the driver with that "ah shit" look on his face would be instructed to pull over, answer questions and allow his vehicle to be searched. Three cars in front of us passed through without a problem but as we approached, "WAAA WAAA WAAA WAAA". I crapped myself. Many Caribbean islands off the coast of Belize and Honduras have become "Narco Islands", where Narcos can go about their dirty business with impunity. They then must transport through Mexico to the largest narcotics market on the planet, the USA.

Mexican drug cartels simply adore fundamentalist Christians and conservatives whose understanding of narcotics use, treatment and market ensure that drugs like cocaine and heroin will probably never be legal, taxable and controlled by the state. If you are addicted to opioid painkillers supplied by Pfizer after let's say, you were wounded fighting for your country in Afghanistan, you are an unfortunate hero, if you are addicted to heroin because you could no longer get a prescription to the drug Pfizer got you hooked on, you are a criminal. And Satan lives in your house. And you should be sent to jail for the rest of your life. But that would just cost the taxpayer money. "I really don't know what we are gonna do with all these gosh darn junkie assholes, Betty".

Colorado became a kazillionaire state when weed was legalised there, and every dollar of revenue earned is a dollar out of the pockets of the narcos. Countries, where all drugs are legal, have reported a significant decrease in drug use and drug-related crimes because the state controls the supply and demand and junkies can be treated. Legalisation does not mean that drugs are morally acceptable, it is simply the greatest tool against the drug lords and organised crime. Do you want less crime? Legalise drugs. Do you want gangbangers off the street? Legalise drugs. You want your neighbour Mexico to stabilise and prosper, to become a market for your goods and not just a source of cheap, sometimes illegal, labour? Legalise drugs. Simple. If it works in Portugal, it will work in the USA.

We were sitting at the front line of the failed War on Drugs with Mexican narco cops searching our vehicle and asking us if we had any drugs with us. It is not a good feeling, having enthusiastic sniffer dogs inspect your vehicle, especially when you are as paranoid as I am, convinced that some narco piece of shit is going to somehow tape 10 kilograms of cocaine or heroin to the Land Rovers chassis before we cross a border. I make it a habit to scrutinise the vehicle inside and out before we cross any borders, and I think that is a bloody good idea. Of course, we were not carrying any illegal substances, and the narco cops let us through.

Mexico is cool, man! We drove on decent roads into Chetumal and filled up with gas at a clean, modern gas station. We then drove around the clean and modern town looking for a Walmart we had seen advertised. We had never been to a Walmart, and we were expecting the worst; plastic food and fat people with two heads. We parked the Landy outside the Walmart and walked through the doors straight into a wall of cold air and the fresh produce department. Oh. My. God. After Central America and, most recently, Belize where you could not buy a fizzy drink in a two-litre bottle, but you could buy a 2 litre of rum, we fell immediately and deeply in love. There, within our grasp, was all the fruit and veg you could wish for, beef, pork, chicken, lamb, yoghurts, hummus, beer, clothing and WD40. What more could an overlander ask for? And the prices were excellent. Just what we needed. This might also be a good time to mention that some Mexican women are beautiful, not that I noticed, Keelan told me. We stocked up on some meat, Corona and Tequila (which I had not had for years after drinking way too many Jose Cuervo shots went I was into clubbing) because we were in Mexico and this how they roll. We had heard of a campsite on the shore of the lagoon and made our way there. The camp was called the Yax Ha resort, and it was paradise. A green lawn dotted with palm trees, a large swimming pool, WIFI, a restaurant and all of this on the shore of a blue lagoon. Just down the road, we found a little restaurant which served a plate of tortillas and a cold coke for $1.00. We knew we were going to be there a few days.

The Land Rovers battery had started giving us trouble and was not holding a charge, we had been push-starting the Landy for the last week. After push starting on a soggy morning lawn, we drove around the city for a while looking for a battery shop. Luisa reprimanded me, "how can the battery be dead, huh, it wasn't like that before?". Her tone was accusatory, and I could imagine her internal monologue, "you did something different and broke the battery, why would you do that, you know we don't have money for a new battery, you just decide that you want a new battery, so you break the old one, I don't understand why you would do that, maybe you have been driving the Landy badly, on purpose, just because you want a new battery, how long are these things supposed to last, what do you mean this one is already four years old, so what, why did you break it, huh?". Her reaction is the same when anything breaks on the Defender, "it wasn't broken before!". In her mind, when she is not looking, I sabotage the vehicle, breaking perfectly good parts, which have lasted 270 000 kilometres and 12 years. I have nothing better to do than cause us expense, one day she will catch me, red-handed, pouring sugar in the fuel tank or sand in the engine, "Aha! I caught you, I knew it, all this time that it was you who was causing things to break. Why would you do that, what is wrong with you?".

I had heard that the Optima batteries were very good and were now manufactured in Mexico. We found a battery store where a technician confirmed that the old battery was in fact "muerto" (dead) and he suggested that we use the Red Top Optima battery at $100.00 US. I said yes, give it, Luisa shot me a hateful look "what is wrong with you?". With the new battery installed we set off back to the camp, I was not happy about the unbudgeted expense, but I was happy that the Landy would now start with a simple turn of the key.

We could have stayed in that camp for a year. Instead, we loaded up on the third day and headed towards Cancun and the Yucatan peninsula in the state of Quintana Roo which, to me, sounds suspiciously Australian. On the way, we stopped in Tulum to visit a Mayan ruin perched on a cliff overlooking a crystal clear blue sea and white sandy beaches. Did the Mayans know that they were living in paradise? Touts and tour guides hustled, and the streets bustled with young tourists having the time of their lives. This entire region is also riddled with Cenotes which are surface connections to subterranean water bodies. The Cenotes are filled with clear freshwater, and there are over 6000 of these beautiful sinkholes in the Yucatan Province alone. "Sinkhole" is not a glamorous word but the Cenotes can be incredible, freshwater Eden's where you might believe, as you float and marvel at the limestone walls and jungle canopy, that you had died and gone to heaven. The Mayans used the Cenotes as a water source and for sacrificial ceremonies.

So far, we had had a wonderful time in Mexico, we felt safe, and most people were friendly and natural. But, you will never forget the first time you see a convoy of Mexican police, commonly known as Federales because as soon as you see them, you know all is not well. The Federales are dressed in black tactical gear, their faces are hidden ominously by masks. They patrol the towns and cities in Ford or Chevy double cab pickup trucks, four men inside, windows closed, two men standing in the back, one handling a 50-calibre machine gun. These men are serious and for a very good reason, in the 11 years that the "War on Drugs" has waged in Mexico, 100 000 people have died, and another 30 000 are missing. The military and police have also been accused of corruption and atrocities, and every time the armed forces cut the head off the Medusa-like drug cartels, another two heads grow. The cartels are barbaric, and the average Mexican pays the price. We had heard many horror stories and, while most of the violent crime exists in this war between the state and the cartels, overlanders and other tourists have been caught in the crossfire in a culture where extreme violence has become the norm.

Harry Devert, a French American biker disappeared near the resort town of Zihuatanejo on the southwestern Pacific coast in January 2014. He had been riding his Kawasaki down to South America and mysteriously vanished shortly after sending a message to his family that he was being escorted by the military to Zihuatanejo. His body was eventually found, dismembered and decomposing in trash bags on a rural road, his motorbike and parcels of narcotics were also found nearby. My theory at the time was that he was suspected of being a US DEA agent, travelling alone. The narcos are absolutely brutal, and the suspicion was justification enough for his murder, in their view, there was a 50/50 chance that he was an agent and those odds were sufficient. This theory was confirmed by a drug gang leader, Andrian Reyes Cadena when he was arrested for Harry's murder in 2015. When the War on Drugs is successful, the unintended result is those gang members who lose their leadership or supply of narcotics turn to other means of income. Being criminals, they know no other way.

In 2016 the bodies of two Australian surfers, Dean Lucas and Adam Coleman, were found incinerated inside their camper van. They had made the mistake of driving at night to Guadalajara, a large city in western Mexico, on the Benito Juarez toll road dubbed "The Highway of Death". They had taken the ferry from the Baja peninsula and were driving through the night to meet a friend when they were, apparently, pulled over by men dressed as highway policemen, robbed and shot before the vehicle was set alight.

We knew that Mexico was dangerous, and we had made the decision, before entering the country, to do as we had when travelling through the equally dangerous Venezuela. We would never travel at night, would surrender any valuables immediately if held at gunpoint, we would remain vigilant of our surroundings and have a plan for dealing with various situations, i.e. hijacking, mugging or corrupt police. The golden rule is to never drive at night and, though we had broken this rule in many countries, we had done so because we had felt safe. The other rule was to be sure to be camped in a safe area by nightfall and to not leave that area until morning, nightclubs and pubs are verboten. We would break one of these golden rules within the first four days.

The drive to Cancun was uneventful. Huge resorts lined the road as we approached, and I read Luisa's mind. We used to be able to afford to stay at some of these resorts, we could have flown in for a week of pampering, buffet meals, air-conditioned rooms, soft beds and sea views. We drove into Cancun just after the sunset. Golden rule number 1 broken. The navigator kept telling us that there was a campsite very close to the highway and we circled the same two intersections for half an hour trying to find the non-existent camp. Eventually, we parked outside a McDonalds and bought the kids each a soft-serve then tried to connect to the WIFI and find another camp. Never knowing where you will spend the next night is, without a doubt, one of the most frustrating and rewarding things about overlanding. McDonald's has a terrible WIFI policy. Every store has a WIFI sign on the door, there is a WIFI network you can connect to, but the only website you can access is the McDonalds website. While we struggled an elderly lady parked her new Honda SUV in front of us, and immediately twenty stray dogs emerged from the shadows, the lady laid out ten bowls, filling five with water and five with pellet dog food. The strays did not fight for the food, instead of sharing peacefully before approaching the kind woman for a petting. I took Jessica over and introduced ourselves to the woman whose name was Angelina. The lady would spend a few hours every night driving around the city, feeding the wretched animals. She worried about who would take care of them when she no longer could. While we were chatting an Australian in a large Ford pickup stopped to admire the Defender. He was friendly and gregarious, a beautiful young Mexican woman, his wife, sat in the passenger seat. The Ozzie was a mariner who owned a fleet of yachts with which he entertained wealthy tourists. He knew of a campsite and invited us to follow him there. He was an interesting guy, high energy and clearly very happy with the lifestyle he enjoyed in Cancun. We followed him through the city for half an hour until he deposited us at the gate of a campsite, we thanked him and said our goodbyes, he gave us his phone number and said he would return the next day to take us to a cricket match.

The campsite was full of large American RV's, essentially buses with air conditioning all the comforts of home. We found a quiet spot next to a small swimming pool and not too far from the bathrooms and set up camp. It had been a long day, and we were eager to sleep, after a quick braai and a few cold beers, of course.

LA LUCHA

The next day the sun cooked, and a dry wind blew. The kids swam in the pool while Luisa and I commandeered the tool shed where we could sit out of the sun and wind and take part in an interview with our new friends from the Centre Steer Podcast, a US-based podcast for Land Rover fans. I don't think they believed us when we told them that we were in the tool shed of a rundown campsite in Cancun, but the WIFI was not strong enough to support video which would have backed up our claim. We spoke for about three hours, answering every question and making an effort to promote We Will Be Free. This was not the first time we had been interviewed, but it was undoubtedly the longest interview we had ever given. Luisa and I both really enjoyed the conversation with the presenters John, Harold and Mark and they invited us to visit them in Pittsburgh.

We left Cancun late and drove only a few hours before deciding to stop for the night. The camp we found was newly built in the middle of dry wood, and the Canadian owner was very excited to have guests. A fire raged nearby and darkened the sky while our host took us on the tour of the facilities. His goal was to establish a luxury campsite far from the hustle of Cancun or any tourist attractions, or shops, or activities. He was very proud of the large and relatively luxurious bathrooms he had built, both of which had large unconcealed entrances and the toilets were so large and the cubicles so small that you could not close the door when sitting. He showed us the pool and told us how long it had taken to build and how he had struggled to get any decent service from the pool company. He then showed us the restaurant/bar and introduced us to his ever-smiling Mexican wife. She was an excellent cook apparently, and as soon as she walked away, he told us how exasperated he was with her family, always asking for money, always wanting to visit, always some drama. He had no other guests, but there was a German overlanders truck which had been left there for storage while the owners returned to Germany for a holiday. He told us about the Germans, the peculiarities of their characters and every last detail about this vehicle and how he would change it because back in Canada blah, blah, blah. I was ready to shove a tuna down the man's throat. As is my custom with motormouths, I walked away after excusing myself, dragging the kids and Luisa with me. The Canadian seemed hurt that we did not want to listen to his monologue, he was clearly the most interesting man. His mom had died leaving him some money, and that is how he came to build this camp. Oh my God, who cares?! After a supervised swim, the Canadian never taking his eyes off us for a minute, I sat down at a table and worked on my laptop, headphones covering my ears even though I was not listening to anything. The Canadian came to me to talk, using hand signals I communicated to him that I had headphones on, I couldn't hear him. He wore the look of a little boy whose favourite toy car had fallen in a deep pond then turned his attention to Luisa who has never learned to treat the loquacious with the contempt they deserve. I could hear him rambling on and on until eventually, a toothless gringo friend arrived with his Mexican family in tow. The family swam while the two gringos drank enthusiastically, ridiculing the Mexicans at every opportunity. Within two hours our host was so drunk he had to go lie down in a depressing little greenhouse built in the corner of the plot. With motormouth out of the way, we lit a fire in our little stainless-steel braai and grilled some chicken. It has become a tradition, if we drive any distance over 100 kilometres, we simply must have a braai and a few cold beers. Similarly, we have another tradition, if we drive any distance less than 100 kilometres we simply have to have a braai and a few cold beers. Unfortunately, due to cash flow problems, we were restricted to a beer each. In the morning we awoke ready to hit the road north. The Canadian sheepishly said good morning, sniffed around our vehicle then returned to his pathetic mint greenhouse where he sat by his window and watched us, possibly thinking that we could not see his bumpy bald head through the tinted glass. I took my toiletry bag and towel and headed to the showers. The shower door would not close, and the showerhead would not spray water. At least the 3m x 3m mirror was almost clean. I put my pants back on and walked around to the women's bathroom and tested the shower.

LA LUCHA

Within 15 seconds the babbling reprobate was standing at the bathroom entrance.

"Hello, hello! Is there a problem? This is the women's bathroom!". His tone was aggressive.

"The men's shower doesn't work, doos!".

"Impossible!". He stormed off to check the water, while I stripped and had a shower in the women's shower, the only females in the camp being my girls and his wife and I am sure he allowed her to wash in the pool occasionally.

"You must have done something wrong!", he shouted, fiddling with the shower rose. "Oh, sometimes the shower heads get blocked with sand", his tone becoming apologetic. "The Mexicans have no idea how to lay a pipe!".

"I don't care!"

"You can come shower here now!"

"Too late, I am almost finished!"

"You can't shower in the women's bathroom!"

"I don't think your other guests will mind!"

He retreated to the mint box.

Luisa and the kids had a shower, and we prepared to leave. Our wonderful host wondering why we would not be staying longer and asking us to be sure to give his camp a good review.

Back on the road, we did our best to avoid the numerous toll roads, the plan was to drive the coast all the way up to a town called Brownsville, Texas. The hope was that we would have an easier time getting into the USA through a quiet, less popular border crossing, our funds were too low to show that we could support ourselves, (I hate reminding you all how broke we were, but that is half this story, how we managed to make it all the way up to Alaska while skint) and we were concerned that a more common border crossing would be more difficult. We had B1/B2 ten-year visas for the USA which we had applied for in South Africa but, those visas are no guarantee that we would be allowed into the Land of the Free and Home of the Brave.

Our gamble was that we would print a few hundred copies of We Will Be Free and sell them at the Overland Expo. Those sales would then give us enough money to print another batch of books which we would then sell at the North West Overland Rally, the profits from which would allow us to print more, etc.

Luisa had negotiated a price with a printer in Phoenix, Arizona. We had to pay the full price up front, and that meant using all our available resources, if we were denied entrance into the USA the entire plan would be dashed against the rocks and Luisa would probably use her secret money to buy a one-way ticket for her and the kids to return home. The printer needed a couple weeks to print the books and needed to be paid now if we were to collect the books on time. We paid.

The Caribbean coast of Mexico is a mix of rich and poor, five-star resorts and RV parks, glistening cities and run-down fishing villages. North of the city of Campeche we drove into a small town called Isla Aguada and had to drive across a sea bridge and return because we had missed the turnoff to an RV resort called Freedom Shores. The infrastructure was past its prime, but we were able to get a site close to the white sand beach where a couple of lovebirds sat, as the sunset, perhaps enjoying some much-needed privacy. They were not teenagers and either deeply in love or in mourning, sitting hip to hip, doting on each other with intense but respectful affection. After dark, a group of youngsters drove their old, facelifted, tinted windowed sports car into a side road, on the other side of a tall fence, and drank beer noisily. Their music was not too loud, and though they could clearly see us, they paid very little attention to us. We changed into our swimming costumes and went for a night swim, then made a fire and settled in for the evening. The camp reminded me of our beloved Brazil, and I could have stayed right there for the rest of my life. The enormity of what lay ahead was a constant weight on both of us adults, failure simply was not an option, and we knew that once we crossed into the USA, the hard work would really begin.

From here we were going to make a long haul for the US border. The Mexican toll gates were really starting to grind our gears, as in Colombia, we were spending more on tolls than we were on fuel. It seemed like there was a toll booth around every corner and each charged an exorbitant 50 pesos, particularly frustrating as the roads were as terrible as Colombian roads. Bear in mind that a litre of diesel was 14 pesos. Highway robbery! There are un-tolled roads, but we needed to avoid any roads where we might become isolated and vulnerable, and we were now killing miles, our goal on the horizon but still 1600 kilometres away.

The Land Rover was running beautifully and had proven to be an incredibly reliable vehicle, regular maintenance being key to any vehicles reliability. The Mexican roads were not as well maintained at all and potholes were merely filled with black tar, the result being that empty potholes were virtually invisible, particularly in the shade. We hit a few, the Landy jolting with a sickening thud with each strike on the rim of an unseen crater. And every time we hit a hole, Luisa would reprimand me. "Didn't you see that?!" "Of course, I did Luisa, but, you know, this driving thing gets boring after a while. You can read books and watch movies on your computer or stare out the window or sleep or make a sandwich. I can only drive. So, I get bored, and I start aiming for the potholes, it keeps both the Landy and I wide awake. It is fun. I do it for fun". After a particularly hard knock, the front end of the Landy began to wobble slightly, I stopped to look for damage, hoping that the rim had not been bent. All seemed well, I assumed that the problem must be either a wheel bearing or a swivel bearing and made a mental note to check both the next time we stopped.

It was hot in May, and occasional thunderstorms brought welcome relief. Passing through Tampico in the rain we were delighted by the beauty of the colourful seaside city and the massive suspension bridge. Everything was at it should be, until the men in black with the 50 calibre machine guns rolled by. The sight of the Federales always made me feel uncomfortable.

We were searching for a Walmart, Luisa convinced that she had had enough chicken for a while and needed some ribs. The Landy was too tall to fit inside the Walmart car park and as we were stopped in the road, hazard lights flashing, asking a water delivery man where we could find the large or delivery vehicle parking, blue lights flashed behind us, and a siren wailed. The police moved us to the side of the road. A tall, thin policeman, whose father was possibly a visiting gringo, and a short policeman so fat that when he climbed out of the cruiser, his stomach was on the pavement a full minute before his feet were. If you had read our first books, you would know how we feel about fat cops – the fatter the cop, the more corrupt. We knew exactly what was coming here on the side street.

"Infracción, licencia por favor", ("Infraction, license please"), a gold ringed hand rested on the Land Rovers window frame, palm up.
"Sorry, no Español", ("sorry, no Spanish").
"Infracción, tu, tu licencia!", A thick, hairy finger points at the road a few times then points at me.
"Sorry", I say. I then hand him my driver's licence with a questioning look.
"License?" I ask.

The cop takes the license and looks at it for a while.
"Sud Africa?"
"Yes, yes".
"Multa". A fine.
"What is moota", I ask innocently. The children look at the policeman, Jessica, with big innocent blue eyes and Keelan with concern.

LA LUCHA

"Multa, Multa!". The policeman repeats the word loudly because volume increases comprehension.

"No, I don't know. Do you know moota Luisa?". Luisa had no idea.

This charade continued for a few minutes, the police at first growing aggravated and then finding humour in the situation. The policeman holding my license rested his hand on the window again, and I took the opportunity to slip the laminated card from between his fingers. They knew that the game was up, told us to leave and started walking back towards the car.

"Disculpe, yo necesito encontrar aparcamiento para el Land Rover, es demasiado alto. ¿Sabes dónde puedo estacionar?". ("Excuse me, I need to find parking for the Land Rover, it is too tall. Do you know where I can park?").

I drove away before they could answer, jaws on the floor.

That was cheeky, I know, I should have just driven away and quietly accepted the win. Luckily, they did not follow us, and we returned from the shopping experience to find the Land Rover unmolested.

Tampico was to be the last city we would drive through before reaching the USA. The roads narrowed, and the terrain became dry and windswept. After a few hundred kilometres the Defenders wobble would become worse and deteriorated until eventually, it was terrible at any speed, which seemed to rule out wheel bearing failure as when those bearings fail they usually wobble worst at around 100 kph. We stopped in a small village and found a large area where we could work on the Landy. The wobble had become so severe that it felt like the left front wheel was about to fall off. I jacked up the wheel and tested laterally which would have implicated wheel bearings, diagonally, north and south for wobble which would implicate swivel pin bearings. Nothing. I then checked the shock absorbers and the steering damper; still, there were no visible problems. I then drove while Luisa studied the tyres, back and forth, back and forth. Eventually, Luisa spotted something. "Do that again, side to side. Ah, shit'. The tyre had a huge bulge dead centre of the tread. I must have ruptured the internal belts by intentionally aiming for potholes. Luisa, ever the blamer, immediately informed me that I was an idiot and that we did not have money for a new tyre. I removed the space-saver spare tyre from the bonnet and bolted the large damaged tyre to the bonnet after bolting on the spare. We drove back onto the road, Luisa scolding me continuously. A speed bump attacked us (it was hidden in the shadow of a tree, unmarked) and I hit the brakes causing the vehicle to lurch to the left. Strange. We drove on for a while, the Landy feeling horribly unbalance and braked for a stop sign. Again, the Landy lurched to the left. What the hell? We pulled onto the side of the road outside a house where women, children and old-timers were relaxing on the porch. I had a think and a poke around the brakes but could not think of anything which would cause the lurch other than the fact that the one front tyre was half the width of the other. I jacked up the skinny front tyre and removed it then took a few bricks Keelan had collected and dropped the front axle, slowly, onto the bricks. I then jacked up the rear of the vehicle and removed the wide rear tyre and placed it on the front hub. The skinny tyre was then bolted onto the rear hub. I dropped the rear then jacked up the front, removed the bricks and dropped the front. Back on the road, the lurching disappeared, and we were able to brake safely again. We had bought the BF Goodrich KM2 mud terrain tyres in Colombia back in 2014 in preparation for the Amazon jungle leg of our journey and our completion of the circumnavigation of South America. They were 33-inch tyres, wide and tall and perfect for driving all the terrains we were likely to encounter, and we were likely to encounter mud and sand, deep mud and deep sand and variations of both. They had been excellent, and despite

LA LUCHA

having driven from Colombia through Venezuela, Guyana's, down through Brazil, down to Uruguay and up through Argentina, Bolivia, Peru, Ecuador and back to Colombia then almost to the USA, still had more than 50% tread left and had never had a puncture. I felt very, very sad. Luisa reminded me that we did not have money for a new tyre. She is very helpful.

Our camp that night was to be our last in Mexico, for now. We found a little camp off the road and on the beach, it was a Saturday, and a very stoned, friendly Polish man welcomed us and told us to make ourselves at home. He asked why I was aggravated, and I told him how one of my tyres was fooked. He called over a friend who suggested that tequila might fix the problem, two girls with small bikinis and large sunglasses agreed. I was open to suggestions. Despite repeated efforts, the tequila did not seem to fix the tyre, perhaps we were misusing it. One of our new friends made a phone call, and two men showed up to have a look. Now they were making a fuss, and I would rather drive with one skinny tyre, a pirate's wooden leg than make a fuss.

"No, nothing that size around here, you will have to go to the city, I have a friend going tomorrow, maybe he can take you".

"Thank you, but never mind, I am sure we will be fine".

The skinny spare tyre was roughly the same diameter as the 33-inch tyres, but the problem with running tyres with even slightly different diameters on the same axle is that the tyres will rotate at different speeds which, eventually, could lead to problems with the spider gears within the differential. Of course, when going around corners the tyres rotate at different speeds, and the spider gears are designed to accommodate that movement. I made the decision to drive the remaining distance to the USA by driving in large, overlapping circles. As long as we were turning right, there should not be a problem. Or maybe turning to the left? The tequila had helped me find a solution but was hindering my mathematical reasoning.

The next morning, we left for the border, listening carefully for signs of imminent mechanical failure. We had to cover 700 kilometres in a straight line and, to my eternal dismay, I found that there were no roads built in overlapping circles to help the Landy on its way. How inconsiderate. We pushed on and made very good time. By 3 PM, we found ourselves approaching the border. I stopped the Landy beside the road and did a quick narcotics inspection. Chassis – clear. Engine bay – clear. Load area – clear. We were ready. Luisa had all the paperwork in order, and we had our minds in the right place. We were going to America! Hopefully.

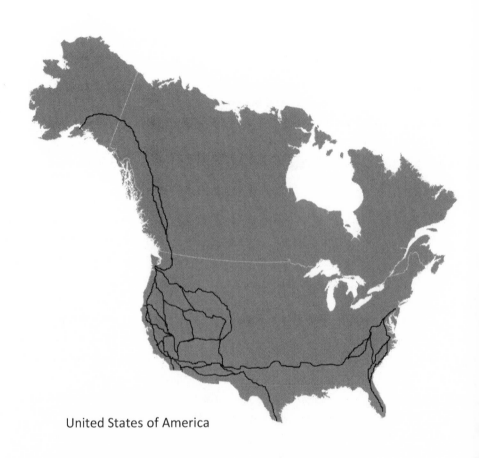

United States of America

4

The United States of America

We approached the Mexican border and immediately drove into the wrong migration lane. We circled back around and drove into the correct lane, parked and headed into the immigration building to check out of beautiful Mexico and cancel the temporary import which would ensure a refund of the deposit we paid to enter the country. With friendly smiles, the Mexicans said goodbye, and we lumped back into the Landy for the drive across the Avenida Alvaro Obregon bridge which stretched across the Rio Grande. Tall razor wire-topped fences, lined the route and multiple cameras watched us closely.

We were now on American soil but not yet in America. We drove down, into a migration lane and stopped next to a migration booth. The official's name was Garcia, I was not sure of his rank. His uniform was dark blue, and he was armed with a multitude of weapons.

"Turn off the engine please, sir".
He asked where we were coming from and stared at us in disbelief when we told him how far we had come. He asked the children to roll down their windows, had a good look at them and looked back at the passports.
"Do you have any cocaine or marijuana or any other narcotic substances", he asked matter of factly.

LA LUCHA

"Of course, not!".
"Please drive your vehicle to the inspection area".

As soon as we parked the Defender, ten smiling, joking border agents exited the US Immigration and Customs Enforcement building and made a beeline for us. Oh boy. The smiles disappeared as they reached the vehicle, and the questions began. Again, we were asked if we were carrying any narcotic substances.

"No? Do you have any firearms?".
"Yes and no, we have a pellet gun, an air rifle".
"You should have told us".
"Yes sir, sorry about that".

The agent asked for the pellet gun, and we handed it over. Carrying the air rifle as if it was a sawn-off shotgun covered in blood and cocaine residue, the agent took the gun into the customs building for a serial number check and whatever else they do with naughty airguns.

We were told to unlock the vehicle and to proceed to the immigration building. I was wary of leaving the vehicle alone, unlocked, and asked if we could wait until they were finished searching before going to immigration. Sure. We were handed a white form and took a seat, watching the border agents sift through our humble belongings. They were very cheerful and friendly with each other and professional when talking to us. After fifteen minutes of searching, the vehicle was declared awesome and clean. They really liked the Defender. What is not to like?

Entering the Immigration building, we were assisted by a young, disinterested man, good looking and clean cut. Other officials came and went, all of them interested in having a look and maybe a few words with these white people who said they were from Africa and who had driven this incredible vehicle up from South America. We were asked where we were going and our answer "Alaska", caused some confusion.

"So, what are you doing here if you are going to Alaska, are you going to work there?".
"No sir, I am a writer and my wife is a photographer and we are travelling the world with our children in our Land Rover. We will be driving to Alaska".
"You are driving from here to Alaska?".

I don't think he believed us. Eventually, we managed to explain that this is how we live, on the road, in the Land Rover, and this is how we had lived for the last few years.
"That's a nice life. How did you get that, right?".
"Ah, you know, hard work and good decisions?".

We each had to pay $6.00 for a tourist card, our photos and fingerprints taken and B1/B2 visas scanned. We were then each issued white tourist cards, valid for six months. This was happening, they were going to let us in! The books had been printed and were waiting for collection in Phoenix. There was one small problem. To ship the Defender to Europe from the US, we needed a temporary import document, but the officials were telling us that they do not issue any kind of paperwork for the vehicle. We asked to speak to the superior, and a sergeant with the physique and moustache of an 1800's bare-knuckle boxer informed us that there was absolutely no way they could issue any kind of papers for the vee-hikkle. With that, we left the office.

We simply could not believe that we were in the USA! Driving on American soil, in Brownsville, Texas. Hell yeah!

LA LUCHA

We drove around Brownsville for a while, amazed at the size of the houses and the width of the roads, the high schools, the cowboy hats. We had heard that the USA was very expensive, so we drove to the first Walmart we could find. Luisa had been warning us for months that in the US we would subsist only on old bread and water and perhaps the occasional slice of cheese.

Everything was dirt cheap! Luisa scooped up a massive pack of ribs for $3.00, some chicken wings $2, a huge fresh baguette $1.00, a readymade salad $1, a case of beers $9, two bottles of wine at $2 each and a bag of charcoal for $2. Apparently, we would be celebrating.

Everything was so new and fresh to our eyes. We had been so deep in Latino culture for so long that, even though Brownsville is 80% Latino, we were absorbing anything American so fast we might suck her right up. In the parking lot, a lady approached us as we loaded our goodies into the Landy.

"You look like you have come a long way". I told her that we were South African, how we had circumnavigated South America almost twice and had just finished the drive up from Panama.
"Well, you can relax now, you are home".

What a profound statement. Why would the USA be "home" for us, clearly, we were foreigners? The lady was Latino, so it could not be because we were white, perhaps it was because we spoke English and looked American. Perhaps by "home", she meant "safe" after the perils we must have braved through the southern Americas. I wish I had asked her to explain, but it seemed rude to ask, the question may have sounded impolite, or arrogant or even ungrateful.

Luisa slapped at the cracked, dirty tablet which had served as our navigation tool since Chile when the old GPS had died and searched the maps she had downloaded. We were looking for a campsite which was not too expensive. The first camp we found resembled a retirement village, but no-one could be found to book us in for the night. The second camp we found was a trailer park where Eminem stalked a girl in shorts so tight you could make out the shape of her coccyx. For some unfathomable reason, Luisa did not want to open the tent there, so we continued our search.

We arrived at a camp after sunset, and the camp manager (and local estate agent) told us to make ourselves at home and asked if we were interested in buying some property. If only we could, we might.

We parked the Landy up on a concrete RV block, opened the tent, took out our little BBQ and started a fire. We were still amazed that we were let in if they had asked for proof of funds we would have been screwed. Our income was low, as were our expenses, but an immigration agent uses a very generic stick to test depth. Perhaps we would have had more problems if we had flown into the country, maybe some land borders experience far less traffic and are therefore less strict. Either way, we were here now, we had no intentions to work illegally or break any laws, we were ready to experience the legend that is the USA.

To be honest, we knew very little about Americans despite having been raised on a diet of American TV and Hollywood movies. If anything, we felt trepidation about entering the US, our opinions being informed of late by the documentaries we had seen. Food Inc., Fahrenheit 911, Supersize Me, Zeitgeist, An Inconvenient Truth, etc. We had met Americans on the road but people travelling are usually very different to people in the safety of their own home countries, and those Americans who travel internationally are apparently a different breed to those who don't. We had been warned about Texas, and we had been told by American friends to get the hell out of the massive, wealthy state as quickly as we could.

LA LUCHA

The ribs were delicious pork, washed down with cold Rolling Rock beer. The kids wasted no time tapping into the high-speed WIFI and Luisa returned from the bathroom with a smile on her face. "You have to go in there". So, I went and was amazed, the bathroom had aircon, and it was super cold in there. I could not remember the last time we had felt air conditioning. In the morning, after a good hot shower, we managed to extract Jessica from the cool bathroom, paid for the camping and set off to explore the town and to buy insurance for the Land Rover, which proved to be an impossible task. The Defender TD5 130 was never sold in the American market and did not exist on any of the insurance companies drop-down lists. I was paranoid that the cops would pull us over and impound the vehicle, if not insured. After a morning driving from insurance office to the insurance office, we gave up the search by land and continued the search by the internet. With no insurance options available, we made the decision to keep on driving and to continue the search for insurance as we went. First, we had to find a solution to our damaged tyre and pulled in at an American Tire where the friendly tire guy said, "no problem, let's have a look" after hearing our story. Luisa had decided to scour the internet for the cause of our "bubble" and discovered that it could well be a factory defect. He measured the remaining thread and calculated that we could get a new tyre of the same size for just under $100. Yes, please. Within half an hour, we had the new tyre on and were ready to roll, after stocking up on a few free bottles of water.

After lunch at McDonald's (when in Rome) and a chat with some friendly locals, we headed out on the wide 69 E, marvelling at the sheer quantity of fast-food restaurants. And cars. Cars everywhere but no traffic jams. The Ford dealership must have had a thousand vehicles parked outside, as did the Chevy, Dodge and Chrysler dealerships. At first, we thought that they must have been depots where cars are stored before being distributed to dealerships, but they were not depots. My mind was struggling to imagine how many cars they must be selling to be able to hold so much stock.

Billboards selling burgers, lawyers and Jesus lined the highway, dead straight and wide. Huge vehicles sped past us, RV's, trucks, pickups with massive load areas, horse trailer and mobile homes. Massive engines powered these beasts up hills and along the straights. Muscle cars were everywhere, Mustangs and Dodges mostly, Luisa liked these and convinced me that I should sell a ton of books and buy her one, black on black. We were on the lookout for the highway police but never saw any police vehicles parked next to the road or under bridges. They were either not there, or they were invisible.

Cruising along at a very slow 120kph, I spotted movement in my left rear mirror (remember the steering wheel is on the right, or correct, side of the vehicle) and a muscle car came blasting past so fast that the heavy Land Rover shuddered. The muscle car was, in fact, a Texas Highway Patrol Dodge Charger and it soon caught up with the vehicle it was after and pulled him to the side of the road. Immediately every driver on the highway moved over into the far-left lane as they passed the police vehicle, an action they would repeat whenever a vehicle was parked on the shoulder. We did not know that we should do the same, and it took a few drivers giving me the WTF look for me to realise that I too should be moving into the left lane when passing.

The 440-kilometre drive to San Antonio took just over four hours, and the rolling hills and beautiful houses were quite unlike anything we had seen before. Luisa directed us off the freeway towards a fuel station where I struggled to put in fuel. I had filled the fuel tank many times with fuel from a jerry can, but I had never fuelled up from a pump, in all the countries we had been to there were people employed to fill your tank. In South Africa, we call them Gas Jockeys and they are the best in the world, some of them. They will whistle and dance and tell jokes as they expertly whiz around your vehicle washing the windows, topping up the cooling system and recommending a pint or two of the best oil for your vehicle. You will then pay them and add a tip, never leaving the comfort of your seat unless you need to buy a pie or take a leak.

We asked a man in a large white SUV how to fill up. "Well, you have to pay first, and then you chose which fuel you want and then put the nozzle in and fill up". He wore a curious smile.

"Where the heck are y'all from that you don't know how to put in fuel?". I told him our story.

"You have gotta be crazy!".

"Only a little bit".

The man welcomed us to America. He told us that he had grown up in San Antonio then moved to San Francisco for about ten years, and now he was back in Texas.

"The US has changed, it is still an amazing country, but it is not what it used to be. There used to be community and people took care of each other, but now…", he paused to think, "it is different, just not the same".

A beautiful blonde woman fuelled up her black Range Rover and listened to us talk. A few people stood and stared at the Defender. We had the look of travellers from away, we were wide-eyed and curious, soaking in everything, our clothes looked different, and we spoke kinda funny.

The man gave me his business card and told me to look him up next time we were in town. We said goodbye, checked that the Landy was closed at the back and that the fuel cap was on before heading towards El Paso. Luisa took us through the city, which was clean and attractive, very masculine. People waved at us as we drove, and others would roll down their windows to chat with us when we stopped at traffic lights. There were Emo kids with tight black clothing and long, sad hair, men with pierced ears, large arms and tattoos, elderly people window shopping, families out for a walk, and teenage girls giggling.

Jessica was over the moon. Almost every radio station played American music, and if we stumbled upon a Spanish language radio station, she would groan and shout "SKIP!". We would scan through the channels each time we lost the signal of the last. Hhhhrrhrhrhrhr, country music, hhhhhrhrhrhrhrhr, Christian music (pop or country, we were fooled a few times), hhhrhrhrhrhhrhrhr, Mexican music (SKIP!), hhhrhrhhrhrhrhrh, rock music, (SKIP! Despite our best efforts she hates rock), hhhhhrhrhrhhrhhrh, a preacher preaching, hrhrhhrhhrhrhrhrhr, pop (STOP! I loooove this song).

Along the highway, we noticed signs saying, "Rest Stop" and decided to pull into one and refresh. Lordy. The rest stop had covered picnic areas with BBQ's, air-conditioned bathrooms, coin-operated vending machines, information centres and murals of cowboys. We contemplated camping there for the night, but there was a sign which clearly stated, "No Overnight Camping", so we pushed on. That is the drawback of having a roof tent as opposed to a sleep-in camper, the tent is conspicuous if we had a sleep-in camper we could sleep just about anywhere.

As the sun began to set, we pulled off the interstate and drove into a town called Junction. I was in need of some rolling tobacco, and we needed a loaf of bread for dinner sandwiches. We drove around the town, curious to get our first glimpse of small-town America. Two churches stood between houses which varied from neat to nasty. There was not much to see.

The convenience store in town was staffed by, what the Americans call a "big" girl and a skinny girl with tattoos covering her arms and hands. The tattoo on her right hand said "James", her son's name. The convenience store was disorganised and dusty, they also did not stock any rolling tobacco or bread without High Fructose Corn Syrup (HFCS). We had been told to avoid the stuff, so we did. The large girl was very apologetic that they did not have what we were looking for and offered to drive us down to the Short Stop, where we would find what we needed. There, I admitted defeat and filled a 52-ounce cup with cold High Fructose Corn Syrup (99c, a 52-oz. bottle of water was $2.50) from a mouldy dispenser machine and bought a loaf of High Fructose Corn Syrup bread. I asked the tall redhead cashier for rolling tobacco, and he responded in a high-pitched voice, "we don't have that kind". A small man with a gigantic purple head and a Superman T-shirt walked in the door and complimented me on the Defender. We left and drove across the bridge to the Chevron gas station which catered for truckers. I asked a man with an extremely large belly if we could park for the night. He looked at me like I was some kind of bug and replied: "well if you have ta, one night". We drove the Landy far from the trucks while watching the children double in size as they slurped the Short Stop pop. Parenting done well. Sitting in the McDonalds trying to get WIFI was too depressing. A well-dressed family sat down to eat, their little daughter begins to cry, "Mommy, I don't want to eat here, this where I ate the food that made my tummy sore and made me sick". Her daddy responds, "Keep quiet child, we are raising you to be grateful". We returned to the Landy, opened the tent and put the kids to bed. Truckers would come and go, and not one of them would return a friendly wave.

In the morning, I crossed the road to take a few photos of Coopers BBQ where two young men worked stoking the outdoor cooker fires and placing large blackened brisket back in the hot boxes. They called these pieces retreads because they were leftover from the day before. The meat looked absolutely delicious. I asked if I could take a photo. The one young man replied, "as long as you don't want me to take my clothes off".

Tip of the Day; stay far away from Junction, Texas.

We left after filling up with fuel and headed back to the I 10 as fast as we could. It was a long, long drive with almost nothing to look at but other vehicles on the road, the occasional farmhouse, rest stop, gas station, cow. Harley Davidson motorcycles seem to be a way of life. It was tornado season, and Luisa was paranoid that we might get caught up in a twister and strewn across Texas. We had been told that if the sky turned green and it began to hail that we should look for cover as that was a sure sign of a twister. Well, the sky turned green, and hail began to fall, but the sheltered shoulder under every single bridge we passed was occupied by an RV, maybe two if the bridge was large. Luisa was not happy, but we pushed on, listening to the radio for emergency updates. A robotic voice would interrupt Jessica's pop song;

"This is a severe weather warning for Jackson County. High winds, hail and rain may be experienced, be sure to find safe shelter".

The robot did not help Luisa to relax at all, and she shrieked with every flash of lighting or BANG of thunder. In heavy storms the Defender will leak from the top of the windows and Jessica will always get wet while Keelan tries to move all the crap off the seat and soak up the water with whatever we have handy. That day was no exception, but the storm did not last very long, and we made very good time, reaching El Paso before 5 pm. We drove through the city, stopping only to put in fuel and continued into New Mexico before stopping in a small, neat town called Deming.

We had read that it was possible to camp overnight in Walmart parking lots and made the decision to save the $25.00 we would have paid for camping at the run down and unwelcoming Roadrunner RV park. The Walmart parking lot was full of RV's, campers and "fifth wheels" (large mobile homes which were towed by equally large pickup trucks). We shopped for some groceries and did some people watching. We had found the infamous "people of Walmart". 50% of the shoppers were ordinary-looking people, thin and healthy, normally dressed and friendly. The other 50% were grotesque, loud, poorly dressed, large and either super friendly or coldly dismissive and 50% of these people were Walmart employees. Many of the latter 50% overflowed the mobility scooters they rode. These were the same people who were so morbidly obese that they were issued handicapped signs and were allowed to park in handicap zones. Our friendly cashier was a woman with a second chin the size of my beer belly and a wild mane of black hair. She asked where we were from. "South Africa". A puzzled look on her face.

"Oh, thought you were from England or Australia".

Back in the parking lot, we fed the children a ready cooked chicken with a salad and a French loaf. This was to become our go-to meal as we drove across the USA. Already we had covered 1650 kilometres in just two days. The Landy was running like a slow Swiss watch, and we were well on track to reach Flagstaff by the 17th May, in time for the Overland Expo where the North American debut of our book was bound to be a stellar success.

We found a quiet spot in the parking lot and opened the roof tent. It was here that I would take one of our most popular photos, the Landy, roof tent open, and the Walmart logo in the background. While I was busy with the tent, a car pulled up, and the occupants had a short conversation with Luisa. "Where Y'all from?".

"Hello, we are from South Africa".

"Uhuh. Are y'all handing out religious books or something?".

"Uh, no, we aren't religious…" (perhaps "nuts" is not the correct word), "types".

"Uhuh, well Y'all have a good night. Nice jeep".

Keelan and I went back into the shop to have a pee while Luisa and Jessica lay in the tent, relieved to be able to lie down after a very long day sitting in a cramped position. When we returned, Luisa looked a little freaked out. "What's wrong?".

"So, while you were inside, this car pulled up next to the Landy and this old lady winds down the window, looks at the vehicle for a while then said either "maggots" or "faggots", I don't know which one is worse".

Welcome to New Mexico. I was upset that someone would insult my family like that and was naturally concerned that this might be the beginning of something more sinister, that perhaps we would not be safely parked outside the 24-hour convenience store.

With nothing to do, we lay in the tent, relaxed and watched people come and go. One of the Walmart employees walked towards the only vehicle parked near us, a relatively new Ford Mustang. He got in and drove away. Everywhere we had ever been, only the rich could afford to drive a Mustang! A retired couple walked back to their large, old RV hand in hand. A security guard made a loop past us every ten minutes, and the parking lot emptied slowly but surely.

That morning we awoke to blue skies and birdsong. After a quick shopping trip to stock up on road food, we headed out towards Phoenix, Arizona. I found a radio station which played classic rock, and we made our way through the desert, driving parallel to train tracks where trains, 100 cargo carriages long shunted goods across the country. This was the America I had come to experience. This was the America of the rebel, the cowboy, the biker and the long-distance trucker. Rounding a large corner, we came upon a border patrol checkpoint. The agent, dressed in green fatigues, gave us a quizzical smile and called the other agents over. They listened to our story, "we explored Southernly and East Africa up to the Serengeti, then circumnavigated South America, almost twice, and then took a ferry from Colombia to Panama, then drove up through Central America to Texas and now we are here, heading to Alaska". "Wow, ok, off you go, drive safe". Nice guys.

On the outskirts of Phoenix, we drove through the Gila River Indian Reservation, where we saw real poverty for the first time since entering the USA. We had only been in the country a few days, but it felt like we had been here much longer. I think it was that never-ending drive through Texas which had dulled our senses. The outskirts of Phoenix reminded me of the neighbourhoods in the movie E.T (the movie was filmed in the San Fernando Valley which has a similar arid climate), and I was jealous that people get to live in those houses and I sleep in a tent every night. Then I reminded myself that I used to live in a house just like those behemoths on a hill, and I had chosen to sleep in a tent every night instead.

On we rolled, into the city. Man, Americans drive fast! We made our way through the city, Luisa shouting directions, Keelan keeping an eye on traffic, Jessica sleeping as always, and I try not to miss my turn off or get in the way of a fast-moving eighteen-wheeler. The highway bridges and retaining walls were decorated with natural and cultural motifs, eagles, Mexicans, Native Americans, cowboys, horses, cacti. The next day we would be collecting the books from the printers in downtown Phoenix, and Luisa had found a campsite as close to the printers as possible, which turned out to be a 30-kilometre drive. The campsite, called The Covered Wagon, was located in a neighbourhood just off the Black Canyon Highway 17, the same highway we would take to reach Flagstaff. The neighbourhood was rough by American standards but wealthy by others. The RV camp did not have any walls or a fence which made us feel safe, strangely.

Before arriving in the USA, we had had a good talk with the kids. They were instructed to be extremely careful to not be either injured or to fall ill, we would never be able to afford US medical treatment or even medicine. I was sitting beside the Landy sorting through our gear, something we do at least once, if not twice a month, and felt a pain in my stomach, near my navel. "Ah, good, I must have done some exercise which worked the stomach muscles". But then I had a think. I had been sitting on my ever-expanding ass for the last three days, doing nothing but driving. I stood up and stuck a finger in my navel. Ouch! I felt around a bit more and came across a soft lump above the belly button. "Ah, shit". Luisa had a feel, and we agreed that it was a hernia. How on earth did I get that right? Perhaps the constant driving and lack of exercise had caught up with me. My dad had had a hernia, and it had swelled to the size of a tennis ball and made his stomach look like a large boob. Why now? If this had happened in Brazil, they would have sorted me out in a day. A sexy nurse would have been kind to me, and they would not have charged me a cent. Hernia operations in the USA can cost up to $11,000, and we definitely did not have travel insurance which would cover that expense. It would be cheaper to fly back to South Africa and hire a hospital for a day or two. Bugger! Luisa reprimanded me. Why on earth would I go and get a hernia, knowing full well that we all had instructions to stay happy and healthy. I would have to invest in a kidney belt, watch what I lifted and keep an eye on the rip. Keelan and Jessica were both instructed to stop punching me in the stomach, Luisa to stop punching me in the face.

In the morning, we drove to the printers to collect the 200 books we had spent the majority of our remaining savings on. The printers were lovely, friendly people who took a deep interest in our journey. The printing staff stopped their work to come and meet us, and we answered the usual questions and even a few unusual questions. We could not wait to get our hands on the books and eventually we were presented with eight boxes. I opened one of the boxes, and there they were, We Will Be Free! To see the book printed and bound, that beautiful cover, the font the correct size and the photos looking good was both a relief and a proud accomplishment. I am very proud of that work which took two years and endless edits to finally be ready for printing. I had written the bulk on the balcony of an almost empty house on the island of Isla Margarita, a Venezuelan territory. The remainder was written on the balcony of a little cottage nestled between coffee fields in Brazil, and the final editing and ending were composed in the dining room of a mountain cottage on the road through the Ecuadorian Andes to Peru.

Originally the first third of the book had been an account of my tumultuous childhood in South Africa, but that was side-lined when I realised that that was probably not the story people wanted to read, not yet anyway. Writing that omitted first third had been important though – I had been able to look

LA LUCHA

back at my life from a different angle, and it was the therapy I needed to make peace with the past and embrace the future. I had come to terms with my father's desertion, my childhood of loneliness, isolation and confusion, my teen years of rebellion, excess, self-abuse, depression and self-destruction and the events of early adulthood which made a man of me.

The book looked fantastic, and I was sure that the cover alone would shift the majority of the units we had printed. I had photographed the Land Rover on our first day in Bolivia, in the high-altitude city of Tupiza. We had had to jump through fiery hoops to finally get the Bolivian visas only for me to be denied entry into the country on my British passport (I had wanted to exit Argentina on my South African passport and enter Bolivia with the British passport in order to avoid problems when entering the USA with the British passport, much later in our journey). We had parked the Defender outside an ancient building which had been converted into a restaurant. Luisa ran off to find an internet café and the kids, and I waited for our food to be cooked. I looked out the window and was mesmerised by what I saw. The Land Rover was framed by the weathered, solid wood doors, a couple of pyramid-shaped lamps, resembling ancient bird cages, hung either side of the doorway. The streets were cobbled, and the building behind on the other side of the road wore a band of blue paint, an anonymous flag within the blue band, a symbol of independence. The unlit birdcage lamps represented captivity, the life we had left behind, the Defender looked purposeful and inviting, she was the key to our freedom, the band of blue represented water, the ocean the freedom of wide-open skies. I had developed the photograph with a dark border, rendering the room we are in dark and foreboding, the Defender is there, standing proud and rugged, waiting and ready to help you escape. You, Will Be Free!

Here is some trivia for you WWBF fans. In the cover photo you can clearly see the number 333 on the driver's door, that number was my participation

98

number for the Brazilian Land Rover meeting held in a town called Sao Lourenco, near Sao Paulo in 2014. Next to the number is what appears to be a face, that is the face of Nelson Mandela, the greatest statesman in the history of Africa and a symbol of South African goodwill, a statement of our solidarity. Mandela, or Madiba as we affectionately called him, dedicated his life to the freedom of his people (that photo would cause some trouble for us at a border crossing later the next year). On the side of the bonnet are the words Legion Land Rover, this is the website of our dear friends the Colombian Land Rover club. The faded flag (or emblem) high on the wall in the background is called La Wiphala, and it represents the native people of the Andes from Colombia in the north to Chile in the far south. The flag also represented the Tupac Kateri Guerrilla Army, a Maoist movement who were the direct descendants of revolutionaries trained by Che Guevara, the communist overlander (we are not communists, but we are certainly rebels). The geometry of the photo helps to portray a sense of discomfort, of unsettlement. Only the vehicle, the title and my name are truly square. I chose this shot in an urban setting for the cover as it is obvious to all that we have travelled great distances and through incredible landscapes to get to this place. It is also the culture of each country we tour which interests us as much, and sometimes more than the geography.

I hoped only that the contents of the book would do justice to the promise of the cover. Parked outside the printer's warehouse in stifling hot Phoenix, I gave Keelan a copy of the book, and he proudly began to read. Holding the book in my hands gave me a certain peace of mind. Of all the things I had done in my life, this book was something tangible, something that no-one could ever take from me. At the very least, it documented our journey from the normality of suburban existence to shades of glory and self-discovery through adventure. I believed the book was exceptional and, over the next two years, thousands of people read the book, and many agree with me, particularly if the sales and online reviews are anything to go by. It was my first book, and it was self-published, it could very easily have been complete crap! (Search "overlanding" on Amazon, We Will Be Free is the first article to appear).

We loaded the books into the rear of the Landy and crammed two boxes between the kids and set off for Flagstaff. The desert heat was oppressive, but soon we found ourselves climbing up out of the Sonora desert with an altitude of 331m, and as we did, the air began to cool. Flagstaff, at an elevation of 2,106m, was positively chilly. The 230-kilometre drive took us about four hours, and we were amazed by the change in the climate and vegetation. From the subtropical desert cacti, we rose up to the bush and emerged in a pristine pine forest. Flagstaff is where we will live one day when Luisa finally convinces me to move to America. The town is well kept and beautiful, in the shadow of the Mount Elden. The houses masculine and modern, built of wood and painted in shades of grey, dark blue and khaki. The roads are perfectly clean, the people friendly and healthy, Alice Cooper has a show on the local radio station. Fires threaten the pine forests during the summer months, and in the winter the area is covered by a blanket of snow. We booked into the Flagstaff KOA (Campsites of America) and prepared ourselves and the vehicle for the Overland Expo event on which we had pinned great expectations.

The Expo was the reason that we had driven up from Panama so quickly. We had to put our best foot forward but I, unfortunately, had only broken shoes which I had worn for the last three years. Yes, we live a life of glamour. Walmart sold me some car shampoo and a pair of blue slip-on shoes. We washed the Land Rover and prepared ourselves and the kids, we would have to work together as a team, Luisa and I selling books and Keelan and Jessica helping out with the camp chores and being the perfect example of well educated, well-raised little angels.

A few overland vehicles shared the camp with us, and we met Emily and Jon, a couple from North Carolina and Frederick and Denise. Jon was a veteran who ran a Land Rover workshop, and Frederick was a retired US ambassador who had spent his life travelling the world in his private capacity and as a civil servant. Both had high vehicles and were an excellent source of information. We asked them what to expect from the expo, and they were able to give us an idea of the layout and what kind of people we were likely to meet. As prepared as we could be, we left on the morning of the first day of the event, stopping first to stock up on quick prepare meals and water. We were nervous and excited, this was it, our moment to turn the tables on our dire financial situation and to reinvent ourselves. Surely the good people of the overlanding community would know a good story when they see one and companies would be banging on the tent to shower us with sponsorship contracts and gear. The press would not be able to get enough of us, and I had prepared a stock of witty and interesting answers to the flood of questions.

We arrived at the event held in a floodplain next to Mormon Lake. The area was buzzing with overland vehicles of every shape and size, motorbikes, vans, trucks. Luisa had organised with the organisers that we would receive a free pass and camping as we were international overlanders, on the road. We were grateful for the complimentary tickets as there was no way we could afford the entrance and camping fees. I parked the Defender,, which was turning even more heads than usual, and we approached the check-in desk. I was struggling to recognise the faces of people who I might have been friends with on Facebook and immediately recognised the Motorhead moustache worn by an amiable man who calls himself, Anthony. After shooting the breeze for a while, he pointed us in the direction of the exhibitor queue where a woman dressed by Mussolini's tailor waited to admonish us. The organiser could not find our information in the box of welcome packs. Were we listed under A2A, or as Luisa Bell or Graeme Bell?

LA LUCHA

We did not know, we had not organised their system. The lady bristled with impatience, I was concerned that the leopard print scarf might be too tight or that the ivory-handled knife, which sat on her hip, held not only by an exquisite belt but also a shoulder strap, might be thrust into our bothersome bellies by angry, manicured hands. Eventually, our information was found, and we were relieved, almost apologetic. We had been allocated a campsite in the exhibitor area, along with the other travellers and we drove towards the area only to be directed by a confused moustache into the general camping area. This would not do. We had Keelan run back down the road and stop the one-way traffic so that we could backtrack and show the moustache the error. He then directed us to the correct area where we found ourselves hidden from the exhibitor area by a wall of Unimog's. Luisa fussed while I set about finding a level hole to park in and to open the tent and set up camp. I am here people, let's go!

The event itself had not yet begun, but there were plenty of people wandering around looking at the various vehicles and chatting with each other. Some groups were cliquey and not too interested in socialising, some groups were there to mingle and a few, like us, had something to sell. That first night was quiet, initially. We sold a few books to people who knew us from the internet, and we befriended a Spanish couple, Anna and Pablo, a couple of Canadians, Jean Francois and Yan, Gregory from San Francisco, Fernando a fire chief from Salt Lake City, a retired US Army intelligence colonel going by the name of Bob and a group of veterans, Team Overland, who employed overlanding to help other veterans deal with the damage which war had inflicted on them. We were not permitted to make a fire, so we kept warm that cool spring evening by drinking beers. Somebody produced a bottle of whiskey, someone, called Bryon, had a beer sponsor. Someone had a bottle of rum from Venezuela, and together we laughed and joked until way past my two beers, 10 o'clock curfew. This group would become a group which met every night to stomp feet, drink, joke and tell stories.

It began to rain, the rain turned to hail, the hail turned into sleet, and the sleet turned into snow. Progressively the soil, trampled by boots and large off-road tyres, softened and became mud. For the next two days, it sleeted and snowed. Occasionally the sun made an appearance but not long enough to dry the soggy ground of the floodplain. Regardless, we persevered and were fortunate that we had a relatively large social media following. We were recognisable, once people ventured past the Berlin wall (the Unimog's) and found us splodging around, telling our story to anyone who would listen and applying sales tactics, soft and hard, in an attempt to move 200 books at $20 each. Not only did we need the money, but we also needed to get rid of the books! What would we do with all these large, heavy boxes? We really did not have anywhere to store them as we made our way up to Alaska, once leaving Flagstaff. If we managed to sell all 200 at full price we would have earned $4000 less the $600 we paid for the books to be printed. We would then print another 200 books and would sell those through Amazon, keeping a few with us to sell as we travelled.

In the general campsite, vehicles were bogged up to their axles in mud as they tried to leave the event, the conditions being too uncomfortable for some. I felt a huge pang of sympathy for the organisers. They had no control over the weather and mobilized their staff and volunteers to try and improve the conditions as best they could, spreading straw on the main walkways and roads, trying to drain the wetter areas and keep all parties happy, particularly the companies which had paid large sums to be able to promote their products. People were demanding refunds, the portable toilets became a sludge, the sleet and snow continued to fall, and we took refuge inside the roof tent annex (the large zip on tent) and battled to make food and cups of tea with the tank of Butane gas we had carried since Argentina (we had been unable to find any gas supplier who could refill our old South African tank. We could also not find a replacement tank which would fit in the tank frame we had permanently attached to the back of the Defender). Bob, the colonel, lent us a hiking cooker he had as a backup in his truck and we were able to at least have something warm to eat. The kids were fantastic troopers as always, and we did the best we could to keep them entertained while we dealt with the cold and wet. At night, while the kids dozed in the roof tent, Luisa and I would relax with our new friends. Matthew and Jared, the veterans from Team Overland, had made a heater from an old washing machine drum and a gas tank, it was the most popular place to hang out at what had been renamed "Snowverland Expo".

We discovered something particularly interesting about ourselves and Americans in those few days. We, as South Africans, are not politically correct. At all. The Americans are the polar opposite. Gregory, from San Francisco, had the Scottish surname McDonald and has Pilipino roots, therefore has Asian features. Sometimes after a shared bottle of whiskey, I called someone "my china". My china is cockney slang popular with Durban surfers, don't ask why I do not know. Plate rhymes with a mate, so in cockney, a mate is a china plate, which eventually, at least in the South African context, became just "China". Howzit my china! It has absolutely nothing to do with ethnicity, but Gregory liked it and started calling me china and vice versa. By the end of the night, the cold, wet, muddy camp area was reverberating to the sounds of "my china!" being shouted every five minutes.

The next morning, I am doing the walk of shame through the mud, hung over and barefoot, in my underpants, seeking the desperate relief only a muddy porta potty can provide. I spot Gregory standing around the Team Overland heater with a bunch of people I have never seen before. "My china!", I shout triumphantly. "Oh, hi, Graeme". All his new, sober friends look at me with shocked indignation. An evil smile plays on Gregory's lips. What an arsehole! "South African".

Our sharp South African sense of humour, shot shotgun shells through the polite veil of American political correctness. We blasted each other and our new friends with hilarious insults and comebacks. This is something we have learned, as South Africans, as part of a new Rainbow nation. Have a look at the early works of Trevor Noah or read the satirical and very funny, "South African guide to being a racist". They knock you on the funny bone with a ten-pound hammer. Why? Because if we take ourselves, our culture and that of others too seriously, we run the risk of becoming polarised, again. Back home, a braai with a group of good friends of many races will give each other such a hard time, based mostly on stereotypes, that an outsider might be stunned. But, it is in our differences that we find common ground. It might even be a Southern Hemisphere "thing". (A few weeks later again drinking whisky, an Ozzie and I had a playful go at each other, insulting each other beautifully, relaxed. The Americans thought we were about to start swinging fists at each. Nah mate, we were just bonding. (I still love that little bastard). If an American tries to swing a bat in the arena of friendly insults, he tends to insult. We can't all be amicably unpleasant.

On the fourth day, the Sunday, as the last remaining exhibitors and campers began to pack, the sun decided to make an appearance. Too much too late, you mean, yellow orb. Despite the terrible weather we had managed to sell forty books which was not the home run 200 we had been hoping for, but it was enough for us to be able to continue heading north. We had heard of a rally being run in Washington state, the Northwest Overland Rally, and we were hoping that the weather gods would smile on us and that we would be able to sell the remaining books. I had given ten books to high profile media and industry people in the hope that they would see our worth and tell their readers or followers about us. Many people we met at the expo were amazed by our journey, but I had the profound feeling that we were "selling" ourselves incorrectly, we were not professional enough, particularly by American standards. We still had a lot to learn, and if you are going to learn the business, an American is a man to teach you.

The cold wind had sucked the moisture from our bodies and the hot, high altitude sun-crisped us on that last day. Luisa resembled an elderly Bolivian woman as she hates the feeling of sunblock and it was decided that we would return to Flagstaff, to the pleasant KOA camp where we could have a braai, chill and clean up. Little Ceasers was our first stop, and we happily paid cash for a few extra cheese, bacon crust pizzas. The kid behind the counter gave us a box of free crispy garlic bread, perhaps out of pity or more likely because we were funny, smelled bad and were obviously starving. Already America was becoming normal to us. We did not feel like strangers in a strange land but felt, almost, at home. There were still surprises though. One example is the sheer quantity and variety of beer which can be bought at a nondescript gas station. Banks of fridges cooling thousands of brands – Indian Pale Ales (IPA's), double IPA's, lager, pilsner, stout. I was happy sucking on a Coors light but soon found new brands to enjoy. Often, we would buy whichever beer was on special and soon developed a liking for certain brews.

With bellies full of pizza, Luisa routed us to the nearest QFC supermarket where we bought huge, delicious cherries, racks of rib, some bread and a salad. By now we had realised that buying bulk was infinitely cheaper than not and Luisa has never met a bulk buy special she could resist. We applied for a QFC members card with which we could earn points, which could be redeemed for cheaper fuel at the QFC gas station. If we shopped at QFC often enough, we could buy diesel at less than a dollar per gallon (3.7 litres).

Our new friend Gregory accompanied us to the KOA, and we cheerfully approached the check-in counter. Luisa, burned purple and dried like a raisin, was the butt of my lame jokes. "Ha, you get Indians, and you get Red Indians, you are a Red Indian". Ha-ha. No. Not funny? The cashier looked apologetically at a Native American who was standing in the queue, then summoned up her most disdainful look for me. "Sir, here we don't say that". Are you kidding? I grew up playing cowboys and Indians. All the comic books I read spoke of red Indians, Louis Lamour dammit! Ah, shit. "Oh, sorry, was I appropriate". I was just making this worse for myself, Gregory stepped away, and navel gazed a flask, Luisa shook her head. The cashier also shook her head, motivating her face jewellery to join in the admonishing sway. "We just don't". We had a lot to learn. I waited outside for the Native American lady to leave and apologised. "I am so sorry, I am from South Africa, I did not know that I was being offensive". "I don't care", the lady said as she passed. And the way she said it was so void of interest, I really believed that she did not care, at all. I did not feel better but had a good talking to myself, we needed to be more PC. Apparently calling a gluten intolerant person a wheatard (wheat retard) is also not acceptable, neither is Keelan's playful nickname Todd Schmidt (Todd sounds like tard which is short for retard and Schmidt which is a politer version of shit as in, "shit for brains"). Jessica's nickname Slow White (because she moves at a snail's pace and is a princess) is equally inappropriate. You could not say a black man is a black man, he is either an African American or "the gentleman wearing a blue shirt", which I grew to understand once I knew more about the racial tensions in America.

I must be friendly and polite and considerate. Write that on the board one hundred times, you mean little man.

Gregory skilfully built a bivouac near the fire while I watched and drank beer to soothe my throbbing liver. Bob stopped by to say hello, and we grilled the ribs slowly before coating them with thick layers of Leroy's Sweet BBQ sauce. A young Australian policeman and his bride joined the conversation, the Americans not able to believe that he had colleagues on the force who had twenty years under the belt but had never drawn their guns in the line of duty. "It's just not worth all the paperwork, mate". He worked down south where the majority of problems they had were either with massive, aggressive Maoris from New Zealand or the Aborigines, who the locals called "blackfellas". Careful. I wanted to warn the fit, muscular young man, who had almost qualified to be a fighter pilot but who had dropped out after a Sheila shattered his heart, that here they would call them "the fella in the red shirt". There is a community in South Africa, a race unto themselves, who are known as Coloureds, this name being used as a bureaucratic classification to this day and a name of which the Coloured community is very proud of. When telling people we met, about the Cape Coloureds, I had to add this quid pro quo which soon became tiresome. We had to be careful that people who did not know us would perceive us as being racist, even if we did publicly call our new Asian American friend "my china". Even now, as I write this, I wonder if I should write about race and if you are reading this it is because I have decided that our innocence is absolute. Dammit, I had a Coloured friend who called me Pinky.

In the morning Greg packed his matt black Nissan and invited us to visit him in San Francisco, we hugged, took photos of each other and together, then said a fond farewell to Bob the Colonel and headed out of town towards the Grand Canyon.

Anxiety is not a word often associated with overlanding, but, if you are adventurous enough to test the limit of your courage, you will experience your fair share of angst. I am not merely referring to the pre-departure turmoil (particularly the intercontinental "let's sell it all and see what happens" journey) but more specifically the crap you will get yourself into when you are tight-fisted and reluctant to admit your sporadic but persistent fear of the dark.

And it is exactly that penny pinching long-term overlander mentality which tends to get us into the most precarious (or potentially precarious) positions. The eternal search for free camping can often yield the most wonderful results but will often also lead to the most terrifying evenings, particularly if you, like me, share an overactive imagination with an easily petrified spouse. Let me explain. When I was eight or nine years old, my older brother and his teenage friends thought it would be great fun to force me to watch a horror movie, their choice was a 1981 production called, The Burning and it has haunted me for years. "A former summer camp caretaker, horribly burned from a prank gone wrong, lurks around an upstate New York summer camp bent on killing the teenagers responsible for his disfigurement". I would never be the same, even as a large boned, relatively courageous and mildly superstitious man, my inner child is sometimes totally beyond control. One evening, on a farm back home in South Africa, I stepped outside to turn off the sprinkler. We had just watched the movie, Signs and the faucet was a good distance from the farmhouse, next to a corn field. As I reached down to close the faucet, the corn shuddered in the breeze. I turned stiffly and briskly headed back to the house. A breeze bristled again through the cornfield, and inner child freaked out. Don't run, don't run, don't run! I ran, convinced that the aliens were on my heels. The faster I ran, the more frightened I became. I reached the door, grabbed the handle and turned it, ready to slam the door behind me and walk nonchalantly back into the living room. The door was locked! Luisa stood behind it laughing a hysterical cackle, while I begged bravely to be let inside. I was 33 years old.

Shortly after foolishly watching, The Blair Witch Project an opportunity for revenge presented itself. Beside a grey forest, a quarter mile from the house, a large gate controlled access to the farm. While I waited in the Land Rover, Luisa (who was also traumatised by her older brothers) would unlock and open the gate, I would drive through while she hurriedly closed and lock the gate, before quick marching back to the truck, her inner child barely controlled. We returned from work one pitch black night, me innocently chatting about the scariest movies I had ever seen, priming her imagination for the coming retribution. At the gate, she asked me to get out and open up, I told her not to be silly. She reluctantly stepped out and quickly opened the gate. I drove through and did not stop, a chorus of petrified, furious screams and running feet following me up the driveway. She was 32 years old.

Overlanding Africa and South America, our fears were mostly limited to wild animals, thieves and the ubiquitous Brazilian werewolf, or Lobisomem, which we were fortunate to encounter only twice. In the USA, our imaginations were ignited by the very landscape where we free camped, the same landscape which provided the setting for a thousand horror movies. Our first-night free camping in the USA was just off the south rim of the Grand Canyon. A kind Native American ranger had told us about an area of BLM (Bureau of Land Management) land just outside the national park where we could escape the crowds and camp for free, "but, be careful, there is no-one else out there". "What do you mean?" "Oh, nothing, I am sure you will be just fine". We followed her directions and were surprised to find a well-used site with a fire pit, a bench and a distant long drop toilet next to an empty ranger's station. Success. While all the other camper tourists huddled together, breathing each other's fumes while parked on an expensive slab of concrete, we were having a true adventure. With the roof tent open and the kids scavenging firewood, we prepared for a night of grilled meat and a few cold beers. Just before dusk, a pickup with tinted windows drove rapidly towards us on the dirt road then stopped suddenly a hundred feet from us. The pickup remained stationary for a few minutes, the blackened windows staring at us, unblinking. Suddenly the vehicle accelerated and disappeared. The ranger whispered in my ear, "be careful, there is no-one else out there". Ten minutes later, the pick-up returned and regarded us once more from another angle for an equally sinister period of time before racing off back the way it had originally come. Inner children stirred, "I am sure you will be just fine".

No traffic passed us for the few hours it took for the sun to set, the fire to dwindle and imagination to create monsters in the blackness beyond the dull light of the fire. Sweeping the flashlight through the darkness only served to remind us how alone and exposed we were. I armed myself. Machete, Leatherman, hunting knife, pepper spray, a stout piece of wood, Dutch courage. As the man of the tent it is my job to stay calm, remain rational and defend. If I show any fear, Luisa's fear will run in circles screaming, stripped of all pretence and begging to get the hell outta there. The dark closed in around us, menacing and thick. We chatted for a while, Luisa sporadically surveying the surrounding forest with the Maglite. "Did you see that?" "I saw eyes". To acknowledge fear is to encourage it. "You are imagining things, love". A patronising tone. Were those eyes, did she just see eyes, what would have eyes out here, is this mad killer bear country, do human eyes reflect torchlight? "Be cool honey bunny, be cool". Listening to Credence did not do much to relax me, neither did Bob Dylan, Bob Marley, a few more beers or The Doors. "Let's go to bed". Climbing the ladders to the tent, a beast of the night ripped at my feet, I felt the missed strike brush on my ankles. WTF, WTF, WTF? Luisa, her panic activated by my own, flew up the ladders into the tent, the last one in is eaten. Ha-ha-ha-ha-ha-ha. Nervous laughter. We lay there, protected by thick South African canvas and the gentle purr of brave, sleeping children, our eyes wide open. We were both 39 years old.

Nothing ripped at the tent, nothing prowled outside except our persistent imagination. Eventually, I gave in to sleep, safe in the knowledge that Luisa would probably not sleep at all, her rampaging paranoia ever vigilant, her pricked ears analysing every breath of the wind, every rustle of leaves.

LA LUCHA

In the middle of the night, the beers awoke me, asking to be let out. My stirring woke Luisa, whose tale of exhaustion reminded me to be fearful. Dammit. Did I really need to dress, climb down the ladder, find a pair of shoes and walk out into the dark, a respectful distance from the Defender? Yes, I really did. I began to relieve myself. Behind a tree, to my right, The Burnings disfigured, deranged mutilator stood watching, blood-caked, razor-sharp garden shears in hand. This was the moment he had been waiting for. He would be standing directly behind me as I turned, would lunge at me from the darkness, superhuman strength and the stench of death. Surely, I would fight him, defend my family and my life; pee on my feet.

That morning I awoke feeling drowsy, relieved and foolish. I stoked the coals and prepared the family breakfast while berating myself. The daylight restored my courage, and I realised that I had not been nearly as scared as Luisa had been, that if anything I was merely tapping into her fear and my concern had simply been a reaction to her terror. Yes, that's exactly what happened. What a silly girl you are Luisa.

The sinister pick up returned just after we finished a breakfast of bacon and eggs, my heart skipped a beat. Fight or flight? Do we throw the tent up, jump in the Landy and head for the safety of the canyon ring road? Five excited young men emerged, smiling from the pick-up. "Hey, is that a Defender? Where the heck are you guys from? What, you travelled around South America and then all the way up here?" "Man, you guys are really brave".

Silly, silly Luisa.

The friendly young men each bought a copy of We Will Be Free (we were selling a copy almost every time we stopped, usually at a gas station) and it began to snow and sleet as we packed up the roof tent and stowed away the camping chairs. Luisa and I decided that what the Grand Canyon desperately lacked was two underdressed South Africans posing at the rim, in the sleet. Keelan was roped in as the photographer, at whom we would yell instruction while standing at a viewing point with nothing covering our uglies but swimwear and with trousers around our ankles. Inappropriate attire, indeed. Keelan did the best he could to keep us happy, keep the camera dry and not to get too wet and miserable for the sake of his parent's insanity. For those of you who are new to our particular brand of insanity, we like to engage in an activity titled, Inappropriate Attire. If I remember correctly we were inspired by a photo taken by a couple of young American Overlanders, Brenton and Shannon who posted an image of themselves doing perfectly timed Ninja kicks at Macchu Pichu. We are not ninjas, so we decided to carry a wetsuit, goggles and a bikini up to the sacred site and to pose, I as if I was snorkelling the lost underwater city of Atlantis and Luisa to freeze her butt off in a bikini. This set off an overlander risqué photo competition which ended with a couple of overachievers stark naked at the Salar de Uyuni. We also posed in swimwear at the Perito Moreno glacier at 5 am, at Torres del Paine and making snow angels in deep snow up in the Rockies, dressed in the same old and weathered swimwear and again after it snowed on top of the San Pedro de Martir mountains in Baja, Mexico.

Shivering and damp, we dressed and climbed back into the foggy Defender, a drive around the rim revealed the magnificence of the canyon, though visibility was not great. We were on a mission and could not find a reason to hang around longer, waiting for the weather to eventually clear. We had met a couple at the Snowverland expo who had earned Guinness World Records for riding motorbikes around the world, and they invited us to visit them at their home in Boulder, Colorado. Our plan was to drive to Zion National Park, up to Moab then across to Boulder.

Our next stop was Lake Powell, a massive and controversial reservoir which was created by the construction of the Glen Canyon dam of the Colorado River which had taken its bloody sweet time to create the Grand Canyon. I bought a geological souvenir at the gift shop where well informed and friendly volunteers waited to tell us about the dam's history and construction. We walked the wall, Luisa refusing to look down into the gulley below, her fear (heights) lay to the right, my fear (deep water) lay to the left. I used to suffer acrophobia until I did the world's highest bungee jump in South Africa in an attempt to cure myself. I also used to surf large offshore waves in Cape Town for a few years, but that did little to cure me of either mild and sporadic aquaphobia or my severe galeophobia, Cape Town being the Great White shark capital of the planet. A Canadian couple, attracted by the Defender, began to chat with us in the parking lot of the Lake Powell information centre. Alain and MJ invited us to share their campsite on the shores of the lake, and we gladly accepted. We had no intention of paying $40 for a campsite but Alain assured me that the site was paid for and we could join them, at no extra cost to them or us. Perhaps people are confused by how money-conscious we are. The expectation is that we must be wealthy to be able to travel the way we do, in a Defender. Perhaps wealth will visit us later in life (thank you so much for buying and/or reading this book). Alain and MJ ran a company near Quebec and have two incredibly handsome and intelligent sons who were waiting back home in Canada. We had dinner and drank a few Coors Light while looking out over the lake, which was populated by houseboats and speedboats and fishing boats, booze cruise boats, kayaks and canoes but hardly any dugout canoes. The camp itself was full of behemoths, RV's and fifth wheel trailer the size of long distances coaches. An 80-year-old man can drive a vehicle the size of a bus, without a special driver's licence as long as the vehicle is a recreational vehicle. Each campsite was built to accommodate these rolling palaces, and people sat in leather armchairs next to simulation fireplaces, watching football while their wives prepare meals in kitchens equipped with granite tops and every mod con available. The river had over millennia carved the landscape into an incredible collection of outcrops, islands, gulley's, alcoves and slot canyons. The sedimentary layers of sandstone bore witness to the passage of time, and the mind-boggling age of our planet, the construction of the dam had been controversial because it was seen as an unnecessary endeavour which drowned unimaginable beauty and the history of the native people who had populated the area for thousands of years. It is claimed that the modern environmentalist movement was born out of the controversy surrounding the construction of the dam.

While talking to our new friends Alan and MJ in the Glen Canyon camp, I complained about how all the kids wanted to do was sit and stare at screens all day long. I told him how I wished that they would make more of an effort to meet other kids, to hike and bike and be active like we had been as kids. Alan, who has two sons, had a different point of view. He said that it would not matter if they were surrounded by friends, they would all be sitting staring at their phones, communicating with people who were somewhere else. He reminded me of the Sony Walkman, which all the old fuddy-duddies were convinced was going to turn a generation of kids into zombies. He reminded me of the opportunities which growing up tech-savvy presented, and he helped me to see the children's internet usage in a more positive light. Which brings us to…

The Internet Tried to Ruin my Children but Failed.

(The following few paragraphs are not chronological).
In the three years, it took us to circumnavigate South America and drive up to the USA, the children were children as children used to be. You know, before kids were born with screens welded to their faces. In South America, where WIFI access is usually wonderfully terrible, the kids had to do kid-ly things when we were parked up to camp. They would explore and play with sticks, play with other children, stray dogs, toys. They each had a bag of toys, Jessica was obsessed with Barbie dolls (she had eight for the love of), playing cards, plastic fast food toys and all the paraphernalia which comes

with dolls and fast food toys. Keelan's obsession was Lego, Hot Wheels, green and grey soldiers and fast food toys. When not chasing a ball with local kids, they would either read or play with their toys or fight over a broken white tablet we had bought in Chile and which we used primarily for navigation. Before we had the tablet, we had had a small iPod which we gave to Keelan when we bought the tablet. We then bought a tablet for Keelan, an extravagant birthday gift which we bought in Cartagena after two years on the road. The iPod was then passed down to Jessica. They were able to download games and play Minecraft, and that was, essentially, the extent of their internet use. The games were a great distraction when we were driving long distances on boring roads and at night when Luisa and I were outside standing around the fire, and the kids were huddled in the tent, waiting for the meat to eventually be ready.

When we initially entered the USA, we were amazed by the high-speed internet available almost everywhere. Keelan, a budding gamer, was over the moon that he would eventually be able to play games online, and Jessica asked for permission to download the Instagram app. "Sure Jess, you have been such a good girl, go for it" and had the uncomfortable "the internet is full of old men dressed as young girls" conversation. Luisa and I were working hard, glued to our screens, often for hours a day, marketing our newly released book. We set a terrible example but did not realise that we had fallen down the rabbit's hole until it was too late.

The first signs that something was amiss were that the kids were no longer as willing to help around the camp as had always been. Where before they had asked if where we were headed that day was a campsite and did it have a toilet, or a swimming pool if it was hot, or if there were kids to play with, now they only wanted and needed one thing – WIFI. Before they had used their devices so infrequently that they only had to charge them once every second day – now if I needed to find my kids I just needed to look in the direction of the nearest power outlet. There they would huddle, regardless of comfort or location. A request to brush teeth and go to bed was met with loud groans. We eventually banned the use of electronics during the day. Luisa, in a past life, used to work sixteen hours a day running our old business and fifteen of those sixteen hours were spent on the computer. It took me two years of writing, re-writing and editing to produce my first book, the kids have grown up watching us look at screens, we have no-one to blame but ourselves. And the seduction of the internet. Even Zion National Park or Moab or San Francisco or Macchu Pichu cannot compete with the world where everything you want is at your fingertips. For Keelan, the games became more and more important, he joined online groups and made friends across the planet, Jessica would spend her hours watching vines and YouTube personalities and pop music videos. Cracks grew between us.

In the morning the kids would be grumpy and unhelpful, we had been a pretty well-oiled machine and could knock down camp in five minutes, but now we had to first have a blowout, and a meltdown, a timeout and threats of boarding school before the kids would begrudgingly do their chores. I would talk to them about internet addiction and try to explain to them the dangers of that addiction. Keelan lost interest in all other activities and grew overweight, Jessica withdrew and became someone we did not know. We grew desperate. Perhaps what frustrated me the most is that I was now not the primary influence on my children and I had almost no control over what they viewed or with who they communicated.

With time, though, our lives began to normalise. Luisa and I agreed that we had to set boundaries and we had to be consistent in the enforcement of those boundaries. We also took the time to remind the children of the dangers of the internet and tried to encourage them to use the web for self-improvement and learning. They had to self-censor, I refuse to check their search histories or spy on them, I must be confident that I have raised them well enough that they will not compromise themselves in the dark corners of the internet.

Keelan's love for gaming grew to the point that he now identifies himself as "an overlander gamer" (he refuses to choose one activity over the other) and he has earned himself a position of respect in the gamer community. The most influential games he has played in the last three years have been Homebrew, an open world vehicle design and construction platform, Foxhole, a top-down tactical shooter (and high on the list because this is where he met most of the friends he still games with today), Day of Infamy, a WW2 tactical shooter, The Long Dark, a single player survival game, Armor 3, a military simulator, but has spent the most time playing Gary's Mod, the ultimate sandbox game. (If he can get his Steam running he can tell me how many hours he has on the game, our WIFI is always terrible. He has a modest 240 hours (he has a friend who has played the game for 4000 hours)). His interest in gaming has led him towards an interest in IT, from a gamers perspective. He designs computers for friends, selecting hardware components from various sources in order to create the ultimate, cost-effective gaming computer. Our morning walk conversations are now divided into two topics; the first, our lives on the road, our goals and challenges and how to overcome the challenges (I do most of the talking as we walk away) and the second, Keelan's gaming experiences, the games he is playing and plans to play, the dynamics of the other society he inhabits and his strategies (he does all the talking as we return). At first, I looked down on gaming as a waste of time and this created tension between us probably because we have so much real-world work to do, which he can help with. But when I took the time to talk to him about what gaming means to him, I learned that he had made friends, real, loyal, kind and compassionate friends through gaming. When we lived in Cape Town, Keelan had a few good friends but when we left he lost contact with those boys and girls as they continued with their lives. Living on the road, he would make friends, but within days or weeks, we would move on. It is the price both our children have had to pay for our goal to show them, and ourselves, the world. Keelan discovered that through gaming he made friends and those friends would still be there when he eventually was able to go online after we had been on the road for a while. They shared a common love for gaming. His clan, the 75th Reapers, is run by a senior gamer who goes by the name King Burns who treats the clan like a family, going so far as to buy online gifts for clan members on their birthdays. The clan has 25 members, and they are a solid unit, after a bit of Game of Thrones type succession and leadership battles, Keelan emerged as a leading member, his kindness and peaceful personality earning him the loyalty of his brother clan members. I learned to respect his involvement in this community. After our successful Kickstarter campaign, we were able to buy Keelan a new computer, I had written two books on an old Acer laptop we had bought from friends in Brazil and which had a Spanish keyboard. I needed a new computer, but I realised that if Keelan was to be able to enjoy the games his friends enjoyed, he would need a new machine. I made the decision to buy the new computer for him and continue with my old Acer, which had served me well enough. We invested in his passion as we have always tried to encourage him to find something that he can be passionate about, something which will help him grow and something which could one day, perhaps, help him build a career.

The boundaries, however, remain.

Jessica's internet usage was far less intricate than her big brother's, but her needs were similar. She needed a community of people her age with whom she could share vines, memes, pictures of puppies, fail videos, and whatever else it is that pre-pubescent girls are into. She could chat for hours with her friends in South Africa, South America, the USA and Malawi. She could watch videos and memes, and she developed a personality based on those of the internet characters she followed. She grew up and ditched the Barbie clothing and dolls, instead of becoming a little pop star. We would watch videos together, and I now know almost all the words to Jimmy Fallon and Will I Am's, "Ew!". She created a series of hand "dance" movements and would sing along to pop songs holding onto her large, pink silicone wrapped tablet, headphones in, hands flipping at the wrist making gestures to match the music, hip-hop rhythmic puppetry. She knew the words to all the new pop songs and developed a sense of humour based on the content she favoured. Instagram and YouTube were her favourites - Bad Lip Reading, The Kosmic 8, Liza Koshy, Deligracy playing Simms, LDshadowlady were characters she followed. Jessica loved entertainment and lifestyle videos and would download her favourite TV series', Grimm, Riverdale, Grey's Anatomy, New Girl and Super Girl.

I am proud that both children chose to use the internet responsibly, their characters have changed, but they are still wonderful, if anything, they will be better equipped to communicate with their peers, even if they do so via Snapchat.
(End).

Alan made us promise to visit him in Canada, and we left the next morning, headed in the direction of Zion National Park.
Utah, we would later decide, was to be one of our favourite states in the USA. Huge blue skies sit above landscapes which are just too perfect. No rock is out of place, and it seems as if some great artist had dedicated the best years of his creative life to designing, creating, airbrushing and maintaining the land. I am pretty sure that the Mormons, who make up 61% of the population in Utah, know who that artist is, and they have a name for him. Our jaws dropped at the magnificence enjoyed by the Church of the Latter-Day Saints. Driving into a town called Kanab, we stopped at one gas station to compare fuel prices with the gas station across the road. While stopped, a young, trendy man ran across the road and made a beeline for

us. He had wide eyes, and we were slightly bemused. "Is that a Defender 130?" Yes, it is. "Golly. Wait here I will be right back". The young man turned on his heel and ran off down the wide main road. He returned a minute later driving a beautifully maintained yellow Series 3 88 Landy. His Dad ran a snow cone stall across the road (but that was only one of his businesses. He was also a retired naval officer, a dentist, an estate agent and a wheeler-dealer) and we were invited to have a snow cone. Luisa and I choose the smallest option, which was huge, and Keelan chose a gallon jug of sugar drenched ice. We noticed that people would dive into the parking lot, park and walk away from their cars without locking them. On closer inspection, we noted that almost every car still had the keys in the ignition and valuables left on the seats. Our new friend David, and his dad, David Snr chatted with us for a while about our travels and then invited us to go have a look at the tv tower. Um, ok. It was late afternoon, and we had no idea where we would stay the night, but by now we had learned to accept what the road gods present us with. These were such clean cut and friendly people that we could not refuse the offer to visit their local infrastructure. Well, that is a weird sentence. David Snr made a few phone calls, and within minutes we found ourselves in a convoy of Land Rover Discovery's and the Series 3 heading up a deep red sand track in low range. The lighter vehicles nimbly climbing over boulders and around steep corners, while our heavily loaded 130 did the same without breaking a sweat, it was only in the tightest hairpin bends that we had to do some manoeuvring. Luisa, Jessica and I did the best we could to finish our snow cones while driving up the track, and Keelan sat quietly in the back seat, deep in the early stages of a sugar coma and the beginning stages of diabetes. At the summit, next to a large tv tower, we looked down on the town of Kanab, and David Snr explained the layout of the town and shared some history. Kanab is nicknamed, "Little Hollywood" by the residents as the town and the surrounding areas were popular with Hollywood filmmakers. Two Planet of the Apes movies, Evolution (a personal favourite), The Outlaw Josie Wales, Windtalker, The

LA LUCHA

Lone Ranger, Maverick and Broken Arrow are just a few of the movies made in the area. No wonder it all looked so familiar, I was relieved that Luisa had brought the Head and Shoulders. One of our new friends apparently had a yard full of Land Rovers somewhere down there, and he was a vehicle insurance broker. "I bet you don't have much business living in the safest town on the planet". Well, no. Insurance was mandatory by law and because there was no crime, there were never any claims for theft, only for damage. The insurance agent was pretending not to be in awe of the 130.

For those who do not know, Land Rover Defenders are extremely popular in the USA, despite only a few thousand having been sold there as the NAS (North American Spec) version. Most of the NAS Defenders were the 90 and 110-inch wheelbase and all had the V8 engine. The rarer the Defender, the more coveted it is and a South African, 2003 model, 130-inch wheelbase with a TD5 diesel engine which had circumnavigated continents were, without a doubt, the rarest of them all. I had heard rumours and had seen Defenders for sale in the US for amounts well above $100 000 US and knew that we were driving an aluminium gold mine. Selling the Defender would solve all our financial problems and we would have enough money to return to South Africa, buy another 130, kit it out and drive around the planet for two years. However, it was not that simple. There were two major obstacles to us selling the vehicle, the first is that it was illegal to do so as the vehicle had to be over 25 years old to be legally imported and, the second, is that we are so deeply in love with our Mafuta, that we could hardly bear the thought of selling her. Ridiculous! Shortly before we had entered the USA, we watched a video on YouTube of US Defenders being crushed by Homeland Security. The Feds were mounting dawn raids, dressed in SWAT gear, to scare the early morning daylights out of people wearing colour match pyjamas. A lawyer, now known affectionately as The Defender of Defenders (but known to his proud mama as Will Hedrick), stepped up to the plate, took on the government, won the fight, put an end to the destruction of the vehicles and had them returned to their rightful owners. (The full story is quite complex and does not add to the narrative of this story but if you are interested, search the internet "Homeland Security seizes Defenders" for the full story and the many opinions which surround it). The grateful Defender owners thanked Will by buying him a Defender. And they say that the Americans don't get irony. The irony was not lost on us that we were driving a rare diamond but had to sell books at gas stations to put fuel in her.

"Hey, do you know where we can get insurance for the Defender?". Unfortunately, our new insurance selling friend did not, and he doubted that we would find a company which might insure us. The conversation continued, I might have cussed, but I did not suspect that our new friends were Mormon, they were not carrying bibles and did not wear black ties and did not try to convert us or held hands in a circle and thanked the God of Utah for granting us safe passage up the mountainside. I stopped cussing (the Americanisation had begun) and David Snr invited us to his home where they did not drink alcohol, but they did make cheeseburgers. I accepted after a short Afrikaans chat with Luisa and we followed the group back down the hill, Keelan bouncing around in the back of the Series. He had not yet regained the facility of speech, but his body had stopped buzzing long enough for him to be able to put one foot in front of the other. We entrusted him with a video camera to film our descent over the boulders and through the deep sand. He produced only footage of his feet, a fire extinguisher, an empty coke can and a Series floor.

Krugersdorp, the town where I spent much of my childhood and most of my teen years, was also home to a very large Church of the Latter-Day Saints compound. Every Sunday morning at 8 am, there would be a knock on the door and a couple of unhappy looking people would try and convince me to become equally unhappy. I was given Mormon comic books with very unfunny subjects. I remember the one comic clearly; the devil was convincing a small boy to play with girl's dolls and he even made the boy dress up as a girl. Hilarity ensued as the family fell to pieces and the boy grew up and ended his own life. Joy to the world. For six years they knocked on my door and for six years I politely told them thanks but no thanks, took their comics and closed the door. Yes, I heard about Jesus, I am a South African for the love of Saint Petrus. We were taught to sing hymns from the day we could talk, we had a class called Religious Instruction in high school where a small Greek woman had her faith tested twice a week. Until the age of eleven, I had been dragged to a church called Rhema where I would waste four beautiful sunny hours every Sunday, sitting in a converted movie house abusing my eyeballs, trying to stare down the light bulbs in the ceiling, attempting to reach the point where my iris had retracted to the size of a pin tip and I was able to see God himself behind the stunning haze of electric light. For me, a living nightmare was a clammy hand kumbaya session.

At age twenty, after six years of having my Sunday morning ruined, I awoke one morning to the persistent and expected knock on the door. I had just gotten to bed after a night headbanging at a Thrash Metal club in Randburg and my body was in need of rest after hours of mosh pit violence. I opened the door wearing my favourite Morbid Angel T-shirt and told them to "Fuck off!". I had been patient for all those years, but enough was enough. I never heard from them again.

And now, here we were in Kanab, USA, headed to Lion's den. If we do not have the courage to challenge our preconceptions, then we have failed in our goal as travellers.

As we drove back into Kanab and into the driveway of our new friend's middle-class home, where we were surprised to see what looked like a mechanics yard. A large warehouse stood facing the house and I could only imagine that the family had been unfortunate enough to have a business built in their backyard. Vehicles were parked in a U in front of the warehouse and included an old school bus, a trailer housing four snowmobiles, a Trans Am, a Chevy Blazer, a Discovery, an ancient Ford pickup, a large kidnap van (as Luisa calls them) and a few ex-military off-road trailers. The Series was added to the collection and I soon learned that all the vehicles and the warehouse belonged to the family. I suspected that David Snr, being a Mormon, must have a few wives and a tribe of kids to transport, but he had only the one lovely wife and four children. When asked about the warehouse, David Jnr gave us a tour. Inside we found every tool imaginable, a fleet of motorbikes, old and new, a large ski boat, a few muscle cars and a couple of 50's pickups. This was not a business. This was a hobby! I had read that Americans only makeup 5% of the world's population but use 25% of the world's resources. I had never been able to figure out how they could be such prolific consumers but here, in front of my eyes, stood the answer. Machines, toys, books, packaging crates, Bric a Brac, antiques and every conceivable household appliance sat one on top of the other, in every corner, on every shelf on storage platforms built two meters below the high ceiling. David Snr liked to attend auctions and had picked up the school bus for a few thousand dollars, as there is a rule that a school bus may not be driven, as a school bus, if it exceeds mileage of 10 000 miles. He had removed the body of the bus from the rear wheels back, had welded the rear window section of the bus back onto the shortened body and had reinforced the frame to carry the Series 3. The plan was to convert the bus into a camper and carry the little Land Rover with them as they went on holiday or camping trips. He had bought the military trailers for a steal at another auction and would use them to haul firewood. Now and then they would complete the restoration of a vehicle and would flip it for a profit.

LA LUCHA

According to Scientific American, it is the American's love of the personal automobile which partly accounts for these excessive rates of consumption. Each vehicle requires oil, fuel, filters, parts, storage, insurance, etc. I could now fathom how our new insurance agent friend thrived. I had been trying to calculate his income based on the average two-car house in the western world. How silly of me. It seemed that in America, a two-car household is bare bones minimalism.

We were asked how we could afford to travel the world and I produced a copy of WWBF which David Jnr took immediately and disappeared into his room.

Now, many people who are not American, criticise the American BBQ and that night was our first experience with this culinary treat. All the BBQ's we had had so far in the States, had been South African Braais, made by us. Our style of BBQ is similar to the South American Asado, slow and elaborate. We had driven many new friends to the brink of starvation, when they join us for a braai, expecting to eat at 7 pm or 8 pm and only being fed huge quantities of flesh at midnight when they have had way too much to drink, on an empty stomach. If an American is going to BBQ long and slow, it will be to make ribs or brisket and he will get up at 5 am to start the fire. The day to day BBQ will be gas grilled brats (a derivative of the bratwurst sausage) and burgers. Ground beef to an American is the burger, if you ask for mince the butcher will only give you two pounds of a quizzical look. Ask for a burger and he will give you ground beef. (Please note, I am generalising based on the commonalities we experienced in the areas we visited. If in Nantucket they call it burger mince, I apologise, I have not been to Nantucket yet and I have not tasted your excellent mince. But if in Nantucket, you asked your local butcher for a burger, I guarantee he will give you mince. Or ground beef). The average American has a few jobs and lives far away from everyone and everything. An hour drive to visit a friend is normal and he does not have the time to visit thirsty South Africans. He wants to walk in the door, have a cold beer, be given a hamburger (tomato ketchup is the basic topping, fancy people add cheese, a gourmet burger has tomato, lettuce, etc) and a brat's hot dog, he wants to eat those and get back on the road because he has to be up at 6 am for a meeting. He lives far from everything simply because everything is far away. If in Phoenix, Arizona, for instance, you wanted to go to Home Depot, Walmart and Costco you would have to drive, and it would not be a short drive. Because America is huge and relatively young, and Americans are logical and enterprising, they build their cities (mostly) low and flat, with wide roads. Seattle goes on forever in every direction, as does Albuquerque, Miami, Orlando, New York. You will see more skyscrapers in Belo Horizonte Brazil than you will in most of those cities. Because the cities are so huge and spread out and so far apart from each other the average American needs a car, or two. Public transport is almost non-existent simply because it would be impossibly expensive and complicated for our friend in Phoenix to visit all three stores and return home without taking three buses and a cab. That, my friends, is why the USA is ripe for the autonomous electric vehicle, which we will be run by Google or Amazon as a de facto public transit system. You know those self-checkout tellers in supermarkets? We are being trained to do the work ourselves so that the corporations no longer have to employ hundreds of thousands of human cashiers. Uber does not want drivers, they want self-drive vehicles which are safe, reliable and cost-effective. In the UK, in 2017, Tesco now has scanners which you collect as you enter the store and scan your items, you put them in your cart, at the self-checkout you scan the scanner, pay and leave. We are entering the age of robotics, autonomous machines, self-service and the universal basic income. At first, amongst the developing nations, that technology will be shoehorned into the developing world.

LA LUCHA

Back to burgers. Brats and burgers are perfectly acceptable as a quick, fun meal, served with a packet of Lays and a glass of cold Coca-Cola. Our host, David Snr, made the entire meal in about ten minutes and Keelan, who had just recovered from the snow cone coma had to be told that three burgers are enough. I then had to be told that three burgers are enough. David Jnr joined us for a burger then disappeared back into his bedroom, shortly before his mom, younger brothers and sister returned from a friend's graduation party. On the kitchen counter lay a stack of invitations to attend high school graduation parties. Each year each graduate would hire a professional photographer and pose for photos in their best clothing, their families would then throw a party for them and people would arrive with gifts. In South America, such a party would last from the morning until the next morning, in Utah the party would last perhaps three hours. Each, full colour, multi-page invitation included five or six photos and a description of the graduate's achievements academically, socially and athletically. Most graduates would then leave to do a mission with the church and evangelise.

After chatting with the family for a while, we were shown to rooms which were comfortably furnished and modern. After a shower, we went to bed and I became paranoid. Was that a camera in the ceiling? I am sure the kids are ok, what if we woke up in the middle of the night and the door was locked, or we were drugged and chained in the basement. Who knew we were here? No-one! Why on earth was safe, secure America making me so neurotic? Perhaps it was because I had recently read a horrifying statistic. There have been 2743 known serial killers in the USA, closely followed by the UK with 145, and my sweet and gentle homeland of South Africa, with 112. Of course, I did not suspect that our kind and generous hosts were anything but kind and generous but, paranoia is not logical.

In the morning, we had breakfast with David Snr and his younger son, his wife and daughter had already left for church as it was a Sunday, David Jnr had not left his room since the night before and apparently, he had not slept until he had finished our book. I became concerned. In WWBF I write about my motivation and life philosophy as a secular person. It might upset our host if he learned that he had inadvertently invited doubt into his home and we had just been told that we could stay as long as we wanted. Although we were tempted to stay, we were also happy to keep going, to keep on exploring glorious Utah. Before leaving, David Snr approached us with his hands behind his back... "I see that you are a wonderful family and are dedicated to each other, the Mormon faith is all about family, we have your book, and now", he passed me the Book of Mormon, "you have ours". What, no, kumbaya? We said fond farewells and headed out of Kanab, well rested, clean and deep in thought.

Luisa read the Book of Mormon to us and we discovered that Mormonism is a new religion for the new country. As American as Brats and Burgers. Wikipedia says, "Mormons trace their origins to the visions that Joseph Smith reported having in the early 1820s while living in upstate New York. ... On April 6, 1830, Smith founded the Church of Christ. The early church grew westward as Smith sent missionaries to proselytise". We were not converted, but our view of Mormons had been changed by a charming, fit, healthy and hardworking family who had taken smelly strangers into their home and who had made us feel at home.

The drive from Kanab to Zion National park was short, at around 55 kilometres, and beautiful. We had the misfortune of visiting the area during a holiday period but, for some reason, all the traffic was coming from the west and the left lane of the road through the park resembled a Los Angeles traffic jam. Our lane was almost void of traffic, which is a good thing as we were spellbound by the beauty of the park. Never before had we seen such natural perfection. Every grain of sand seemed to have been carefully arranged. "No way, that's impossible", "oh my God, look at that", "that's ridiculous". To quote the mighty internet, Zion National Park was formed as, over time… "rock layers have been uplifted, tilted, and eroded, forming a feature called the Grand Staircase, a series of colourful cliffs stretching between Bryce Canyon and the Grand Canyon. The bottom layer of rock at Bryce Canyon is the top layer at Zion, and the bottom layer at Zion is the top layer at the Grand Canyon". I cannot imagine any place on this planet, which could be more perfect or pristine. RV's, Harley Davidsons, pickups, convertibles, tour buses and every other vehicle imaginable (ok, there were no Tuk-Tuk's) tortoised their way east through the park. The park peaks looked down on us with disdain. We were insects, ants, dung beetles, grasshoppers, filling the air with a foul smell and the noise of our silly machines. An eternal time lapse would show that pristine environment evolving, deepening, crumbling, rising to achieve perfection over a 150-million-year period. Human habitation began 8000 years ago. In that time lapse we would appear, taking ownership, building roads and tunnels and lodges and information centres, restrooms, cinemas and spas 0.0005333333 of a second from the end. In a million years, when we have disappeared, long after the last remnants of our plastic society have disintegrated, the peaks will still be there, looking at each other, retelling that story about those clever little insects. Those industrious little bugs were probably the most interesting thing to happen there, since that time the fire fell out of the sky and killed the big lizards.

Yes, Zion made me feel tiny and insignificant, ugly and temporary. The hordes seeking satisfaction did not help me to feel any better about the human species. There exists a theory that when a man looked at the magnificence and immensity of nature, he felt tiny and ridiculous, like a bug. He could dominate the animals which surrounded him, he could beat other men and his woman and chop down a great tree, but even if he dug all day at Mother Nature's skin, all he would have is a big hole in which he could fall and break his little, weak neck. The man created a god for each of the powerful things he did not understand. These gods, who spoke to the man while he was digging the hole frantically, told the man that these gods had made the earth and he would be master of the earth IF he worshipped the gods of the sun, the moon, the wind, the sea, the river, winter, fire. The man convinced others that it was the gods which had created all things. He told them, that only he could talk to the gods and that they would all be punished if they did not obey the following rules which the gods had given him. He created a place to worship these gods and told the people that they would have to bring precious things to offer the gods so that they would not become angry. He gave the people hope for a life with the gods, where they would forever be with the ones they loved, no-one would ever truly die IF they all followed these rules. A drought, a flood, a violent death, an earthquake, a comet, a good hunt, a good crop, were all proof of the gods' displeasure or happiness. The man learned that he could enslave his fellow men with the invisible whip of vengeful gods. But, he elevated the people because they were created by gods and were second only to the gods, the earth was their possession and existed only for their use. By having gods, man became a god.

Leaving crowded Zion, (named after a special hill in Jerusalem) we passed beautiful homes and hundreds of US flags and headed for the I15 which would take us to Bryce Canyon. Unfortunately, Bryce Canyon was so full of visitors that the park was closed, and we instead turned left on the I70, destination Moab. Stopping at a gas station for a much-needed top up, we met two overlanders who we met in person (after being internet friends for a long time) at the Overland Expo. Anthony and Astrid had, a few years earlier, been set to head out and explore the planet in their Land Cruiser, but Astrid had been diagnosed with cancer. She bravely fought the disease and continues to fight to this day. I hope that we will one day meet them again on the road, that would be an incredible victory for them both. Anthony has the gift of an incredible sense of humour and an incredible

Motorhead moustache, both of them will keep you entertained for hours. They explained to us that it was a holiday and that we would struggle to find anywhere to stay in the national parks and even private campsites. Hence our decision to hit the road to Moab. After a good laugh and a chinwag, we set off and arrived at Moab that evening. Driving down into the famous town past the Arches National Park.

Enquiring at the campsites in town, we found that we were going to be charged $30 to park on a piece of concrete. Luisa had the great idea to drive to every campsite in town and compare price vs facilities vs availability of WIFI vs friendliness of the staff. It was great fun after a long day on the road. As we were headed down the main street, we passed a white Defender belonging to Clarence, a Boulder resident who we had met at a campsite in Phoenix, then again at the Overland Expo. He told us not to worry, he knew of a place outside the town where we could camp for free. Bingo! We followed Clarence's very well laid out Defender and after 20 kilometres turned left onto a gravel road. Within ten minutes of driving, we found a spot to camp on the side of a hill with a view of the golden sun setting over the red road of the Arches National Park. While campers sat cheek by jowl on expensive pieces of concrete blocks in town, we were in paradise with not a soul in sight. Clarence produced some excellent cold beer as we set up camp and started a fire for the braai. Clarence had travelled the area extensively and we were disappointed to find that the trails we wanted to explore would most likely be full of crowds in modified Jeeps and other off-road vehicles. We proposed trying a particularly difficult but achievable trail, which Clarence had done the year before, but his wife put her foot down and squashed the idea. Luisa then jumped up and down on what was left of the idea until there was nothing left but an excuse to have another beer.

We sat and solved the world's problems until the sky was deep black and sparkling with a billion stars.

That night, my dreams were of mountains, snakes, sand and deserts. The morning was crisp and clear as we packed. The kids were warned, when wandering away from camp carrying our old spade and fresh toilet paper, to be aware of rattlesnakes and other critters which would bite them in the bum when settling down for the morning movement. This was our element, off the beaten track and self-sufficient. Moab, (the Biblical name Moab refers to an area of land located on the eastern side of the Jordan River, or the name is derived from the Paiute word, Moapa, meaning mosquito) is an outdoorsman's paradise. One of the remarkable things about the USA is the land managed by the Bureau of Land Management (BLM). BLM land is controlled public land which, depending on the area, are available for various activities. You can usually camp for free on BLM land for a period of up to two weeks, thereafter you must move but can move to another site in the same area. Each state we visited had a well-equipped BLM office where we could attain maps of the surrounding areas, which included campsites and off-road trails. The town of Moab is unremarkable, but the surrounding areas are spectacular. Having waited out the majority of the holidaymakers, we were able to tour Arches Park in relative solitude, hiking various trails and taking photos. The kids can hike to the moon and back when they are motivated, but motivating them takes patience and creative parenting. Both had hiked to the top of Torres del Paine in Patagonia, Keelan doing most of the hike barefoot because he is a large hobbit, and once they find their pace they tend to settle in and enjoy the hike.

I threw my imagination back to the 1800s when Native Americans and settlers were still fighting for control of the vast land. I could imagine being a German or Irish settler who had come to America, dreaming of a new life in a new world, free from the shackles of oppressive Europe. Here he could own land and dig for gold and raise animals, but he had to be prepared to fight for it. A European laying his eyes on this part of Utah for the first time must have been astounded, intimidated and astonished. This was not a place for the weak. I imagine that those men and women who were brave and enterprising enough to make the journey to this hostile world, are the very reason that America is the powerful country that it is today. The majority of Americans who are descendant of those pioneers will have the DNA of the alpha male, of those who believed in freedom, exploration, the right to wealth and limited government. Those pioneers left Europe to escape the governments and royalty which oppressed them, they went to the new world to escape crippling taxation and they were prepared to take up arms to defend their new liberty. America is a very young country and many Americans today hold onto the beliefs of those first Americans of yesterday. I imagined being a cowboy, my profession of choice when I was a kid. I would be a good guy, and I would be the fastest gun in the west, maybe a sheriff or a bounty hunter. Herding cows are all good and fun, but the real money lies in bringing back the bodies or heads of those who broke the law. Now, if you imagine a Bon Jovi song as the soundtrack, please don't, this soundtrack is more The Good, The Bad and The Ugly. My diet would be rabbit and steak and jerky and whiskey, pretty much what it is today, and the little lady Luisa would be at my side, kicking ass and looking fine in leather chaps and a white blouse, her red hair braided beneath her cowgirl hat. Oops, my mind might have wandered.

After a day of hiking, trails and exploring, we returned to Moab and met up with Clarence who had another free camping spot to show us. We drove out of town towards a canyon and as we entered the descent into the canyon, it began to rain, thick and heavy drops which quickly turned the road to mud. Within half an hour the rain stopped, and we were amazed to find ourselves camping next to a river and a road, frogs croaking and our voices echoing off the canyon walls. Another night, another braai, more of the planet's problems solved. We awoke to the enthusiastic croaking of the frogs and a perfect blue sky overhead. One high altitude jet flew above us, leaving a thick, white chemtrail. Another jet, then another and another. The jets continued to criss-cross the sky until, by late morning, the perfect blue sky was no longer visible, at all. Them Utards (as the Idahoes call them) must be an uppity bunch if the New World Order has to spray so much tranquilising chem into the atmosphere. America is a busy place, everyone on the move.

We said goodbye to Clarence and Moab and headed out of town towards Boulder, Colorado. Driving in the USA is a national past time, the road trip an integral part of the national psyche and pop culture. How many American road trip movies have you seen? Dozens I bet. Utah reminded me of the movie Breakdown, Kurt Russel and Kathleen Quinlan are on a road trip when his Jeep breaks down. Being a Jeep that is an entirely probable scenario. Kurt's wife is then kidnapped by a bunch of rednecks and poor Kurt must transform from a mild Californian into a kick-ass Californian. In Easy Rider, Dennis Hopper and John Fonda cross the country on Harley's after a drug deal in Baja, Mexico. They meet a drunken Jack Nicholson in a town jail, where they spent the night for the crime of having long hair. They then introduce Jack Nicholson to Marijuana (a very Beatles/Bob Dylan moment) before poor Jack is stomped to death under the stars by, you guessed it, Rednecks. The movie ends abruptly with our Harley heroes being shot with a shotgun while being overtaken by Rednecks. Bates Motel. Thelma and Louise. Road-trippin' in the USA.

We climbed up from Utah into Colorado, past beautiful towns dedicated to snow tourism. The road climbed higher and higher and, for long periods, was accompanied by a large river which ran uphill. Luisa and Keelan laughed and told me that I was losing my mind. "Look", I said, "we have been driving uphill for the last hour and for that entire hour the river has run parallel to the road, at the same elevation, and is flowing in the same direction as we are driving. If the river was running in the other direction, then I would not be confused, but it is not". Luisa explained, rationally, that the river must have run downhill very quickly at some stage and it was that momentum which was carrying it uphill. Luisa has an incredible grasp of aqua dynamics, but I had to question that logic. "Surely water can't do that, it would pool and become a lake?". Ha, she laughed at me again, Keelan joining in the mockery. "Look, assholes, the river is running uphill, look now!". They laughed at me some more and I felt extreme frustration. I used to lie a lot when I was a kid, creating incredible stories which my parents ignored. One day I witnessed a car accident while walking home from school. A driver lost control, drove up onto the sidewalk and rolled the vehicle. I could not wait to tell my mom, but when I told her she, naturally did not believe me and the more I tried to convince her, the less interested she became. I learned an important lesson that day and vowed to become a credible witness. That river flowed uphill, I shit you not.

The pass which led to Aspen from the I70 was closed due to heavy snowfall and we decided to give the famous town a miss, instead of continuing until we drove into Boulder.

Boulder is one of the wealthiest, most liberal towns in Colorado and is home to a beautiful university. As we drove the neighbourhoods looking for our friend Chris' house, we were astonished to see frat houses, exactly like those you have seen in a thousand movies involving short skirts, large breasts, beer kegs, drugs and comedic mayhem. In the USA, art imitates life and us naïve Africans were gobsmacked. We thought the silver screen versions of these houses were exaggerations, they are not. Alpha Kappa Alpha. Beautiful athletic girls rode bicycles, groups of young muscular men occupied the sidewalk and preferred to stare at the Land Rover rather than at the girls. Girls they see every day, African Defenders they do not. Perfect neighbourhoods, the model of the American dream waved their red, white and blue flags to welcome us. There were no fences except a few, obligatory, white picket fences. No guard dogs, razor wire, electric fences, rent a cops or burglar bars. I do not know why I am comparing Boulder to a South African town, perhaps because that is how I wish South Africa would be. Neither Chris nor his wife Erin was at home, but they had messaged us the lock code for the front door. At first, we were nervous. Surely, we can't just open the front door and make ourselves at home. The cops would show up in a hot minute and blow us all to kingdom come. Surely. We tentatively opened the door. No alarm. We left the door open and waited outside for five minutes. No cops. We eventually decided to let the kids sit inside while we sat outside and threw down a few cold beers. The neighbours came over to say hi and have a look at the Defender. What lovely people! Now, if ever you meet us while we are travelling, please be aware - we usually do not smell great, especially if we have been wild camping for the last few days. Our clothing is musky, and we have the smell of campfires, sweat and dust. I assume that is how we smell, I cannot smell myself, my family or the Land Rover. Apparently, one cannot smell their own home because we are so accustomed to the smell of ourselves. Many times, we meet people who invite us to their homes and they immediately offer us a shower. "Oh, no, we are ok, I think. Does anyone need a shower?". Note to self, you always need a shower. I like to think that we smell of adventure, of the wild, of macho, but civilised people don't actually like that smell if they did you would be able to buy Eau de Overlander from Dior. We might even smell a bit homeless. I have to bottle that.

Chris and Erin, who are estate agents and therefore work every day, eventually arrived to find us stinking up the front porch. They are used to smelly overlanders, having once been smelly intercontinental, round the world, overlanders themselves. Nevertheless, they invited us to freshen up. The basement of their home had been converted into a guest "apartment" and we soon unpacked our essentials and washed away Northern Arizona, Utah and this corner of Colorado. Smelling fresh and looking not quite as tanned, we joined them on the porch of their home to share a few more drinks and to shoot the breeze and answer all the new questions we had about the USA. Craig and Emily, the overlanders who had brought our spare fuel pump over the mountains from Chile to Argentina, saving us a massive import expenditure, joined us for a small reunion. I began to realise something that evening... Luisa and I are moderate, social smokers and smoking in America is a big no-no. Sure, there are still a lot of people who smoke, but it has become social suicide to smoke at any gathering which does not bounce to the beat of Kid Rock (running for president soon, muthaf@ckers). South Africans are much like Europeans in that we tend to be smokers, but I could feel that there was a definite negative reaction to smoking, everywhere we went. I smoke roll ups which, combined with my macho bush smell renders me irresistible to women without teeth, not the demographic I was aiming for. People seemed genuinely disappointed when we had a rare smoke. I have five roll-ups a day on average and have not touched pharmaceuticals in five years, I'll take Drum over Prozac or Oxycontin any day of the week, thank you. Not that our friends minded our dirty little habits or had any of their own, they have seen the world and know that we all have our crutches.

We slept the sleep of the dead that night and woke to take long walks in the beautiful countryside which lay a stone's throw from our friend's home. Deer watched us plod along and we spotted a coyote, which was a lot smaller and less impressive than I thought they would be. Apparently, there were mountain lions in the area and Chris told us a story of how a deer had been hunted and killed by a lion in his backyard which was not fenced. Boulder does not do fences.

We spent a few days exploring Boulder, doing some repairs on the Landy, promoting We Will Be Free, making new friends and eating great food. Chris and Erin were great hosts and Chris inundated me with questions about my Defender, not allowing me to answer the first question before asking the next (shortly after we left he took my advice and bought a Defender 130 in South Africa, had it modified as I suggested and has used the vehicle to explore Africa during his holidays). We met many South Africans in Boulder and soon realised that there is a very large Saffa expat community. I focused on my work while Chris tried to convince me to go to a bunch of meetings and sell books. I would have if the meetings were in some way or another related to our activities, but they were meetings of estate agents and insurance reps and rugby clubs. Chris derided me for not being business minded. "It is a slow boil Chris, that is my strategy", he thought I was nuts. We extended our stay to attend a "bring a truck" event which was arranged to help raise funds for a local charity. We opened the roof tent and allowed kids to climb inside and play, a few of the little ones becoming so comfortable that they fell asleep and had to be dragged out by their parents.

We were also very lucky to be able to spend an evening with a Lesotho expat, Graham and his very charming wife, Connie. They made a braai for us and gave us gifts of droewors and biltong, which we devoured. Graham's house is surrounded by Land Rovers and he is an incredibly kind and intelligent man. Together they helped to run the Overland Expo event and he had contributed his knowledge to many overlanding books and magazines. I spent some time with Graham, while I serviced my Defender in his back garden and it was a pleasure to learn so much from such a knowledgeable person. My only regret is that my terrible sense of humour cracked a joke which might have been taken the wrong way. Graham, you know I suffer from foot in mouth disease.

Just before leaving Boulder, Luisa and I decided that it would be a great idea to buy some Marijuana from the local dispensary. Since weed had become legal in Colorado, the state had earned billions in taxes and in the weed tourism industry. I used to be a pothead, but Luisa put a stop to that and ever since then, I have learned that I do not enjoy smoking pot. I get very,

very paranoid. Also, the weed I used to enjoy was grown in a field somewhere in Swaziland and was a mellow high. You could smoke big, fat joints all day long and never feel completely out of it. These days, weed has been GMO'd to the point that the plants drip with THC, yellow flowers and crystals and the heads are extremely potent, causing me to almost have a panic attack of anxiety when I do smoke, once every year or two.

The kids were with us in the Landy and we decided to park outside a liquor store and run around to the dispensary, the kids can see us buying booze, that's ok, but the green stuff? No way, Jose. We had been to the dispensary earlier in the week but did not have our passports with us so could not enter the establishment. "Ground control to Major Tom, you need your passport to leave this planet". After having our passports inspected, we entered a room which smelled herbal and sticky, a tall, well-built man who could have been a pharmacist, a policeman or a school teacher, took a long time to decide exactly which kind of high he would prefer. The options were endless and the prices astronomical. Back in the late Nineties, I once bought a shopping bag of weed for about $10.00 in my old hometown, Durban. Here a gram cost $50.00. Sweet mother. Eventually, it was our turn to choose our poison and for some reason, I was paranoid, which was not surprising, I get paranoid watching people smoke weed on TV. "I need the old school stuff, super mellow, no paranoia, please". The nerdy girl behind the counter suggested I try Fat Albert, very low THC, low potency, almost medicinal, and it was on special. "One gram please". The girl dispensed some Fat Albert into a small brown pill cylinder. So exciting, we had never bought legal weed before! We handed over the cash and ran back over to the Landy where the children sat waiting impatiently. "What took you so long?".

We hugged Chris and Erin and thanked them for being such great hosts, we even left a few boxes of crap and our surf gear with them, promising to try and return to collect the excess gear sometime in the future. Boulder was even more beautiful than Flagstaff.

We left because there was an overland event taking place near Seattle and that was an opportunity to make up for the poor sales we had had at the Overland Expo. Between Colorado and the Pacific Northwest, lay the Rocky Mountains and we were a stone's throw from the Rocky Mountain National Park. The next town we entered was very different from Boulder, much poorer and far more rural. Girls in tight jeans and pink cowboy hats exited a Jeep, sat on fat tyres and entered a bar. People drove battered pick up's and the houses seemed run down, lawns uncut, old cars abandoned in unkempt fields.

We entered the national park and were immediately impressed with the sheer beauty of the mountains and the valleys. As we drove up the mountain, we encountered snow on the ground and eventually drove below massive banks of snow, meters high, where snow ploughs had dug to liberate the road. We stopped at a lookout point and instantly began a massive snowball fight. Defeated I retreated to the Landy and watched Luisa and Keelan pelt each other with hard packed snowballs. Down in the valley, we met a large moose, his antlers at least two meters apart at their tip. We explored the spectacular park for most of the day, before heading out to find camping as all the park camps were full. It was not cold at all, despite the high banks of snow and we were not worried about a cold night down in the valley. Searching for camping in the valley we came across a few over-priced camps next to a lake.

At one of the camps, a weathered and weary man stopped to give us directions. He and his wife had retired, but all their money had been lost in the 2008 crash, now they worked running the campsite, which was full. He hated his wife, within five minutes we learned that she was very fat, not very smart and particularly cruel. He wore khaki clothing and a large, grey, tobacco yellow moustache. They were from Texas and missed Texas, their son was a hero and had served four tours in Afghanistan and Iraq, but he was not the same anymore. He had almost lost his mind from all the things he had done and seen over there, and he was on a disability pension. His son lived with them now, but it was not easy. He used to be an amazing kid, top athlete, football player, did very well in school and had excellent grades. Now, he had changed. He had become a recluse, a survivalist, he often took his Samurai sword and a crossbow and would disappear into those wooded hills over there for weeks at a time, living off the land. "Anyway, that's a nice rig you have there, South African, huh, you folks aren't allowed to own guns, but you need them, dontcha?". We chatted about South Africa for a while, the man made me feel a bit uneasy, his mouth was always creased in a smile, but his eyes did not smile, at all. "Well, there is BLM land over there and some camps, keep an eye out for moose and bear, don't worry, you should be fine, you have a gun, right?" No, sir, no gun. He looked at me as if I was half-mad. No gun? That's just irresponsible.

The BLM land was easy to find as it was located in the wooded hills which the old man had gestured towards and which was visible from the road. We drove past cleared site after cleared site until we found one that was level, free of litter and had a log fence surrounding it, a measure to keep the moose and bear away. We had found another site, but the freshly eaten carcass of a deer lay in the middle of the camp, perhaps eaten by coyote or mountain lion. The hills were dead quiet, no birds sang, and the leaves did not rustle. Luisa and I made a fire and fed the kids, while they sat in the tent, a beautiful night sky shone above us. "Hey, let's try that Fat Albert". Good idea. I quickly mixed and rolled a little joint, Luisa had a few tokes, and I finished the rest. We waited. I began to relax, and my shorts felt clammy, I needed to take a dump. Luisa started talking about bears, we heard a rustle in the woods. "What do we do if a bear comes into the camp; apparently, the moose are even more dangerous? I have got the pepper spray, here, have a can. You have to spray it in their eyes but make sure the wind is behind you, I wonder if they can climb into the tent? What do we do if it tries to climb into the tent? Have you got your knife? Good. And your machete? Good. That old man was really spooky. It is a shame about his son, there are a lot of guys like that, you know? Veterans who come back with PTSD. What do we call that is South Africa again? Ah, yes, recognised. That was spooky. So, what, he just runs off into the wild and does what paints his face with mud and hunts? That's fucked up. I mean that guy should be in therapy, not running around with weapons, he was special forces, right. Imagine he was watching us right now, imagine he was listening to us, sitting in a tree, thinking we are Taliban or something. That's spooky. What? Oh, whatever, stop being such a baby. This stuff has made me tired, I am going to bed, make sure you lock up, don't leave any food lying around. Jeez, that old man really freaked me out".

And that, ladies and gentleman, is why I don't smoke weed. Luisa has no chill. She intentionally freaks me out then goes to bed, leaving me alone with my imagination. And that night my imagination was running around in the dark, wet and hunted, waiting to be skinned alive. I sat and watched the fire for a while. Listening. Listening. My heart was pounding so fast that the veins in my ears bulged and the throbbing made it difficult for me to hear anything but my own blood rushing through my body. Chill, just relax, there is nothing out there. Then why did they build a log fence to keep the animals out? Look, over there, that part of the fence is broken, a bear or moose could easily step over that. And that gateway in the fence on the other side of the Landy? Something smaller could walk through there, and you would not even know about it until it was too late. "You have a gun, right?". Why did he ask me that, why would I need a gun? Maybe he was warning me. Maybe his son has killed people out here before, and he has had to help hide the bodies and vehicles. He wouldn't give up his son, the hero, for killing a bunch of fools out in the wild without even a gun to protect themselves, hell even if we had a gun that probably would not save us. Shit. Drink some water.

My mouth was so dry I could hardly swallow, my tongue felt like it had swollen to the size of a large, dry rat. Drink water, lock up, go to bed.
I stood up and, bravely, walked around the Land Rover to lock the doors and canopy, determined to show no fear. I climbed the ladder quickly and almost fell into the roof tent, thick canvas, my fortress. The family slept, Jessica snoring softly next to me. Her snores morphing into a slow grunting. Or was that a bear? Or a man pretending to be a bear. Is he toying with me? I lay there for what felt like an eternity, listening intently, every fibre in my body tense and ready to explode in defence of my family. Oh, no, I needed to relieve myself. Badly. Another eternity passed.
Eventually, I mustered all my courage, I knew he was out there waiting, I knew that he was the cat and I was the mouse, but this mouse would not be swallowed without a fight. I would confront him, let him come! I stepped down out of the tent, my Remington hunting knife in hand. I stood next to the fire which was still burning brightly (a sign that I had only been in the tent for about twenty minutes, though it had felt like many hours). I stood, my arms stretched out at my sides, a challenge, knife in hand and waited for him to come. He did not. Nothing happened. I started to feel a little foolish. I walked towards the fence, the broken part, testing my courage, and relieved myself. Still, nothing moved. I had a sip of water. I slowly began to relax. Never, ever again.

The next morning, we packed and left for a town called Estes Park, which is a stone's throw from the park entrance and is home to the Stanley Hotel, the hotel that inspired Stephen King's, The Shining. We stumbled across a Land Rover mechanic in the town, and we spent an hour taking a tour of his herd. The rest of the day was spent exploring the area and, after a visit to the BLM office, we found a camp up on the side of a mountain. The view from the camp was incredible and, though the camp was technically closed, we were able to find a good spot for the Landy to park. Close to where we camped a very tall, long-haired Asian man sat playing a traditional Chinese lute. He was dressed entirely in black and wore combat boots and a long Chinese moustache, the kind with no middle, his name was Mike, we called him Mike on a Bike. His motorcycle was pitch black as was his luggage, but his hammock was blood red. He trimmed weed to make money but had just moved out of his apartment and was trying to figure out his next move. Between his little camp and ours, and across a small dirt road, was a semi-permanent camp constructed of tarps which apparently belonged to a Texan. Mike told us to stay away from the Texan; apparently, he was the kind of guy who converted hammers into sharp weapons and who was not likely to be very fond of foreigners. We walked with Mike to have a look at the view, and I walked close to the Texans camp as we returned, which made Mike nervous. Mike did not seem to be the type who was easily scared, I was interested in meeting the Texan. Tex returned from wherever he spent his days and immediately made a large fire and turned his car stereo up loud. He must have recently had his heartbroken because he played one cheesy country love song on repeat for six hours "12 gauge. O 4, four on the floor". The song began to torture us and Tex could not decide whether he wanted to listen to it really loud or soft. He also seemed to have lost something in his truck as he opened the door every five minutes, adjusted the volume and then dug around for a while before slamming the door. People began to move their camps to get away from him, and he would shout at them as they left, as if upset they were going "too loud huh, damn, too loud!". Now, we had been to Texas, and we know that not all Texans are mad, but we certainly had found many of them that were absolutely bonkers. Don't mess with Texas, Texas is always watching (believe it or not, that the last line was actually a sign in a highway rest stop). Tex eventually cried himself to sleep, and we were able to do the same. Without the sobbing, of course. In the morning, Tex was gone, and Mike

LA LUCHA

was still wandering around. We said our goodbyes and took a photo of us Vikings with the "Mongolian" as Mike on a Bike liked to be called.

Our route to the Pacific Northwest took us back through incredible Utah and into Idaho. As we approached the Colorado/Utah state line, we passed a sign. "Marijuana is illegal in Utah". Oh, shit, we still had most of the Fat Albert, which was very expensive if you remember, and despite my vow to never, ever again smoke the stuff, I had somehow convinced myself that the second time I tried it, I would be less freaked out. Luisa held the brown vial in her hand, at the first sign of a roadblock on the border she would throw it from the vehicle. As we approached the state line there appeared to be a commotion, Luisa readied herself to dispose of Fatty, but as we approached we saw a young couple, crying and holding each other next to their campervan. A dead dog lay close to them on the road, and an eighteen-wheel truck was parked fifty meters up the road. Perhaps they had stopped to let the dog out to do his business, and the dog had been spooked or was chasing a rabbit, but he met his untimely end. The couple looked devastated, and we debated whether to stop and try and help them, there was not much we could do for them, and it seemed kinder to allow them to grieve privately. We continued our drive towards Salt Lake City, Luisa found an excellent radio station which played incredible rock and indie music we had never heard before, the soundtrack to a subdued drive, we had all been affected by that small tragedy on the state line.

Our new friends Alain and MJ were heading in the same direction, and we found an almost perfect campsite where we could meet up and enjoy a few days working and tidying the Land Rover. The Park City RV campsite lay at the foot of a large hill, next to a stream and a stone's throw from the 2002 Winter Olympics park and about 45 kilometres east of Salt Lake City. Park City, though relatively small, had all the "big box' stores, Walmart, Costco, Best Buy. Luisa had recently filed a claim for all our tech which had been destroyed while travelling, which included my state of the art Sony Vaio (which six years after purchase still has higher specs than most off the shelf laptops) which had been murdered in Brazil, various cameras, tablets, etc. Our tech goes through hell, we should be using military-grade hardware, but who has money for that? Luisa spent the next three days studying the internet for deals on computers and tablets, her greatest fear, greater than death or poverty, is buying something today, then finding that it goes on special or is cheaper somewhere else. Fifty tabs open on her pink Sony Vaio (bought in a tax-free zone in Paraguay and is now held together with duct tape), she searched the entire country for a new computer. In the morning we would drive to Best Buy, and she would study each laptop on display. Best Buy also has computers which are not on display, marked down computers which were returned or repaired or shop soiled and which they sell for up to 30% less than "new" machines. Each Best Buy has their own selection of marked down computers which they keep locked in a cupboard and Luisa phoned or emailed every Best Buy in and within 100 kilometres of Salt Lake City to find out what they were hiding from her. She scoured the internet for refurbished laptops with ten-year guarantees and wanted me to look at every option available and then tell her which one to buy. When I selected the one I thought she should purchase based on hours of conversation, reading specs and a process of elimination, I was told: "no, not that one, I don't like the colour and they may have it cheaper somewhere else". I needed to make the decision so that I could bear the responsibility if the wrong machine was selected. After three days, I gave up and told her she was on her own. Eventually, she could not commit and only bought a tablet each for Jessica and I (early birthday presents, Keelan's birthday was coming up and we planned to find him a gaming laptop) and a Bose wireless speaker. You can't have buyer's remorse if you don't buy anything.

Alain and MJ joined us at the camp, and we hiked, made brats and burgers, drank Coors Lite and ate cupcakes. Their sons, Jeremy and Nicholas had joined them for this leg of their tour. Jeremy was primed to take over his father's empire and build his own, while Nicholas was studying to become a Canadian policeman, a process which requires a college degree and a thirty-week diploma course and training at a police college. The family is a tight-knit unit, and they enjoyed telling us about how incredible it is to live in Canada. Alain's concern for our future deepened, and at one stage he suggested that he might approach the Canadian Prime Minister, Justin Trudeau (who he knew personally) to help us to get Canadian citizenship. We were not quite ready to give up our travels, but one day we might consider it and take you up on that offer, Alain. Canadians and Americans have a bit of a love-hate relationship – the Canadians enjoy European style socialism, have a strong economy, incredible nature, excellent and affordable healthcare, low crime and a relatively small population.

Salt Lake City is surprisingly chilled and laidback, we were expecting a conservative Mormon city but found the city to be friendly and open. Another new friend who we had met at the Overland Expo had invited us to visit his home. He, Fernando, lives in a lovely restored home in the suburbs with his partner Elizabeth, two dogs, a Sportsmobile and new Land Rover Discovery, a BMW 1200 GS and is a local fire chief who is studying medicine. Fernando is Uruguayan by birth but did not eat enough meat to remain in the country, so they deported him to the USA when he was but a lad. Fernando was a perfect guide to the city, and he could answer many of the questions we had, particularly regarding the epidemic of opioid abuse and homeless veterans. The city has many homeless people and veterans make up a large percentage of their number. Often soldiers would return from war to a hero greeting but found it difficult to adjust back into society, often they had suffered injuries at war and had become reliant on opioid painkillers, which they replaced with illegal narcotics once their prescriptions had expired. These men and women often lacked medical insurance and were cared for by clinics set up by volunteers like Fernando who spent much of his spare time serving the community for which he cares greatly.

Hot, sunny Salt Lake City would be our home for the next few days, and we were invited to attend the British Field Day meet up in the Liberty Park which was to be held over the weekend. We asked permission to open our tent and to sell our book, a request which was granted and on the day of the show we set up and prepared the family for action, we each had our role to play. We had never had to talk so much! Keelan was often surrounded by a group of people, as he animatedly told stories and gave a tour of the Landy, starting in the front of the vehicle and walking people around before asking them to "exit through the gift shop". A pile of books sat on the front fender, and we found ourselves signing books and replenishing the pile often. We lost track of time as a steady stream of people came to meet us, word spreading around the event that there was a crazy family of South Africans giving tours of their awesome machine. Jessica sat in the tent and played with the little kids who clambered up the ladders, Keelan entertained the crowds and Luisa, and I tried to keep up with the man child's work ethic. All too soon, the event came to a close, and we took stock. We had sold forty books at $20 a book! This called for an extravagant celebration at Wendy's burger joint after we had said our goodbyes to Fernando, Elizabeth and our new friend Bill from Great Basin Rovers.

The Wendy's burger joint we choose was just off the highway heading west but could not have been further from green Liberty Park and her collection of iconic British vehicles, if it had been on a concrete moon. People with dirty clothing, tattoos, piercings and questionable health, joined us for a greasy burger and cold fries. We were finding the wealth gap in the USA to be massive. A middle-class neighbourhood anywhere else in the world is a working-class neighbourhood in the USA, perhaps because wealth used to be shared quite evenly throughout the country but a three-bedroom house and a couple cars, the sign of the middle class in other industrialised nations, does not equate to the same here. The "hood" is not a collection of shacks, it has white picket fences, lawns and flags flying in the breeze. How do you know that you are in an affluent area then? The answer, other than the type of cars and general tidiness, lies in the supermarkets which operate there. If there is Whole Foods or QFC supermarket, the area has expendable income. If there is only a Walmart, best you keep on trucking. This is also where you will find the infamous strip mall, a length of shops lined next to each other parallel to the main road. The strip mall is where you will find a bottle store, a tobacconist, a tattoo parlour, a hairdresser and five empty stores. We had visited a proper American mall in Salt Lake City, and we found it to be just like any other we had seen around the planet.

I suspect that when other nations build their malls, they use those of America as the benchmark to surpass. Malls are dying in America. With the rise of online shopping, Americans are staying away from malls with their high overheads and subsequent prices. Amazon and Walmart are going head to head to gain the lion's share of the US consumer spending, Amazon is set to win, and automation is the future, drones and self-drive vehicles will deliver countrywide to fulfilment centres and to your door. Those 1.5 million working-class Americans who work for Walmart will gradually be whittled away until only a corporate handful remains. Amazon will do the same. The top 1% are consolidating their hold on the economy, and once they have it all, they will not be giving it back. Not one administration since Eisenhower has done anything to protect the American public from limitless corporate ambition and competition. The elites know that technology is progressing at such an incredible rate that soon the world and her social systems will be very different from what they are today. If you look at the technological progress which has been made in the last 100 years, you will see that it all really began with the industrial revolution and that we are now at the beginning of the technological revolution, robotics and artificial intelligence (AI) will soon render many of us obsolete as a labour force. I am not talking about R2D2 collecting your trash or cleaning your house but rather the kind of robotics and AI which self-diagnoses, maintains and improves, the machines which will build your self-drive cars and the batteries which power them. Some of us fear robotics and automation, many of us already know that we are on the brink of new social systems which will change everything we know about who we are and what we are, but many of us refuse to accept what is coming.

Now, if you opened this book thinking it might be helpful to read about an adventure in a Land Rover, but now you are being confronted with opinions which you did not ask for, I sympathise, but let me explain. My goal is to travel the planet and learn. To learn as much as I can and to teach my kids what I have learned. I have no real bias, patriotism or loyalty except to my fellow man, no matter what shape, colour, size or sexual orientation. As global overlanders, we have the distinct advantage of visiting countries and seeing them as outsiders while slowly immersing ourselves. We can look at a society from three perspectives, our perceptions before we visit, our experiences while we are there and our impressions once we leave. We can see the changes which are taking place across the globe, we can see those changes as we move, we are exposed to many different forms of information from mainstream media, on the ground information from people we know and through social media. I am not expected to be loyal to any government, but I expect myself to be fair to the people, people who we have found that more than anything else, see themselves as being good. Americans are the most giving people on the planet and contribute far more to charity than any other people, almost double as generous in fact. We experienced that generosity first hand. But something has happened in America over the last twenty years, something which Americans themselves despise. Enter Donald Trump.

LA LUCHA

Trump announced in June 2015 that he would run for the presidency of the United States of America, and it was while we were in Salt Lake City that we first heard the announcement. Everyone laughed and dismissed him. What could possibly qualify this real estate tycoon to be one of the most powerful and influential people on the planet? He called Mexicans rapists and criminals. He tapped into the fears many Americans felt. We know better, we had spent months in Mexico, and most Mexicans we met were hard-working, decent people. But many Americans thought that they had been robbed by the previous administrations, the wealth and prosperity they used to enjoy was slowly being eroded, and the reasons to support Trump were many and varied. The conspiracy theorists saw Trump as a government outsider, they wanted less government, not more. Barrack Obama, was to these people, not a patriot but instead someone who wanted to change the cultural landscape of America, to allow refugees and migrants who would steal the jobs from generations of Americans, the Democrats seen to be attempting to implement socialist practices such as universal healthcare which would tax the workers and sustain the lazy. Fundamentalist Christian America held hands with the right-wing, and both groups had lost faith in the Republican party. Make America Great Again was Trump's rallying call and that message resonated with many Americans. And they hated Hillary Clinton almost as much as they hated Barrack Obama, Clinton perhaps more so, she represented everything that they hated, and Bernie Sanders was not much better. Trump has none of the qualities of a good politician, and it is for that very reason that people began to stand behind him, they did not love Trump, they hated the alternative. Perhaps if the Republicans had a decent alternative, the Trump MAGA movement would have been stillborn but dopey Ben Carson, slimy Ted Cruz and chinless Jeb Bush, were no match for a huge population sick and tired of, "business as usual". Mainstream media hated Trump and "middle" America hates the mainstream media. Conservative personalities like Bill O'Reilly, Sean Hannity and Rush Limbaugh threw their weight behind

Trump when they saw his populist appeal and the debate raged on the airwaves.

Most of the Americans we had met laughed the announcement off, Trump was just trying to get publicity, as he always did, and he would not even make it to the first round of debates.

Oops, I did it again.

5

Leaving Utah

We were incredibly impressed with the state and had enjoyed almost every minute we had spent gawking at the incredible natural beauty. Idaho was next on the agenda and had a huge task to be able to live up to the standard set by the states we had already visited. We were pumped to cross another state line, and after driving 3 hours on the I84, we crossed the line. A truck overtook us and started drifting back into our lane, way too soon. Luisa screamed, and I hit the brakes and the hooter. The truck jerked back into its lane then continued to swerve between the lanes before settling back into the right-hand lane and powering up a huge hill. We stopped in a small town to buy groceries at the local Walmart and, while looking for parking, drove towards a group of three Latino men. Two of the men were talking and started throwing fists at each other, neither backing down, trading blow for blow until they noticed the Defender staring at them. They must have thought that the vehicle belonged to authority because they stopped hammering each other and continue to chat as if nothing happened. We found a parking spot a good distance away from the men and did our shopping before heading back on the freeway in the direction of Boise. Luisa spotted a campsite just off the main road, and we stopped at the gas station and convenience store where the camp reception was located. The camp was surrounded by flat fields, and a dirt road led off in the direction of a hill. A huge, matt black pick up pulled up and a bald young man, whose size and appearance would not be out of place in a WWE wrestling leotard, lumped out of the vehicle and into the store. Another pick up pulled up, and Axle Rose's younger brother climbed out. Idaho is so rock 'n roll. We joked a bit with the receptionist, asking for an African discount, hahaha, and, without prompting she told us how her daughter had just been released for dealing Methamphetamines (Meth) and her son had just gone in for the same reason. "Oh. Jeez. That's terrible". We paid the $20.00 and parked on a concrete block, surrounded by gigantic RV's and Fifth Wheels, and adjacent to a large green lawn. We noticed that Americans reacted to us either with interest or completely ignored us. As we sat on a bench, under a tree and above a perfect lawn, grilling dinner on our small braai, a man with a young son came to greet us. He was in town for a shooting competition and was interested in our opinion about guns. Well, I like guns, always have, and if I had the option, I would own a 9mm handgun for self-protection and a Tikka 30.06 rifle for target practice and for hunting if the dire need ever arose that I would have to hunt for food. Keelan also enjoyed shooting, and we had bought him a pellet gun in Brazil with the strict instruction that he could never shoot anything with a heartbeat. The conversation turned to the crime situation in South Africa, and we discovered, again, that people we met here either knew nothing about our country or they knew almost as much as we did. I told the man that I have huge respect for Nelson Mandela but not for the modern ANC. He asked me about farm murders and whether the farmers in South Africa should be allowed to defend themselves. Of course, they should, better yet, they shouldn't have to. We spoke about gun murders in the USA, and he told me that more people are murdered in the USA with hammers. I thought back to our heartbroken Texan friend and the sharpened hammers. The reason, I was told, that more people are murdered with hammers than with guns is that hammer murders tend to be a crime of passion. I would have preferred to not have had the conversation after a long day driving. I wanted only a cold beer and a piece of grilled chicken.

LA LUCHA

After packing up and a cold morning shower, we fired up the Landy and headed out, back on the I84 towards Oregon. The road was very quiet, and we hardly had any traffic to contend with as we entered Eastern Oregon then travelled directly towards Washington State, passing close to where the Bundy brothers and a local militia would occupy the Malheur National Forest in early January 2016, asking for snacks and receiving sex toys. Coincidently, Shawna Cox, one of the key militia members arrested, was from friendly Kanab and she sued the Federal government for $666 billion because "she suffered damages from the works of the devil".

Plain was our destination, the little town up in the mountains three hours east of Seattle. We arrived for the event a day early, a rare achievement for us, usually we come skidding in at the last moment. We had driven 2100 kilometres to reach the Northwest Overland Rally, and we were lucky enough to bump into the organiser, Ray, as we approached the field where the event was to be held. An old battered Series 1 Land Rover stood in the field, loaded with tools and equipment. "My family and I are going to drive that Landy from London to Singapore", Ray told us without a hint of boast. 'Where is the roof tent, you must be taking a trailer, how many kids, three! You must be mental". (The next year Ray and his family did drive that temperamental little Series all the way from the UK to Singapore, carrying very little luggage. Tough!). As the set up for the event was not yet complete, we drove down along the banks of the Wenatchee River and were accompanied by a couple of Spanish travellers, Pablo and Anna, who had been driving their Mitsubishi around the world, on and off, for the last fifteen years. We made a braai and talked shop. Pablo had already published a couple books and had them translated into English. I enjoyed his writing style; poetic and descriptive. Anna is the sweetest woman you could ever wish to meet, gentle and tough, as most long-term overlanding women become. I still had a lot to learn about the publishing industry and I learned more from Pablo than he may have intended to teach. The next few days were the exact opposite of the Snoverland Expo. The event had a far more relaxed atmosphere and daytime temperatures reached 43 C, overlanders were dropping like flies and the bikers especially had a tough time dressed head to toe in protective gear (the rally was a combination of an overland rally and the Touratech motorbike rally in 2015). We had been assigned a position a few rows back from the main display area and, mainly because of the heat, there was very little foot traffic past our little Landy bookshop. Luisa and I took turns manning our "booth" and exploring the rally, looking for people like us. I found Brad and Sheena from Drive Nacho Drive fame and we took a break to walk down to the cold flowing river and refresh. Word soon spread that the river was the place to be and hordes of sweating overlanders were soon making the pilgrimage to the aquatic Shangri La. Our friends from Team Overland were also at the rally and we spent an evening cooling off with strong beer. An old, drunk lady showed up at midnight, driving a golf cart to complain to all and sundry about the noise. The rally is a massive boost to the local economy and there was no loud music or fireworks to disrupt the peace, only laughter. Someone stole the drunk ladies golf cart and drove it across the field and parked it in a ditch.

At night the organisers would have kids run around and hand out raffle tickets and with the sun setting and temperatures dropping, the crowds would emerge from their canvas saunas to sit and have a beer while one of the staff whipped everyone up into a frenzy. There was a statewide severe fire warning, but the organisers were allowed to make a bonfire in the middle of the field. It was all just too charming. We gave a book to raffle, my marketing plans are impeccable, one reader at a time. In the morning we were amazed to see Ray's wife, Marianne cleaning up around camp, including the plastic receptacles from hell (in that heat particularly). Ray's family earned the respect of everyone there for their hard work, class and humility. We have been to a few rallies now and the Northwest Overland Rally suits us the best, we loved it. On the last day, the family and I had the opportunity to give a talk about our travels. I once had to do a presentation to a few hundred people with my body and face covered in pussy boils, the result of contracting impetigo in a filthy African river, after that experience, public speaking does not scare me in the least, how could anything be worse than that experience. Our only fear was that no-one would show up for the talk but at the last minute, the presentation filled. We had everyone laughing and gave a tour of the Landy as well as having a long chat with a friend we had never met before, Dan from the 4x4 Podcast. He was moving up to Alaska to serve the military and had had us on his podcast for an enjoyable interview.

After a long weekend of the scorching sun, we eventually left Plain and all our new friends, a few books lighter, and headed towards Seattle. At first, we stayed at one of the vendor's house and then moved to a pleasant campsite run by unpleasant people in Gig Harbour. The plan was to try and get some resources together for the final push up to Alaska. Our book sales out of hand had been quite good but not good enough, winter would soon be approaching, and we needed to get moving. We toured the Olympic National Park for a few days while trying to figure out how we would get the funds together and we came up with the idea of attending car shows, the rallies had not been very good for sales but, if the British Field Day in Salt Lake City was anything to go by, we were in with a win. Little did we know that the Greater Seattle area would become our base for a few months and we were about to embark on one of the most challenging and spectacular challenges of our journey.

6

Going Nowhere Slowly

We bummed around the Puget Sound for a while staying with friends of friends and even doing a presentation for the Gig Harbour Rotary Club. We house-sat a home in Tacoma, the home of a lovely Defender owning military family, and it was there that Luisa read about the weekly exotic car show held in a town called Redmond, east of Seattle. Redmond boasts a few exotic cars simply because it is the home of Microsoft, Nintendo of America and AT&T Mobility, amongst others. We reached out to the organisers of the car show and told them our story. We are a South African family travelling the world in a Land Rover Defender. We would love to show off our vehicle and maybe, if possible, sell a few of our books. "Sure", they said, "you are more than welcome".

We set off for Redmond one busy Friday morning and eventually found ourselves camped in the parking lot of the Marymoor Park and arrived in the centre of Redmond early, ready for a day of non-stop talking. The organiser gave us a huge smile when he saw us coming and directed us to park on the sidewalk, directly in front of the display window for a large fashion outlet. Lamborghini's, Porches, Ferrari's, Aston Martins, Jaguars and other supercars surrounded us. We thought we did not have a chance of attracting any interest. Until we opened the roof tent, that is. We were suddenly surrounded by groups of people, kids clambering into the tent and impeccably dressed adults inundating us with questions. Keelan was in top form and guided groups around the battle-scarred Defender, telling our stories from his point of view, enchanting the crowd. We would have sold all our books that day, if only we had a credit card machine, nobody was carrying cash and a few people had to go draw money from the ATM, some never returned, but most did. As the show was winding down, at about 2 pm, Keelan came to me and gave me a small but heavy box. "What is it?" I asked before opening the box. "Look", he said. Inside the box were five smaller, rectangular boxes and each box contained a new Samsung Galaxy tablet, the very latest version. "Are you kidding?". Keelan told me the story. He had been showing a group around the Land Rover and a dark-haired man had asked what we use for navigation. Keelan produced our old, cracked Samsung tablet which we had bought in Chile and explained to the man that we downloaded free maps and used that to get ourselves across continents. The man asked a few more questions and then disappeared, only to return twenty minutes later, giving the box to Keelan, who nearly had a heart attack on the spot. Keelan introduced me to Mark, a senior marketing director at AT&T who had been incredibly impressed by Keelan's open, friendly nature and engaging storytelling. We were flabbergasted. Each tablet was worth $400, and this kind man had just given us a $2000 gift. Only in America, my friends. We took some photos with Mark and gave him a signed copy of We Will Be Free, it was all we had to give. Mark left, and we packed up the Landy, buzzing. Keelan and Luisa each unwrapped a new tablet (Jessica and I already had new tablets) and the rest were put away for future use. "I told you, Luisa, we have a story to tell, people are interested, we are going to do this!". It was the confidence boost we all needed, after months of doubt and hard work, we all realised that we were on the correct path.

Our luck seemed to have improved and the next day we met a couple who were hosting one of the state campsites. Jim and Linda were recently retired and loving life. Jim was an ex-fireman and Linda had been an IT professional. We chatted to Jim as we sat in the campsite, planning our next step. Jim is an incredibly warm and caring person and he was intrigued by our story. We left early the next morning and moved to another state camp by the ocean and were very surprised when Jim and Linda rolled into our campsite. They had been passing by and spotted the Land Rover, this is what they told us, I think Jim wanted to help us and when he noticed that we had left his camp early in the morning (we had gone to their fifth wheel to say goodbye, but they were not there or were sleeping and we did not want to disturb them) he had made a few calls to the other state camps to see if we had shown up there. They had a house standing empty in a town called, Mukilteo (home to the Boeing factory) and wanted to know if we wanted to house-sit the house for a while, while they were not there. Naturally, we were very grateful and accepted the offer. That night we slept in their beautiful little home and soon we were part of the community. The neighbours took us in and made us feel at home. Keith and Anna, Mike and Sue, Tim and Nicole and a doctor who looked like a young James Spader, lived in homes which shared the cul-de-sac and they made us feel like we were part of the furniture. It is incredible how quickly we adapted to being Americans.

The kids and I would take a long walk to the supermarket every day, past the high school and beautifully manicured homes. On the third day, there was a knock on the door and Luisa answered to find a policeman, hand on the holster, asking us what we were doing in the home. Linda had cancelled the trash collection and the trashman's suspicion had been aroused when Keelan asked him why he was not taking our trash. The trashman called the cops and the cops scared the living daylights out of Luisa. Once Luisa explained the situation, the cop relaxed, and she gave him a tour of the Land Rover, answered all his questions about our travels and advised him to take his bride to be to Argentina for their honeymoon, explaining that once they exchanged their dollars on the black market, everything would be half price.

LA LUCHA

Luisa was incredibly impressed by the experience if only the police back home could serve their community as well. The police had come to check the house because there had been a few cases of people breaking into people's homes why they were on holiday, then squatting.

We were not planning to stay in Mukilteo for very long, but one weekend had a conversation with our new friend Mark from AT&T when we returned for another round at the exotic car show in Redmond. Mark had recently run a very successful online campaign with his team and he was thinking about working with us to launch one of AT&T's new devices, the LG V10. "Yeah, sure we are interested". "Where are you going to be for the next few weeks?". He asked. "We will be wherever you need us to be!".

The implications were massive. If we could be part of an advertising campaign with one of the largest corporations in America, our problems would be solved. We would get unprecedented access to the US market; the pay would probably not suck, and it would launch us onto the national stage. That Monday, we received an email from Mark confirming what we had spoken about, giving us some background and information about the LG device. The idea was that we would make videos and take photos as we travelled, using the LG device and providing the footage daily to the AT&T team. We were ecstatic and made plans to stay in Mukilteo, while the negotiations continued. Of course, we were also realistic, having learned too many times in the past not to count our chickens before they hatch.

We settled into a routine of working on the Land Rover and promoting our book online during the week and attending car shows on the weekend.

We ordered two hundred more books, which cleaned out most of our recent earnings, and soon learned that not all car shows are equal. The All British Field Meet at the St. Edward State Park was a fun event and the Landy won two awards for just being awesome (the judges of the one award were local cub scouts) and we met many like-minded people. The 4th July car show we attended near Seattle was not really our cup of tea and the Tacoma car show was not a great event for us. The Wings and Wheels event held at an airport in Gig Harbour introduced us to many of the vintage vehicle owners we would meet again and again at the various car shows we attended. We might have become overexposed in the greater Washington area. Still, we were doing well enough selling books to cover our expenses, which essentially was our grocery and internet bill.

Italian Mike from the Mukilteo cul-de-sac made the mistake of telling Luisa that he was an ex-Fed Ex-manager and that he paid half price for shipments, soon he was inundated with packages flying to and fro. I opened a bank account at Bank of America who essentially required only my passport and within two hours Luisa was on internet banking distributing our hard-earned cash to the masses. America knows how to do business. Luisa discovered Amazon Prime and one-year unlimited money back guarantees, REI and Costco. Customer service is incredible, and everything gets done and usually, it gets done well. Not happy? Talk to a supervisor, problem solved. Your black paint too black? No worries, we are so sorry, here you can have your money back. Safeway will deliver groceries to your door? Oh, we need ice cream. Buy one, pay $3.00, buy six, pay $4.00. Luisa is an American and proud of it.

One thing we had very little experience of was American football or the NFL, yes, we had seen Any Given Sunday (and wondered who in their right mind would put Cameron Diaz in the same room as Al Pacino) and we had an idea as to what the rules were. Our new neighbours, Tim and Nicole invited us to watch a Seahawks (seeeeeeeeeee HOKS!) game. They made brats and burgers and we sipped on a few Coors Lite. It took a short while for Tim to talk us through the rules and we then settled in to watch the action. Football is probably the only thing that Americans do slow. A BBQ may only last an hour, but an NFL match can take five hours to come to an end. Remember, we are rugby fans and rugby is eighty minutes of action, with a ten-minute halftime, you scream at the tv, you jump up and down, your heart is in your throat and you sit on the edge of your seat, especially when South Africa takes on New Zealand. Football is not rugby. You must keep your eye on the screen, following the action, but you also have time to chat to a visiting friend about that new guy at work and how your truck just isn't pulling like it should. Maybe you will have a talk about adverts on TV. In football when there is a stop in play, the networks will switch to adverts and the transition from game to advert is so seamless, you hardly realise that you are watching an advert. The whole experience of watching the game was laid back and social. By contrast, when Luisa and I watched a rugby match a few days later, the neighbours came running over to find out what all the screaming was about.

Mark had us on tenterhooks waiting for the email to follow the last. Things move slowly in the corporate world and there were many people involved in the decision-making process, we had to be patient and be ready when the time came. Unfortunately, the Landy developed a mechanical knock and we found that the rear half shafts had worn quite badly. A friend who had worked as a welder on nuclear submarines tried to weld the shafts to the drive members, but the weld did not hold. We ordered a new set of half shafts from the UK, but after two weeks the incorrect shafts were sent, and we had to wait for a new set to arrive. It was almost a month that we were unable to drive the Landy and that meant we were not selling books at car shows. And with Luisa's rate of spending, we were soon running low on cash (Luisa would argue that it is my rate of consumption which is the problem). Again, we were impressed by how things were done in the US. In any other country, our valuable spares would have sat at customs for two weeks, or more, and we would have to pay large import duties. The USA understands that business is business, keep the goods moving, simplify the systems, boost the economy. By now we were in September 2015 and the window to visit Alaska was drawing close. Soon the snow would begin to fall, and temperatures would plummet. We needed to move or not go at all.

We spoke to Mark at AT&T and he advised us to head on up to Alaska when he needed us he would let us know and a plan would be made. Damn, we really wanted this thing to kick off sooner rather than later, Alaska could wait, but we agreed that it was now or never, packed the Landy, locked up Jim and Linda's lovely home, kissed the neighbours and set off for the Canadian border, a two-hour drive away.

7

Canadia, Ey

We arrived at the USA/Canada border just before dusk. We had applied for the Canadian visas while in Mukilteo and had been relieved when they arrived, valid for five years. We chose a small border east of the main border crossing, we did not want to sit in queues and compete with trucks and we have always found that smaller borders are easier to cross. We drove straight out of the USA into Canada without even seeing an American border official. We pulled into the Canadian immigration car park and went inside to be greeted by a surly, officious Canadian border official. She grilled us for a while, being passive-aggressive and smirking when she could have smiled. We asked whether we should have handed in our tourist cards when we left the USA. She said no, but did not explain why not. "Are you sure we don't have to hand in the cards, ma'am?". "I have been working here for twenty years, what do you think?". I think you are uptight and need a holiday, somewhere sunny and friendly. We doubted that she would let us into Canada, despite our freshly printed visas. Eventually, she scanned each passport, after studying each for ten minutes, and told us to fuck off and welcome to Canada, but not quite with those words. We headed back to the Landy but decided not to take Cruella Deville's advice and instead walked over to the US border control office. There we explained the situation to a friendly and professional border agent. "Canadians", he said, "don't worry, you have done the right thing", and he took our white tourist cards. The border agent was muscular and good looking and later we would realise that we were lucky to have met him. We hoped that when we returned to the US, they would give us new tourist cards valid for a fresh six months of America. Hell yeah!

We drove east on the 1 Trans Canadian Highway and then up a muddy forest road to find a camp near Jones Lake. It was so late in the year that many of the camps had closed for the season, which meant we could camp for free. The road up to the lake was not a test of the Land Rover at all but it was easier to drive up in low range 3rd gear than it was to keep swapping through the gears in high. A film of mud covered the Landy when we eventually chose a campsite and as the sunset, the rain began to fall. We were wary of bears, so installed the kids in the roof tent and Luisa cooked a pasta dinner, as the persistent rain slowly drenched our camp. We still had the butane in our tank, which a helpful dork had put in the tank instead of propane in Argentina, the little blue flame struggling to warm the pots, let alone cook our food. We had tried to refill the gas tank in almost every town we passed through, but no-one would touch our South African tank. I had been complaining to Luisa, back in Jim and Linda's house, that I missed the road, that I could never settle down for a long period of time, that I was happiest out in the wild and a grumpy bitch indoors. Luisa took a video of me standing in the rain, trying to stop the water from leaking into the side of the tent. "Are you happy now?" she asked. I was not, and this was not a good sign of things to come as we headed north into the approaching winter.

That morning, the muddy road to the lake was as slippery as an ice rink with large muddy puddles which the Landy laughed at. Again, we drove in low range, down, down, down and emerged back on the 1 highway looking like we had spent a week in the forest. Up we drove and soon we were in the most beautiful wilderness, the sun broke through the clouds and we were astounded by the alpine beauty of British Colombia.

Canada is a huge country, sparsely populated and wild. Almost 75% of the population lives within 170 kilometres of the long, straight US border. Much of Canada is beautiful wilderness which will chew you up and spit you out if you don't treat her like a dangerous lady. I had been watching a lot of bushcraft videos, Ray Mears, Dick Proenneke, and John Nieman Tools (now Northmen). I had restored my old axe which had travelled with us for so many years and had become fascinated by the idea of living off the grid, far from anyone or anything, building a home by hand using only hand tools and my dear Land Rover. I would need a plot of land, near a lake full of fish. If the land was sloped, I could build my home into the hill, Hobbit style, and if the land was flat and wooded, I would build a large log home and a stable where my chicken, rabbits and sheep would live. A dairy cow or two would be grand. A good hunting rifle and a supply of shells would keep the cool box full of deer and black bear (yes, black bears are good eating). I would make biltong and would learn how to preserve fish, fruit and vegetables for the long winter months. The summer days would be spent preparing for winter and the winter months would be spent exploring with snowshoes, hunting and living off winter foods. I would have a blacksmithing cabin, where I would forge my own tools and learn how to make exquisite knives, axes and other tools. I would learn to farm and could eventually withdraw almost entirely from society, allowing only my favourite humans to know where we could be found (I say we, but let's be honest, I mean me. The wife would probably last a couple winters, Keelan would need to find some girls to keep himself warm and both he and Jessica would freak out after longer than three months without the internet).

As we drove north, through the pristine boreal forest, I would daydream about building that home where money was not as important as hard work or food or sunshine. I would need only to buy the land, tools and animals, almost everything else I could make myself, my bed would be bearskin, my blankets beaver pelt, my clothing the forest Armani of softened deerskin. I would make my furniture by hand and would learn how to make moonshine and beer. Canada is overflowing with animals, thanks to very strict hunting rules, but where I will be there will be no-one to tell me what I could or could not do, besides, I would only take what I needed. Once every two months, a supply waterplane would deliver selected books and notepads, tobacco, whisky, a case of Guinness, girlie mags, flour, soap, spices, salt and a huge bar of chocolate.

My driving daydreams would be interrupted only by a short conversation, a passing car or a small town. In the USA, we would usually sell a book or two every time we stopped at a gas station to fill up the tank. Those book sales paid for the fuel, food and accommodation and we were hoping that the Canadians would be as interested and generous. It did not seem like that was going to happen. Yes, the Canadians would strike up a conversation with us and after half an hour of talking, I would tell them about our book. Where an American would say "jeez, I need that book!", the Canadian would look at me as if I had just kissed his wife, say "oh, that's nice, have a good trip". Ok then.

Our first stop was Prince George, a clean, modern city so remote I wondered if it was supplied by airdrop. I was to learn what remote really was in the next few weeks. We found a campsite on the way out of the city and settled in for a braai. As Luisa and I sat chatting, a pick up pulled up at the store across the road, plumes of steam rising from the bonnet and hot water spraying the ground below the engine. I asked if I could help and we found that one of the coolant hoses had burst. He could not get mobile phone reception and we offered him the camp WIFI password. The man and his friend were on their way home from working in a lumber yard in the north. "It's ok, my girlfriend will get the trailer and come to get us, it is only a five-hour drive". Only Canadians, Russians, Australians and Americans can say those words with a straight face. They had been driving solidly for three days already, five hours was a short trip. The men each drank a beer and then went to sleep in the truck.

Canadians are really trusting. Each supermarket will have a pick and mix area hidden amongst the aisles where you can fill your own bags with nuts, fruit and chocolate. Being on a tight budget we would descend on the pick 'n mix and try everything and, being foreigners, we had no idea what M&M's, assorted chocolates, liquorice or nuts tasted like. "Mm, kids, you have to try this one. Ooh, that is nice, have you tried these? Thank you for asking, no, I have not! What is that over there? I suggest we try some. Yes, I do believe they have an excellent selection of snacks in this fine country, I believe we should now purchase some". Luisa, at first, pretended that she did not know us, but soon joined in the fun. Please note, we are only serial "tasters" in chain supermarkets and would not try the same trick in a family-owned mom 'n pop store. We are of the people. Our daily diet consisted of a breakfast of yoghurt and fruit, lunch of pick 'n mix and a ham and cheese sandwich and dinner of braaied chicken and salad. For snacks, we had the pick 'n mix we had bought and either carrot or snap peas or fruit.

The idea was that we would motor it up to Alaska quickly and then take our time as we drove back down. A new friend, Christophe, knew Alaska and Canada very well, having lived in the area and being an insatiable explorer, put together an extensive list of must-see places. We intended to get up to Prudhoe Bay at the tip of the Pan American highway and to then explore Christophe's list at a leisurely pace from the north to the south, keeping ahead of the snow.

The Defender developed a leak in the transfer box and every day I was having to crawl under her and top up the oil, other than that she was driving beautifully. Her BF Goodrich tyres had already done 70 000 kilometres, but the tread looked good, as did the sidewalls. The TD5 engine never missed a beat and every morning she would start on the second crank.

At Katanga, we reached the junction in the road where we turned onto the route 37, the road up to the Yukon. At the junction, the road crossed a bridge and below the bridge the Skeena river flowed into a narrow gorge where First Nation people fished salmon by hand, plucking the delicious fish from the water deftly. Route 37 is also known as the Stewart Cassiar Highway and it reaches up into some of the most isolated areas in British Colombia. On this road, we would see large amounts of wild animals, mostly moose, elk, bison and black bear. The road was old, weathered and quiet and I soon learned to keep an eye on the wild verges of the road where animals grazed and hid. Approaching Kwitancool Lake, I spotted movement 200 metres ahead and slowed the Land Rover. A black bear stepped out on to the road, followed closely by a cub. I had seen enough wildlife programs to know that black bears usually have twin cubs, so I slowed down further even though momma bear and her nervous cub had already crossed the road. Sure enough, a second cub darted out of the forest and headed across the road to join her family. We were expecting the Kwitancool Camp to be a rustic affair, long drop toilets and campsites etched out of the forest. It was not. The camp was packed with RV's and fifth wheels, motorhomes and campers. People fished and rode bicycles, made fires and chilled. We found a spot near the pristine lake and befriended the neighbours who donated wood and cold beer to our evening, we did not ask for either, but they had plenty and were happy to share. To even the score and stoke the karma we gave our new friends a copy of, We Will Be Free. The sunset late and we went to bed with stomachs full of grilled chicken, listening to the lake lapping at the shore. Though the camp was relatively modern and well equipped, it did have a long drop toilet which, by mid-morning, stank to high hell. You had to sit and do your business as quickly as possible, holding your breath or breathing through your shirt, trying not to think of the hell that lay below you.

Back on the road, we enjoyed great weather and we're making good time. We had missed the bug season and though the nights were cool, they were not cold. The next few days consisted of covering large distances and chilling in small-town libraries, where we always found comfortable chairs and free WIFI. Finding camping was never a problem and we either parked in a parking lot next to a lake or found an unmanned state campsite where we could make ourselves comfortable around the fire as the night crept in around us. The Canadian long drops were terrible, clean, but the smell could curl your toes after a long summer of traveller dumps. We had a saying that nothing is as strong as a Bolivian woman, now we added that nothing on earth stinks like a Canadian long drop. Occasionally we would be joined in camp by another camper, but most were heading South, while we headed north. "A bit late dontcha think?".

As we headed towards the Yukon, the landscape began to change as the evergreens spruce, pine and fir were outclassed by the autumn yellows and oranges of the millions of birch, poplar, cottonwood and aspen trees. There was evidence of large fires, but much of the road was bordered by the brilliant autumn colours. We have never seen so many trees, billions cover Canada, which surely must be the lungs of the planet, and the Canadians care for their wildlife and though there may be some exploitation, the Canadians are dedicated to the preservation of the natural habitat. The original pioneers had used the rivers to explore deep into the wilderness, using the river network and large canoes. Trading in furs was a very lucrative but dangerous business, and those pioneer families had to be tough as nails. We were entering the "Taiga" or boreal forest, which is the world second largest biome (after the oceans) making up 29% of the world's forest cover and which stretches across the northern reaches of the northern hemisphere across Canada, Alaska, Russia, Mongolia and Scandinavia. This is the land of the survivalist and bushcraft. Every day I used my axe to chop wood for the fire, but I was not felling trees, I was merely making pre-cut logs smaller. The Canadian park service kept the camps supplied with large cut logs, which were sprayed with a special orange spray paint to prevent theft. As the nights began to get colder, the further north we headed, we would make a large fire and would park the Land Rover close to the coals once we had cooked and the flames had died down. The residual heat would drift up towards the tent and would keep the chill at bay. The only drawback to warming the Land Rover like this was that we soon stank of smoke, which we could not smell but others could.

We made it up to the Yukon territory and turned left onto the Alaskan Highway, those last few hundred kilometres of the Cassian Highway had been relatively rough and undulating with large sections of burned forest and very little traffic. The 1 Alaskan Highway was in much better condition and we found a camp at the Mallard Marsh campsite, east of Whitehorse. The Alaskan Highway had been built during World War 2 to connect the "Lower 48" with Alaska, which the Americans had purchased from Russia in 1867 in what could only be described as the greatest real estate purchase in history. The Americans paid 7.2 million dollars for 1.7 million square kilometres of land. I like to imagine the course of history, had Russia not sold that land but instead hovered above the US during the cold war. It would not have ended well.

When possible, we listened to the Canadian Broadcasting Corporation radio station and the hot topic in late 2015 was the refugee and immigration crisis in Europe, stemming from Syria and North Africa. The Canadian broadcasters were strongly in favour of allowing refugees to enter Canada and, generally, the CBC is so liberal it makes left-leaning NPR (National Public Radio) in the USA sound like Fox news. The violence in Syria was despicable and while one narcissist destroyed his country for the sake of his own power, other narcissists joined in and bombed the hell out of the civilian population. Ever since World War Two, the military strategy of "total war" has murdered millions of innocent men, women and children, while the United Nations stands by with its finger in its butt. But Russia's Putin needs regional dominance and the USA is at war with ISIS and the Taliban and the Sunnis hate the Shiite and oil is god, Iran backs Hezbollah, the Palestinians build tunnels and lob missiles at schools, Israel responds to the death of each Israeli by killing a hundred Palestinians, the Turkish are oppressing the Kurds while the Kurds fight ISIS and America backs the Kurds while the Syrians fight ISIS, the Russians fight ISIS and the Kurds, ISIS implements a perverted version of Sharia Law in the areas it controls, lobbing off heads at a rate which would have impressed Pol Pot. Germany, who for decades had been dealing with a steep population decline, decides to accept a million refugees, under the guise of human compassion and North and sub-Saharan Africans decide that now is the time to move to Europe, swelling the ranks of the Syrian refugees desperate to cross the dangerous Mediterranean. Sweden accepts more refugees and migrants than it can accommodate. Deranged lunatics use the refugee crisis as a Trojan horse and assault the good people of Europe with assault rifles, suicide bombers and trucks. Je Suis Charlie! People from distant cultures struggle to assimilate into liberal Europe, the right-wing experiences it's most significant growth in decades and anti-immigrant, anti-refugee Trump gains momentum in the USA presidential race.

Canada needs immigration, the country is massive and requires a workforce and people who are able to live in remote places. I doubt they would deport anyone who is not a criminal or is breaking the law. There is an interesting story about a white South African, Brandon Huntley, who claimed asylum in Canada in 2009. His lawyer informed the immigration committee that Mr Huntley faced daily abuse from black people, had been assaulted on numerous occasions and had been threatened with death. The Canadian immigration board granted Mr Huntley with asylum but then retracted the decision after the South African government protested. Mr Huntley appealed and was eventually granted asylum in 2016. The white farming community, in particular, has been systematically victimised by organised criminal gangs, who rape, torture and murder and it would be those farmers who are the best fit possible for Canadian citizenship, they are as tough as nails and can grow food anywhere. We had no intention of applying for asylum and sincerely hope that we would never have to.

The city of Whitehorse is the capital of the Yukon territory and the only city in Northern Canada. It is also a city of immigrants, not according to the official statistics though, I think someone forgot how to count. Perhaps the most visible people were those in the service industry and almost none of them were either First Nation or of French or English stock. The local Bigway supermarket seemed to be staffed almost entirely by Chinese and there were more Sikh than we had seen since South Africa. Because of its location in the Whitehorse valley, the city has a milder climate than comparable northern cities with a very reasonable average low temperature of -19C in January the record low a mild and toasty -56C. The average high in January? – 11C. All the cars we saw had a two-point plug sticking out of the radiator grill, the plugs were how the engine heaters were plugged in before the car was parked for a significant period. If you forget to plug the vehicle in, you would be guaranteed a frozen engine. I wanted to install one of those heaters for the Landy, she hates the cold, being a European African, just like us. After a raid on the pick 'n mix, we drove the 446 kilometres from Whitehorse to the Beaver Creek border, passed town with names like Destruction Bay and Haines Junction. There are over two million lakes in Canada (surely, they can spare a little one full of fish for me and mine) and a few of those lakes lined our route. The roads were full of animals who had almost no fear of humans, they would graze and swat flies with their tails and look at us like we were bugs, they were so comfortable and brave. The American hunters who travelled through Canada every year would wear drool cups under their chins and had to lock up their high-powered rifles, lest they are tempted the shoot the shit out of those huge, fat, mocking, loping, grazing Canadian trophies.

We reached the USA border and after a short interrogation and inspection of our passports were given the balance of our six months in a year quota. Obviously, the immigration system had been updated when we had handed back our white tourist cards. Luisa asked for six months, but the immigration lady said, "sorry sweetheart" before handing us new tourist cards.

We had made it! After more than four years after we had set off on our Argentina to Alaska "expedition", we were in Alaska. We had driven up from Argentina in seven months (after a circumnavigation of South America and visiting every country in the Americas except for El Salvador) and we had calculated that we could have done the entire world "circuit" with the treasure we had spent and the miles we had covered, about 125 000 kilometres. We stopped next to the sign saying Welcome to Alaska, danced around the sign and took a hundred silly photos. What an incredible journey it had been. We had pushed ourselves and our resources to the limit, but we had made it. Eventually!

Overnight camping in Deming, New Mexico

Target Shooting in Gig Harbour, Washington

Keelan reading We Will Be Free

Keelan takes over the wheel

Jessica's favourite food - cupcakes

Gauchos in Baja California, Mexico

JellyBean enjoying the sunset in Baja

We made some amazing friends while in the US of A

The road leading up to the Ranch in Baja California, Mexico

Good Guy Steve & Bahia in the Alvord Desert, Oregon

Scientology Church on Sunset Boulevard, Los Angeles

A ride along on a Ural with Anthony Sciola at the Overland Expo

Dusty Graeme at the Alvord Desert, Oregon

Family hug at Crater Lake, Oregon

The Landy looking awesome on the Alvord Desert in Oregon

Wild camping in the mountains of California

The rebuild begins at Ron's in Homestead, Florida

Time for a change from the old build to something new

Working on the Landy in Steve's workshop in the UK

8

Northern Exposure

Alaska was immediately different from Canada. The landscape was almost the same, but here we saw post boxes every 2 kilometres in some areas, we had heard that land is very cheap in Alaska (no wonder, the USA bought the state for the same price as a large house in Malibu (not adjusted for inflation)) but the buyer has one year to erect a structure on the land, or he would risk losing it. Some homes, visible through the trees, were modern and well kept, others were zombie apocalypse trailer parks, overflowing with broken vehicles and old tyres. It was hunting season, and large RV's and fifth wheels crowded the roadside parking areas. Large men in camouflage hunting clothing and high visibility vests rode all-terrain vehicles out into the wild. There was not an animal in sight, the clever creatures had long since emigrated to Canada where they were given a nightly massage and story before being tucked into bed. A few all-terrain vehicles had the carcass of Black Tail Deer or Elk or Caribou or Black Bear bleeding in the back and in Tok we saw a pick up at a gas station with a massive set of antlers protruding from the load area. Tok itself looked like it had just been imported, roads, buildings, gas station and churches, direct from Idaho. We booked into the Sourdough campsite and made a fire. Luisa was sick of grilled chicken and wanted a stew, her body needs vegetables occasionally, though I still cannot figure out why. One by one, we trudged off to the ablutions and had our first shower in almost a week. The smell of soap is incredibly strong when you are the great unwashed and when Luisa stepped out of the shower, her hair freshly shampooed and perfume on her neck, I reacted like a bull in musth, pawing at the ground and snorting. She would not let me touch her, holding her nose because, now that she was clean, she could actually smell how badly we stank. I was banished to the showers where I had one of the best showers of my life, before pulling on the last of my clean clothing. The Alaska Mountain range curved off in front of us, 650 kilometres long, the famous Denali mountain, the third most isolated and third most prominent peak in the world, standing tall roughly in the middle of that curve. Just north of Denali lay the Stampede Trail and "The Magic Bus" where Chris McCandless came to a premature end. I could not believe that it was only a twenty-mile walk from the bus back to civilisation, but I had to go see for myself. I had been critical of Christopher McCandless setting out into the wild without the bushcraft skills to be able to survive, I had done similar things in my youth, hitchhiking across the country, sleeping in trucks and abandoned buildings, Alexander Supertramp, but I needed to walk those twenty miles in his shoes.

It began to snow in Tok that morning. We had stayed awake past midnight in the hope of seeing the Aurora Borealis. The camp owner had said that the spectacular lights had been seen the night before and we may get lucky. No luck. The snow fell briefly, and the clouds blew away. We packed and headed towards Anchorage. One of my favourite TV shows as a kid was Northern Exposure, the town Talkeetna was the inspiration for the fictional town of Cecily and Talkeetna lay just north of Anchorage. We would have to visit there on our way up towards Fairbanks and our ultimate, but not the final, destination, Prudhoe Bay. Funds were running low, but we were hoping that being back on US soil, our luck would change. We had some cash in the UK, the early online book sales of We Will Be Free were finally being translated into cash for us. The only problem was that we did not have access to the cash as it was in a relatives account. Regardless, we headed down towards Anchorage, surrounded by mountains and glaciers and the most incredible autumn colours. We passed through towns with more churches than houses and pulled into a camp alongside a river where a slightly manic but incredibly friendly young veteran helped us to get settled in for the night. We chose a spot in the forest and, while I prepared the fire in the moist forest campsite, Luisa retrieved a bottle of Sparkling wine which she had hidden from me. We had been filthy and tired when we arrived in Tok, but tonight my wonderful wife wanted to celebrate being in Alaska.

We drove into Anchorage the next day and headed down to Kenai where we had a date with a doughnut. We had met an American girl in Canada and she had told us that when we made it to Alaska we had to head to her foot truck in Kenai where she would give us the best doughnut we had ever tasted, she was not wrong. Fresh from the fryer, they were delicious. There were some camps near where they were parked and a canvas tent which a brave soul had occupied through the entire winter. He had good whisky and a wood-burning stove in there so was warm and happy, no matter the depth of the snow. We camped in a state campsite, completely alone, or so we thought. I chopped wood and Luisa did some repairs on the kitchen area of the Landy, the children helped to gather wood and we explored the area. We found a lone Toyota Corolla parked behind some trees and thought that perhaps someone had abandoned the car until someone sat up suddenly in the rear seat and looked at us intently. We crapped ourselves. Luckily it was just another Alexander Supertramp who had come to Alaska seeking adventure and he was taking a nap after a long drive.

I had started wearing both my Leatherman and my Remington hunting knife on my hip, if a bear did attack us, I would at least have something sharper than my tongue to hurt his feelings. I also felt safer, manlier and way more adventurous with a knife at my side. I would have preferred a gun, but that is just the cowboy in me who wants to stand like Sheriff Rick from The Walking Dead, hand on holster. I took to standing with my hand resting on my knife, a manly pout on my ugly mug. Luisa would mock me. "Hey, tough guy". "Back off woman, there's bear in them woods".

In the morning, we suffered through another long drop session and headed towards Homer. The road down was spectacular (I am running out of interesting adjectives to describe the northern scenery), bordered by snow-capped mountains and icy blue water. Again, there were two types of homes, beautiful, well-maintained houses with excellent gardens or apocalypse zombie trailer dumps. Homer itself lies 350 kilometres south of Anchorage on the Kenai Peninsula and is also known as "the end of the road" and "the cosmic hamlet by the sea". We joked bitterly that it must be called Homer because it is full of homeless people. Alaska has a huge homeless population and up there, there is a thin line between camping and being homeless. Many of the homeless in Alaska come from Native Alaskan homes, not all, and many homeless are chronic alcoholics, but certainly not all. We had seen people living in cars in Walmart parking lots and we had camped beside them. A man had struck up a conversation with Luisa as they stood outside their respective vehicles near Wasilla, north of Anchorage. They spoke for a while, he was a veteran who had come to Alaska to find work either in the fishing or oil industry. He had registered with the employment agency, but because he had a disability (he was injured in Afghanistan) and had PTSD none of the companies wanted to employ him. He was now trying to change his status from veteran to civilian, but that was impossible as he had registered with his social security number. He was waiting for the Alaska Permanent Fund pay-out (a fund worth about $55 billion and financed by oil reserves which pay dividends to Alaskan residents) and he would receive $2000 in 2015. Luisa did not realise that the man was homeless, she thought he was a fellow traveller. We gave the man some food, a bottle of coke and a copy of WWBF, perhaps the book would raise his spirits.

Homer and the Kenai Peninsula, in general, had its fair share of homeless people and we met many inside the warm, modern Homer library where anyone could spend a warm day in a comfortable chair, reading a book or searching the internet. As we approached the library (we knew that we would find a comfortable chair and WIFI) Luisa noticed a sign advertising that there was going to be a book fair that Saturday. Flanked by the kids and holding a copy of WWBF, I approached the librarian. I realised that we looked a bit rough and smelled like a fire, but I was sure that if I spoke with integrity and maintained a decent distance from the counter, I would be well received. I had been a salesman in my twenties and thirties and was confident that I had this cold call nailed. "Hello. Perhaps you can help me. I would like to register to participate in Saturdays book fare", I handed her the copy of WWBF. "We are a South African family travelling the world in our Land Rover and these book sales help us to keep the wheels rolling". The pretty, sweetly scented young librarian looked at me as if I was a pesky homeless person, her body language eroding my confidence. "Hang on, I will ask the director". My hair was long and tied back casually, my beard long and grey, I wore brown Dickies work pants, an old black K Way winter jacket over a faded black hoodie I had bought in Chile, my Merrill shoes which had climbed Torres del Paine in Patagonia were old and worn. The children were dressed in weathered Craghoppers winter gear but were equally scruffy. I realised then that everywhere else in the world homeless people dress in rags but here they dressed in clothing better than mine, donated by REI, Northface and a hundred churches in the lower 48. The director came out of her office and asked me, almost bluntly, how she could help. She looked at the kids with pity. I repeated my spiel and waited for an answer. The director, a tall, graceful woman wearing a simple but elegant gold necklace and a silk blouse, looked at me for a moment, then at the children, then back at me. "I won't call the police", and handed back my book, unopened. I won't call the police. That response demolished me. I looked around. "Oh, um, thank you, ma'am". I was stunned, shell-shocked, a loud buzzing in my ears. I slipped the book under my arm, took the kids by the hand and walked slowly towards Luisa who was sitting beneath a large window, a beautiful bay behind her, mountains in the distance. I sent the children to sit by their mom and sat down in a soft leather chair, feeling dazed and completely confused. I stared at the book in my hands. We Will Be Free. What a complete and utter fool I had been. I had believed in myself so stubbornly, despite all the voices who said I should not, that I was irresponsible, that my children would grow to hate me. I had believed that what we were doing was so courageous, so incredible that we could not fail. I had believed in myself so much that I had convinced my wife and children, who love me so dearly, that we would not only survive but that we would prosper, that they should believe in me. Here I sat. Responsible for a family who had once lived in a beautiful home by the sea, who had eaten beautiful meals which I had lovingly crafted, who had everything they would ever need. Now, we had very little money and we were very, very far from home. Snap out of it! For the sake of my family, I could not show weakness, I had to be strong even though inside I was slowly disintegrating. I only had twenty dollars in my wallet and sometimes even the strong can be weak.

Keelan came over and put his hand gently on my shoulder. "Mom needs to talk to you", he said quietly. I imagined that the kids had just told Luisa what had just happened, and I prepared myself for the inevitable. Luisa was glowing, her smile wide delighted. What on earth? "AT&T just emailed, the campaign is on!". What?! Mark had sent an email with the title "working the dollars now". The campaign in which we would travel and promote the V10 device had been approved, the campaign where we would be broadcast into every home in America was financed and negotiated and rubber-stamped and ready to roll! "Where will you be in two weeks?" Mark asked. We will be wherever the hell you need us to be!

From the bottom of the bucket, we were now on top of the world. I was right to believe in us, in myself. A wave of emotion swept over Luisa and the kids and me, we all knew how important this moment was. We Will Be Free. I felt punch drunk but excited, to experience such extreme emotions in the space of ten minutes was simply unintelligible. We sat for a moment and let it all sink in. "Ok! We need to head back south". "But we just got here, when are we ever going to have the chance again to visit Denali, or drive to Prudhoe Bay, or hike the Stampede trail or do any of the things we planned to do?", "Think of it like this. It will take ten days to get back to Washington. What if we have a breakdown or something happens, and we need a few days to get back on the road? Once we have done this campaign, we can go wherever we want. We have hit the jackpot". "Don't count your chickens before they hatch". "They are hatched, the chicken is out, and it is yellow and fluffy and pecking the corn and taking a crap on the straw! We have it in writing, this is happening". "I know, but let's not get too excited". "Fine, whatever. But, can we agree, we need to go back, and we need to leave today?". "Yes, I agree". "Tell Mark we are on our way".

Looking back, it was then that I decided to title this book, La Lucha! The Fight, because this truly was what our lives had become. We had stepped into the ring, had been knocked down, again and again, but we stood up again and again. Now, we were winning!

As we left the library, holding hands and laughing, I looked over at the pretty librarian and flashed her a goofy smile. "See ya later. You have a lovely library by the way". She gave me a puzzled smile and a timid wave. She must have thought we had all been smoking crack cocaine in the fiction section.

Buzzing with excitement we drove out to the Homer Spit where a few of the Deadliest Catch fishing trawlers docked. We took some photos, we saw a beautiful eagle and an eerie house, we tried to focus on the raw beauty of the environment we were surrounded by, but there was nothing else on our minds but the AT&T campaign. We had to step up to the plate and be professional travellers, this was a massive opportunity but also a massive responsibility. We needed to shape up, get the kids involved, plan a route, organise ourselves and our gear, we had to be ready for this opportunity and we had to deliver. We had no great desire to be famous, that is not what drove us, we desired to be financially independent, we wanted to continue to tour the planet and we wanted to be secure. Working with, and having been thoroughly vetted by AT&T, would give us the credibility to work with other corporations and it would stand us in good stead when we negotiated contracts with publishers. Our social media accounts would explode, and we would be able to write our own pay check. Yes, we would lose a huge amount of freedom and yes, we would now have corporate masters, but that would only be for a short period and the attention would mainly be in the USA, everywhere else in the world we would hopefully still be able to travel with a degree of anonymity. Had we been independently wealthy, I would probably never have written our books with the passion that I have, we would simply not be the people that we are today, because we have had to fight, we have been forged in fire.

The drive back to Washington was going to be a 4300-kilometre trek and we had to leave immediately. A moose tried to kill itself, and us, as we drove back up the Kenai Peninsula. Before we had left Washington, we met a lovely family, Tim and Shannon and their son Noah, who had given us a gift in preparation for our journey north. Tim, an ex-Special Forces marine and Land Rover fanatic, noticed that we did not have any spotlights on the Landy. He knew that the crisp light of an LED light would help us to see animals hiding in the dark verges of the boreal forest and installed a set on our bull-bar while I sucked on a beer and tried to help. The LED lights were small and square but increased my night vision by 70% at least and it was thanks to those lights, and dear Tim, that I spotted the moose as it screamed Banzai! and charged out into the road. I braked hard, swerved away and narrowly missed the stupid, presumably Japanese, moose. Those lights were to save us a few more road kill moments as we headed south, often breaking the golden "never drive at night" rule. Thank you, Tim, Shannon and Noah.

By nightfall, we had made it to a town called Cooper Landing, where we had been invited to visit a Land Rover enthusiast and friend of a friend. After a cup of coffee in the morning, we headed back towards Anchorage and camped in the Wasilla Walmart parking lot, surrounded by rubber tramps. We had a cash shortage and had asked a relative to send cash from an account we had in the UK, but could not access from Alaska. We needed the money for food and fuel and our relative sent the money to Canada because she thought Alaska was part of Canada. This is pretty depressing to admit, but we did not have enough money on hand to buy the fuel we needed to get back into Canada! Out of the blue (if I was religious I might suspect the hand of a kind God), I received a message from a man called, John Bidney. He had seen one of my recent Facebook posts which mentioned that we were in Alaska and he wanted to meet us. John is a fantastic human being. He had moved his family from New York to Alaska, searching for a life less ordinary. You could not wish to meet a more gentle soul and we were surprised to learn that he had trained for a year to compete in a Mixed Martial Arts fight. The fight did not go well for John, but he had achieved a dream. We can respect that.

John chatted with us for a while and we gave him and his kids a tour of the Landy, which smelled terrible but always looks great. John then bought not one but two books which gave us enough money to get back to Canada, where the wired cash waited. We would have eventually made a plan but thanks to John we were now able to buy a cooked chicken dinner and fill up the tank with diesel. It was too late to leave Wasilla, so we chatted for a while and then opened the roof tent, an uncommon sight in a Walmart parking lot. A cool night forced us to cuddle under our down duvets and keep warm. Two nights had passed since we had received that incredible email in Homer and we still had not left Alaska. I wondered how I would explain to people why we were leaving so soon, I could not talk about the AT&T campaign until it had been formally announced and I knew there would be those who were going to give us a hard time about not exploring Alaska, "jeez, you spent two years driving around every country in South America, but you can't even get up to Prudhoe Bay, you suck".

The next morning, we have some clothing and food to our new rubber tramp friends and headed back towards the Canadian border. Again, the Canadian immigration agent was a sarcastic arsehole, what is wrong with these guys? Canadians are incredible people, but the immigration people are most likely profiled and selected while in high school. "Jimmy is an arsehole, he twangs girl's bras and makes old Mrs Pritchard cry. He told her that she was fat and lazy and had to marry a janitor, 'coz her pipes are blocked'. He made the new girl cry by putting thumbnails on her seat and he was caught spanking the monkey in the teachers' lounge. His grades are awful, he strives to attain only a pass mark 'to make a point about the failure of the education system'. He listens to Def Leppard, Roxette and Bon Jovi. I recommend that he becomes an immigration official".

Ps. If you, dear reader, happen to be a Canadian immigration officer, we are most definitely not referring to you. Actually, picture the guy or girl you hate the most at work. Yes, we are talking about them. Not you. OK?

Despite "Jimmy", we were back in Canada and driving to Whitehorse. Even though we had to abandon our Alaskan itinerary, we were determined to return one day and give the state the attention she deserves. In Whitehorse, we were able to claim the cash which was sent from the UK and we returned to the lake and made a fire. Luisa wanted to talk about the route, she always wants me to make decisions. We have a relationship based on Luisa's feminist philosophy, we are equals, but she is more equal than I am. Until a decision must be made and then I am the most equal. "You are the man", she says. OK, so I make a decision. "Wrong decision, try again". I then make a new decision and repeat the process until I make the decision she wants to make but does not want to take responsibility for. "You made the decision, this mess is your fault, now fix it!". I should have known she was going to be difficult when she refused to make me a cup of tea for the first five years of our relationship. I, on the other hand, am the perfect husband. I make her breakfast in bed which she angrily tells me to take away, "you know I can't eat first thing in the morning!". So, I eat it. I used to buy her flowers twice a week and have cooked dinner so often that I have permanent knife calluses on my right hand. Yes, I am the perfect husband. Luisa brought out the map while I murdered a cold beer. "There are two routes we can take to return to the USA. The first is the route we came up with and the second is the Alaskan Highway, which is 250 kilometres longer. Choose one". I chose the wrong route. "Try again, you muppet". I chose the correct route, and she let me continue playing with the fire.

The Alaskan Highway (or ALCAN as it is also known) was built during World War Two with the sole purpose of connecting the Lower 48 with Alaska. If the Japanese invaded, they would either have to launch a naval attack on the US mainland or enter the North American continent via Alaska. I had a history teacher who once told me that war was excellent for progress, as nations are forced to pool their resources and invest in infrastructure and new technology. The Alaskan Highway was built within two years and was 2,700 kilometres long, it was not a highway though, it was mostly gravel road with log bridges and many sections had to be rebuilt by the Canadians once they took possession of the road after the war. As always, we were born too late, what was once an adventure to drive, is now mostly excellent pavement. We were not complaining though, we had to move quickly, we had a date with destiny. At Watson Lake, we chose the turnoff which led us onto route 97, which took us out of the Yukon and back into beautiful British Colombia. The Alaskan Highway was built in the great plains east of the mountainous coastal region, which made life a heck of a lot easier for the men who built the road and travellers like us who drive it. We passed a small town once every few hundred kilometres, where we would fill up with fuel and hunt for the library so that we could top up on warm comfortable seats and, hopefully, important emails. The locals, many First Nation, did not pay a lot of attention to us, in summer the roads were full of people in fancy vehicles rumbling up and down and through town. If spoken to, the locals would react with open and friendly conversation, the winters are way too cold to be an arse, I suppose. Imagine being stuck in a house for months with an unsocial twat, murder rates would soar.

The nights were getting colder as we drove, but the Alaskan Highway is a lot easier to drive than the Route 37 and we were making good progress. The number of animals grazing next to the road was simply astounding. We had always thought that Bison was near extinction (buffalo live in Africa, bison live in North America), but they certainly are not, not in Canada anyway. These big brown beauties used to number about 60 million before they were hunted to near extinction in the 1800s, a slaughter which led to the starvation of many Native Americans. The Bison (who look like a bodybuilder who hates leg day; huge shoulders, necks and chest, teeny, tiny little butts and legs) were hunted by settlers for their fur and, in many cases, to deprive the indigenous Americans of their most important food source. Killing the Bison forced the Native Americans to live in the reservations allotted to them, as this was the only place they could find food. By the end of the 1800s, the herds of millions were reduced to a few hundred, but now, after a century of protection, their numbers are up to a few hundred thousand. Humans. The bison we met in Canada had not forgotten how we had murdered them in the past and were not impressed with our presence. A herd on the verge of the road would cause a traffic jam of motorhomes and cameras, at least shooting with a camera does not hurt or kill. The bison would slowly lumber and chew at the sweet grass which grew in abundance where the forest had been cleared along the road. One brown, suspicious eye on the fawning humans, the other on their young. A bull reminded another bull that he was the big boss and a skittish calf bounded towards the safety of the forest. Moose, elk and deer mocked passing American hunters.

A long road lay ahead of us and I filled the hours trying to stay awake, daydreaming of my off the grid cabin in the forest, near the trout-filled lake. In Washington, I had watched an old video on the internet, Finnish carpenters building a traditional log cabin using only hand tools. I had watched, lazily hypnotised by their work. First, they stomped into the forest wearing tennis rackets on their feet. They made a joke only they could understand, probably about Mikko, the worst fisherman in the village. Using a circular girth guide, they measured each tree for the correct diameter while charming, children's television music played in the background. The men looked at the camera always with a bemused smile, "He ajattelevat, että kameramies on käsissä naisia ja hänen vaatteensa outoa", the narrator explained. Gotcha. A horse pulled a sleigh loaded with felled pine through the forest, an old man trimmed the logs square and stripped the bark with a draw knife. I wanted to be as skilled as that old man, dressed in dungarees, black knitted sweater and flat black cap, chopping at the log with a one-sided axe. I need that axe. The men laughed at me and laid the stone foundations, laid the log walls, honed windows, filled the floor with offcuts of wood, stuffed the gaps in the walls with moss, built the roof with logs and tiled it with handmade shingles, then ate a hearty lunch of pickled fish and vodka, while quietly mocking the cameraman and Mikko a little more. Their house was ugly but beautiful, my house would be a Viking longhouse, a fire pit in the middle where I would roast suckling pig while drinking draughts of beer and singing Scandinavian hunting songs. To myself, probably. I would have a flush toilet fed by a wind pump and a well inside the home, I would need a cool room for my food and a big bed for me and my girly mags, Voluptuous, all-natural. I would need a desk in the corner, near a large window where I would sit and write with a quill, I would need a few pots and pans and a workshop to repair and manufacture. Working, reading and talking to myself would get me through the day and I would adopt an orphaned bear (I would discover that I had a special way with animals), grow a long beard and help passers-by in the forest. Hang on a second...

I suppose I consider an off-grid lifestyle, working with my hands to build my home and living off the land much more rewarding than modern life in the busy, demanding industrialised world. There are a few cities I love, but after a while, even the most charming city loses its appeal. The living is expensive, you must trade your hours, days, weeks and years for a house, a car, clothing, toys, furniture, a watermelon cooler. Yes, you have wonderful friends who you meet for coffee, drinks, dinner, dancing. I prefer the solitude and calm of coffee, drinks, dinner and dancing around a campfire. In a city, you are an ant, surrounded by millions of other ants, industrious, competitive, always on the move. Some ants are bigger than others, some are small and weak and barely survive, the soldier ants keep the workers in line, with the promise of keeping them safe, and all the little ants work towards the dream of one day being at the top of the mound, from where they can see what it might be like to be free. When city folk go to the country, they feel the need to run everywhere and climb on everything and take a million photos and dominate the environment. "Man, I killed that canyon". That canyon does not give a shit about you, you showed it nothing it has never seen before. The earth is perfect, it is sublime. It gives us everything we need to be satisfied, not just that silly, juvenile emotion – happiness. Satisfaction comes from achieving something, building something, prospering despite the challenges. Satisfaction is not waking up in the morning after going to bed too late, rolling over, turning on your phone and seeing twenty-two Facebook notifications and 1200 likes of your picture of your boobs on Instagram. Those drops of heroin disappear as soon as you ingest them, now you need more.

In modern society, we value ourselves by our online popularity, something which means less than fuck all when the power goes out. I know this because almost every morning I wake up after going to bed too late and immediately reach for my validation machine. Ah, Pages Manager, twenty comments and 200 likes ooh, that feels good, oh yeah, that was a witty comment, damn, I must upload more images like that. Nice. Or, shit, I didn't load anything, I was not witty, I have not been taking enough photos, am I still relevant? Are we fading? I really need to sell books!

Hello, Mr Jones, from the past. Welcome to the year 2017. What? You expected flying cars, world peace, an end to poverty and disease and war? Did you expect a society based on the principles of the enlightenment, science and reason? Oh, no, we don't have any of that stuff. What we do have, this is going to blow your socks right off Mr Jones, are these devices. Yes, they are slick and shiny, aren't they? Well, we call this a phone. Yes, it is very different from the big black thing you have on the desk at your office, but wait until you find out what this thing can do. Well, yes, it can send and receive telephone calls, but it can also send and receive video calls. Incredible, right? It has replaced the VCR, the television, the cinema, the voice recorder, the movie camera and the stills camera, the radio and record player, the library, the post office, your wife and your children. All your friends, many whom you never have and will never meet, live inside this device in an eternal world called Social Media, which lives in another universe called the Internet. Even God is on this social media, it is true! If we "share" a "post" enough times, a child with cancer can be saved. Modern miracles, Hallelujah! Kind and clever corporations have built little microphones into this device not only, so you can listen to your music and television shows but also, get this so that they can listen to us. They also read our mail and have access to all our documents. What is that you ask, is that not an invasion of our privacy? No, you silly man, we give the corporations permission to listen to every conversation we have, we even let them watch us through this little camera, ingenious, isn't it? In return, they give us what we call apps, very useful things we could not possibly live without and they save us the trouble of actually going to look for the things we need. An example. I mentioned earlier the man with a flat black cap who was trimming that log so well. Well, I could not for the life of me remember what a flat cap was called, I asked this device and it told me that not only are they called flat caps but there are many styles available and I could have one or two or three delivered to my door the next day. Incredible, right? When I asked about the device, another question a few hours later an advert, yes like the ones you see on a billboard, popped up and reminded me that I was interested in flat caps. Wonderful, I know. It gets better. If I leave this "phone" here on the table and have a discussion with you about boots, hiking boots, how mine are old and I need a new pair, the next time I visit my friends on that Social Media thing, there will be an advert for hiking boots waiting for me.

Give me convenience or give me death! What does the government have to say about all this? Well, the government and the corporations are very, very good friends, people communicating openly through social media is a very dangerous thing; indeed, we might start to get crazy ideas. So, they are teaming up with the corporations and can also listen to what we do and say, they can even watch us through these devices. No! That is not wrong. This world is a very, very dangerous place and there are people out there who want to hurt us, they hate us, and they want to take away our freedom. I trust my government, yes, they have done questionable things in the past, but I trust them more than my enemies. What do you mean I am deluded?! I am from the future, you are from the past, I know more, I know better! WTF, I can't even.

Welcome to the echo chamber, which is my mind.

A long drive can drive you mad, but with nothing else to do than admire the scenery of the world passing, monitor the temperature and fuel gauge and try not to be killed by a random moose or tired driver, your mind can wander where it wants to. I knew what was waiting for us when we returned to the USA. We were going to be working hard, being social, networking, focussing on producing material, being all the things, one needs to get ahead with expensive dreams in an expensive world. This drive through Canada was a holiday for my mind, a mind which kept me awake every night asking every annoying question it could think of, trying to find ways to be exceptional, to succeed, perform and progress. But when all the heavy thinking has been thunk, the mind can be allowed to wander to where it really wants to go. My mind wanted to go to the wild, to build that cabin, to direct the body to do some of the toughest work a body can do, to struggle against the elements and to very quickly learn what is needed to survive. My minds favourite movie is Cast Away and what many people might imagine as hell, I could imagine as paradise. With a few skills, Tom Hanks could have built himself a lovely home with a hammock on the patio. He could have made a guitar, a fireplace, a bathtub, a dartboard, a pool table and a fishing boat. He could have eaten a variety of foods and surfed the waves which trapped him. Instead, he chose to sleep in a cave and obsess about a fading woman with all the charms of a fertiliser company calendar. When the movie came out I was working hard, helping Luisa to run our Cape Town-based immigration firm. After forcing my body to wake up, I would drive into the city before the sun rose to wait in line with people I despised to get to a counter, where a person I despised, would be despicable. After hours of horrible people and soul-deadening bureaucracy, I would get in my beautiful silver car where I would spend the next few hours trapped, listening to some ugly idiot on the radio (beautiful idiots are on TV), either singing a tepid song or jabbering on, enthusiastically telling stupid stories to brain dead people.

LA LUCHA

I could not listen to my favourite music; the lyrics of good songs will only remind you how trapped you are in a disjointed train of metal debt. With nowhere to go, I sat quietly fuming in traffic, reminded of how I was just an ant, and not even one of the incredible ants, just a dull, often drunk, seldom happy ant. When I eventually returned home, I might have an hour to go surf with other ants who also felt the incredible need to reconnect with nature, but there were more ants than waves, another traffic jam. Dinner. Drink. Sleep. Repeat. Cast Away helped me escape, I would fast forward to the plane crash and be asleep by the time he was rescued.

Escaping to the wild, not only surviving but thriving, I would no longer be that little, deluded ant. I would be the king ant of a tiny empire. I would be a man. I would be all the things that are best about humanity, without waste, without greed, without destruction, in control, alive. But, I realised, more than anything, I love my family and that is where my wilderness fantasies come crashing to the ground. My wife and children are not survivalist loners, they need interaction, friends, people to love and talk to and share good times with. They want movies and popcorn and careers and social media. Perhaps this is why we are overlanders, each one of us can get a bit of what they want, but children won't stay at "home" forever. Luisa, you have been warned.

Driving past McLeod's Lake, I felt like we had stumbled into my daydreams. Crisp, clean water surrounded by forest and mountains invited us to give up on this crazy idea of driving around the world and instead to find our paradise on her shores, or at least on the banks of one of her tributaries. With a decent-sized town nearby, we would not be complete hermits, the children could find spouses and Luisa could go shopping for treats like marshmallows and tampons.

We camped just outside Prince George, we had found a state park which was officially closed, but camping was nonetheless permitted. It was a wet night and we made a meal of pasta while discussing the crossing back into the USA. We had already spent almost five months in that incredible country but, our understanding of the law was that we were possibly only permitted six months in a calendar year. If we only had one month left in the US, we were going to have a very hard time to do the AT&T campaign. As it stood, they would have to hire an immigration firm to be sure that we were legally permitted to do such a campaign. Before we left South Africa, we had applied for and had been granted ten-year B1/B2 business visas. We also had to drive across the country and ship the Land Rover from New York to the United Kingdom. We were completely at the mercy of the immigration officials and were incredibly nervous. With a 900-kilometre drive to return to Mukilteo, we left early in the morning, eager to get back into a house, clean up (it had been a week since our last decent shower) and get the ball rolling on the AT&T campaign. I was sick and tired of being broke and Luisa hates not having a nice pile of cash in the bank. She had believed me when I had told her that I could provide for us as a writer and "professional" overlander, so far, I had done OK, but CNN wasn't exactly kicking down the door. They would soon be, and we had to take the time to seriously consider what we chose to do publicly once the campaign was done. I did not want to become the overlanding Kardashians, but this was our chance to make some serious money, the kind of cash that can last a lifetime. One immigration official held in his hands our entire future, no pressure.

The drive was tedious but beautiful, we had driven this route on our way north and it was surprising how different the world can seem when you are heading in the opposite direction. A single day, 900-kilometre drive in a normal car is hard work, but behind the wheel of the Defender, it is a monumental feat. Those of you who own or have driven a Defender for a decent length of time will know what I am talking about. It certainly does not help that I am bigger than most rugby players. The driver's seat touches the door and the steering wheel is only a few centimetres from the driver's window. The window winder handle juts into the side of your leg, as does the door handle. The B pillar is where your shoulder should be, and the driving position is upright with legs bent at the knee, just less than 90 degrees. There is no cruise control and after driving a few hours, I have to stop and stretch my legs due to the excruciating pain in my buggered up right knee (I had a motorbike accident in '95 which shattered the lower half of my right leg). The heat from the gearbox and exhaust heats the handbrake and seat boxes into scalding metal and you can't rest your left leg against the handbrake because it will cook the flesh. You can drive either with the window wide open, arm out absorbing cancer, or you can drive with the window closed, your arm removed and stashed in the cubby box. This does not mean that driving the legendary Defender is without its luxuries. There is a vent (on older models) which opens above the bonnet and allows cool air to blow directly on your knees, which conveniently seems to speed up the cramping. The air conditioning system is also designed to cool your knees and only your knees. When it rains, a refreshing stream of water will drip on your right foot, the foot which cannot be moved while driving. The radio plays music to your knees (Defender is all about the knee), which your ears can't hear when you are running mud-terrain tyres because you once drove through part of the Amazon jungle and you have not since changed your tyres. The windscreen is so narrow that when you pull down the sun visor you can't see the road. I have driven more than 200 000 kilometres in our Defender, my body is now twisted and contorted to accommodate the vehicle but, I will happily drive her another 200 000 kilometres.

With my left calf cooking to perfection on the hot handbrake, we pushed on down the 97, the kids keeping themselves entertained with games on their new Samsung tablets, reading their school books and sleeping, Luisa either dozing with one eye on the road or going through all our paperwork, preparing for the border crossing. We stopped for a pizza and the all Asian staff gave us half-price pizzas which had not been collected. Perhaps it was a family franchise, the lady behind the counter seemed distressed that the pizzas had not been collected and the entire crew was elated when we took the bait and ate what might have become their dinner. Luisa and I had a debate between mouthfuls; should we find a place to camp or should we drive into the night, we were only 280 kilometres from Mukilteo. The idea of a hot shower and a soft bed was too tempting to resist, and we decided to break the golden rule and continue to drive at night.

The kids had almost grown up in the back seat of the Landy, we had been on the road for over three years and Keelan had changed from a chubby little 12-year-old into a slim and trim man-sized boy. He was outgrowing that back seat very quickly. Jessica was a little girl when we left, but now she was almost as tall as her mother. When we had started travelling, both kids could lie together on the bench and sleep, now Keelan needed to contort to be able to sit comfortably. Their comfort was not improved by the amount of crap which was stored behind the seat, on the floor and on the seat between them. Now that we were carrying a couple boxes of books with us there was less space in the load area and groceries were foisted on the children. If we were going to make a success of this venture and be able to travel the planet together over the next few years, we might have to consider purchasing another vehicle, maybe a Discovery or an old Series. Of course, another vehicle would double our fuel, maintenance (services, tyres, spares, etc) and paid camping costs. We would have to have two drivers at all times and the cost of purchasing and outfitting a second vehicle would be high. Of course, the 130 already had everything we needed, more than we needed, and a second vehicle could be a huge advantage when travelling to remote areas. I liked the idea of a Discovery 2 with a TD5 engine, the same as the 130, which meant we could share spares between engines. We could raise the Discovery suspension a couple of inches, give her some nice big tyres and some underbody protection. Keelan and I could then use the Disco to drive trails and roads the girls did not want to, and they could set up a base camp with the 130 and do whatever it is they would do until we returned, tired, dirty, hungry and thirsty. Luisa then jumped into my new car daydreams and said that the new vehicle should be painted pink with black skulls and because it would be a comfortable vehicle, she and Jessica would drive it and enjoy the soft leather seats, electric windows, functional air conditioning, excellent stereo and car-like performance. I became jealous, very jealous because I knew that that would be exactly what would happen if we did buy a Discovery.

We all suffered equally in the Defender because we had no other option, but a new, comfortable vehicle would cause a civil war in the family. Luisa and both children would drive in the comfortable Disco, and I would be left to drive the Defender alone. We could sell the 130 in the USA for a stupid amount of money and then buy a Discovery in the UK for peanuts, but then we would have serious space issues and an off-road trailer is more expensive than a decent second-hand Ferrari. Another option would be to change the rear seat configuration in the 130, removing the bench and installing a couple of seats which would give the children independent space. The problem was that we would lose the storage area behind the bench seat and the kids would be unable to change their seating position, Jessie was still small enough to semi-lie down and often sat sideways on the seat with her back against the door and her feet on the bench. One solution was to carry far less gear, but we had already reduced our belongings to the bare minimum, recovery gear and winter clothing was not always used but indispensable when you needed it. Another solution was to ship the kids off to a boarding school, but I would rather die than be without them, even though I know that in a few years Keelan would likely fly the coop, which would render a second vehicle superfluous and by then everyone would be softened by the comfort of the Discovery. The ultimate solution, naturally, was to be rich, we could then run a fleet of vehicles or commission purpose-built vehicles. We could spend eight months of the year overlanding and four months living in my off the grid cabin by the lake, writing, eating salmon and entertaining guests. Well that's it then, we just need to be rich, how hard could it be? Hello, is that AT&T?

Persistent rain began to fall as we approached a tiny town called Hells Gate, the road twisting and winding through mountains and forest, parallel to the raging Fraser River. The LED driving lights proving to be indispensable as they time and again illuminated a suicidal Bambi or a kamikaze elk. The Defender was performing beautifully and seemed to have more power than usual, perhaps she too just wanted to get back to the states and have a few days of relaxation. After driving for so long, I and the machine became one and together we drove the winding road with a smooth rhythm, powering out of corners and turning early into the next, using both sides of the road where visibility was good, the wide rims and tyres providing stability and traction, the disc brakes slowing the large but relatively light vehicle evenly and without drama. Luisa does not like it when I drive like a man who has driven many thousands of kilometres of mountain passes. Luisa likes it when I drive like a scared little girl, but when Luisa drives, she drives like a slightly drunk Michael Schumacher, but because she is in control, she is comfortable with speed. My goal was to drive seamlessly, to maintain momentum and turbo pressure, to use fuel sparingly and reduce gear changes, it is an art, I believe. When Luisa drives there is no art, only brute force and very heavy feet (it is worth noting though that Luisa once drove the Landy from Mozambique to Dar es Salaam while I was puking out of the window, ill with a virus). I was aware that I had been driving for almost ten hours, but I was not tired, I was enjoying the winding roads and lack of traffic and knew that eventually, we would pop out of the mountains onto the freeway which led us to the border.

LA LUCHA

The rain was still falling when we did eventually emerge from the Fraser Valley onto the Trans Canadian Highway 1, south of a town called Hope. We were still a long way from Mukilteo, but I was wide awake, and we knew that the Sumas Canadian/American border crossing was open 24 hours. With rain pelting the Landy, we turned onto the 1 and headed to Sumas, arriving at shortly after midnight. This was the moment of truth. If we were not allowed back into the USA for whatever reason or were not granted a new six-month tourist visa, well, we were screwed.

9

The Moment of Truth

We drove to the border, wide awake and prepared. The children knew the drill well, they were expected to be on their best behaviour, to sit quietly, to not argue, to not say anything silly. They knew how important this crossing was for us all. We parked the Defender in the inspection area, with not a soul in sight and walked confidently into the immigration office after locking the Landy. A stocky man with cropped red hair sat behind the counter, chatting to another US border agent, the kids taking a seat on a bench as Luisa and I approached the counter. The agent greeted us somewhat tersely, "how can I help you". We handed him our passports and the agent, taking the passports, asked us to step back, a few feet. That was strange. We then realised that we had not showered in a while, we had been cooking on open fires and had spent the last twelve hours cramped up in the Land Rover. We obviously stank! This was not a good start at all. I clumsily explained that we had just finished a marathon trek back from Alaska and could not wait to get back into the good old USA. The agent took his time and studied each passport. "You have stamps here from Argentina, Bolivia, Colombia, Malawi, Guatemala?", "Yes, sir, we are driving around the world in our Land Rover". He studied us carefully for a moment. "You drove through all these countries?", "Yes, sir". He scanned my passport and read the information on his computer screen. "How do you pay for this?" "I am a writer and my wife is a photographer". From now on that was our profession which we entered on immigration forms. "Do you have sufficient funds to support yourselves while in the USA?". Ah, shit. We took out four credit cards knowing that the agent had no simple means of establishing whether those accounts were overflowing or overdrawn. "We had a house in South Africa and we sold it", said Luisa. This was an unscripted lie and I had a very stubborn rule about not lying, especially to immigration officials, but Luisa was obviously desperate. Instead of playing along I stupidly opened my mouth. "Ah, no, sir, that is not entirely correct, I think what my wife is saying is that we did not have a house to sell, we sold our business back home". The agent's eyebrow shot up and I could feel Luisa mentally beating my skull in with a hammer. That was stupid. "Well, which one is it?" Luisa countered. "No sorry, my husband is correct, sorry, we have been on the road for ages today. We sold our business". "Ok", he said slowly. Luisa continued, changing the course of the conversation. "I have a booking here for the Land Rover to be shipped from New York in February next year, so if you could grant us the six-month tourist visa that would be great". I had really put my foot in it, but we had not agreed to talk about selling the house we never owned, if anything telling immigration that you had sold your house was a red flag, it meant you had nowhere to go back to and possibly intend to live and work in the country illegally. Regardless, if we did not get the six months, or were denied entry, Luisa would probably never forgive me. "You need six months? The system shows that you have already been in the USA for five months this year". "Yes, that is probably correct, but we have ten-year visas for the US, issued in South Africa. I didn't know there was a time limit, I know we can't work, but I did not know there was a limit. Is it different because I have a British passport?". This is exactly what we had feared, but I knew enough about immigration procedures to know that by posing a question which might be impossible to answer, particularly at a small border, at midnight, we might put the agent in a position where he would have to make a judgement call. We were not trying to break the law, we had done our research and knew that the immigration officials had the final say as they judge each entry case by case, if the six months in a year stipulation was hard and fast, we would know better than to ask for another six months and the request would be immediately and flatly denied. What we had in our favour was that we were travelling with dependent children, we had been on the road for quite a few years, had driven to many countries on three continents and we did indeed have valid ten-year visas and I had a British passport, the British being the USA's strongest allies. We were intending to work with AT&T but had not yet signed a contract and knew that the corporation would take the necessary steps to ensure that we did not break any immigration laws. I would have to pull that card if we were left with no other options.

The agent flipped through the passports for a while longer, a crease in his brow. He seemed unable to make a decision. Just then the well-built, bald agent who we had handed our tourist cards to when we had left the USA a few weeks before, walked into the large white room and greeted us warmly. "Hey guys, you are back. How was Alaska?" "Oh, hi, it was fantastic, really beautiful. It is good to be back in the lower 48, though. How are you?". He was good. He was our John Bidney in dark blue. This conversation broke the ice that was hanging over us like a glacier. The red-haired agent turned to the bald agent, who wore the rank of sergeant. He explained that we had asked for six months, but the record showed that we had been in the USA for five months already. The bald agent walked over and had a look at the passports, tapped something into the computer system then handed the passports back to our agent. "No, they are good, you can give them the six months". Boom! Just like that, a mountain of weight lifted from our shoulders. We acted cool though, no jumping up and down, poker-faced. "Thank you, sir". One by one we had our photos and fingerprints electronically taken, the agent careful not to get to close to us. Four, white tourist cards were issued, each valid for six months and our passports

215

returned. "Enjoy your stay". "Thank you, do you want to inspect the vehicle?". "No. You're good". With that we said goodbye and calmly walked back to the Landy, fireworks going off inside our bodies.

Once in the vehicle we quietly gave each other fist pumps, Luisa stored our documentation and we drove back to America. Whack! Luisa hit my arm as hard as she could a huge grin on her face. "You arsehole! You are so lucky that they let us in, I swear, I could have killed you". Whack! She hit me again. I did not mind at all. We were back, and we had six months!

The rain continued to pelt down as we drove the last two hours through small towns and on various freeways until eventually at 2 AM, exhausted but relieved, we pulled into Jim and Linda's driveway, parked, kissed the Landy and went inside to shower and sleep. I was still wired from the drive and after a long, hot shower put on some deodorant and clean clothing then sat on the couch, a cold beer in hand, while my little family slept, at home in someone else's house. We had driven almost 9000 kilometres in just over two weeks, the Land Rover had performed excellently, we had seen some incredible sights, met a few amazing people and had life-changing experiences. Before I went to sleep, I sent Mark at AT&T an email to let him know that we were back in town and ready to roll. I was eager to get going on this project to turn our fortunes around.

This is going to be interesting.

For two days we waited for Mark to respond to our email, two very long, nerve-wracking days. Eventually, I phoned him, and we had a quick chat, he was working on the final details and by the end of the week would be able to give us some concrete feedback. Luisa was getting nervous, as was I. We knew that we had not yet signed any contracts and had not had the opportunity to meet the marketing team, share our ideas and knock their socks off with our amazing story. The campaign was due to launch in just over a week and we were hanging high and dry.

I kept myself busy, servicing the Land Rover, hanging out with the neighbours and promoting We Will Be Free online. The first Amazon reviews had been written and it was a huge relief to receive five-star ratings from people who had never met us. I had hoped that the book was good, now I knew that it was, those reviews gave me the confidence to believe that the book was worthy, that we had a story to tell and had told it well. The week ground by slowly and we were relieved to eventually receive a message from Mark saying that he wanted to meet at a restaurant in Redmond, he would then hand us the devices so that we had some time to experiment with the camera and built-in editing software. We arrived at the restaurant ten minutes early and waited for Mark. We had so many questions and were eager to get started, to show him and his team what we could do with the phone. For the V10 campaign, we had planned to drive across the USA, staying off the highway as much as possible, documenting the entire journey in a series of videos and photos, to be provided daily to his team. We could use satellite positioning so that people could follow our progress and we could finish the campaign at an AT&T store in New York. We had discussed some of the details with Mark and now we just needed to finalise the negotiations, we were not going to break their bank, that was for sure. Mark arrived at the restaurant. Empty-handed. Perhaps he had left the phones in the car. We greeted each other, sat down and began to talk. We immediately sensed that something was not right and after half an hour of Mark saying a lot but not saying anything at all, I asked him directly. "Is this campaign going ahead?". He looked at me for a moment and told us that there had been a development which had affected him personally and he had resigned from AT&T. His wife, fifteen years his junior, had just taken a position as head of marketing for Samsung USA, which presented a conflict of interest, he had had to pack his office that afternoon, his car was full of boxes. "That is unfortunate, what on earth are you going to do?", I asked the question I was supposed to ask. Clearly, Mark losing his job was much more important than us not doing a little campaign with one of the largest corporations in America. But it wasn't. He would be just fine, he would find another job at the drop of a hat or start a business or spend more time playing golf. We were in immediate need. Mark explained that his team would still be running with the campaign and that they would be in touch with us regarding the "go forward". Luisa and I both knew that this was not going to happen. Mark was our sole contact and he had driven the entire project.

Believe me when I tell you that writing about this is extremely difficult and incredibly depressing. The entire process had been a roller coaster of emotions from the initial elation when the campaign was proposed, to the many hours spent planning and waiting for an email or a phone call and then this slow-motion free-fall back to earth. I could see that Luisa was crushed, she had been sceptical from the very beginning, a defence mechanism built over a lifetime of soul-crushing disappointment, and we had both tried to remain grounded and realistic. In that one minute our futures were irrevocably altered, when would we ever get an opportunity of this magnitude again? Never is the obvious answer.

We left Redmond that night in a punch-drunk haze, no-one spoke, the rain fell on the windscreen as we drove in the dark. What could I tell my family? They had believed in me. Did I not respond to the emails correctly, was I not professional enough, did they read We Will Be Free and find the book too controversial? Was my social media presence too abrasive, did we fail to impress them with the images and video we had made on the road to Alaska? Perhaps there was still something that could be salvaged from all of this. Mark had said that he would love to work with us in the future, maybe when he moved on to a new corporation. I believed that he never intended to cause us any inconvenience or pain (which is what we were certainly feeling), he had seen something new and interesting, had identified an opportunity and we were in the right place at the right time. How much could I have done differently? What could I still do to make the campaign become a reality? Doubt can crush a person, it can destroy your belief in everything that you know is good and strong and special about who you are. I had failed. I had reached for the stars and had fallen hard on my face. I had given everything we had to this dream that we could do the impossible, we could travel the planet with our children, that I could use the skills I had, learn new skills and lead my family to prosperity and success. I had tried, and I had failed. But I had tried. Is that not worth remembering? We had tried. We had tried the very best we could and had worked as hard as we possibly could. I felt like I had failed.

Mark had been honest with us and had tried his best, I believe, to make the campaign a success. I never doubted his integrity and, when all is said and done, I owe the man gratitude. The AT&T opportunity was exactly that, an opportunity, and we were very unlucky that it did not go our way. A few weeks after our last meeting with Mark, we received an email from Mosaic, AT&T's advertising agency, asking if we would be available in early summer 2016 as they might be interested in working with us then. We replied that, of course, we would make ourselves available and we had some excellent ideas how we could make the campaign something incredible, but needed whatever commitment they could give us if we were going to make any of our own commitments. The conversation continued until early 2016, but no details were discussed. In late 2015 I was watching a football game with some new friends and an LG V10 advert came on screen. Joseph Gordon Levitt, the dour long-haired kid from Third Rock from the Sun, had grown up and was doing our job (much better than I could it must be said) selling the phone. He then later did the campaign for the V20 smartphone, playing the drums and being adorable. Fucker.

LA LUCHA

The fallout from the AT&T failure was huge. I had to unpack and rebuild myself. I had to embrace the fact that we had been worthy of the project, that our book was great, our journey incredible. I had to eat humble pie and start again, and I had to motivate Luisa, who was beginning to lose faith. Motivating someone else when you can barely find a reason to get out of bed is impossible, I had to put on my big boy pants, roll up my bottom lip and lead by example. My maternal grandfather did not die a painless death, but he died an atheist. I am made of the strong stuff!

10

A New Adventure

We returned to our strategy of attending car shows and selling books and were soon able to afford to head south. The plan had been to head across to New York, but I needed to focus on bringing We Will Be Free to a larger audience. Luisa suggested that we look for a house-sitting opportunity where we could focus on finding ways to make some money without working illegally. The car shows were usually an excellent source of income, we could sell up to twenty books in a day, which supplemented the books we would sell to people as we travelled, usually a book or two a day. We were not suffering, but we were not making enough money to be able to afford the shipping and flights to the UK where we would probably have to apply for ancestral visas for Luisa and the kids and where I would have to get a job. It was possible that we could get a long-term house-sitting assignment and I could work as a barman, or bouncer or as a postman or a tree surgeon, a park ranger or a house painter. Luisa had kept the immigration company running as a small-scale operation and there was an opportunity for her to run the business in the UK. I would rather be a postman than do the immigration work again. After a year of work, we should have saved enough to drive the Landy to Asia and back, I wanted to do a book tour of the UK and Australia, but Luisa told me that I was mad.

LA LUCHA

In July we had briefly met a man called Carl and we had become good friends, online mostly, though I did like to phone him at work to remind him that his life sucked, in the nicest possible way. Carl and I shared almost identical political views. He had organised a meeting of Defenders in the Alvord Desert in eastern Oregon and we were invited, perhaps to do a talk and sell some books. We needed to hang out with some good people and agreed that we would meet him there. Carl, as an industrial designer, has an incredible eye for detail and we knew that this event would be unlike anything we had done before. Luisa set a course and we headed in that direction, climbing up out of Washington which had almost become home. Jim and Linda had been so open and kind to us and we are forever in their debt, not that they would ever expect anything in return for their kindness. Jim and Linda were an example of the best type of Americans, Americans who see themselves as good people, people who take care of their families and their neighbours. Jim and Linda had a wonderful family and grandchildren who are being raised with love and care. Jim and Linda came across us when we were at a low point and they took it upon themselves to help, even though we never asked them for anything but conversation. We were going to miss our Mukilteo family, people who had opened their hearts and homes and who made us feel like part of the community.

Oregon is incredibly diverse, from the forests of the Pacific coast to the mountains and plains to the east and the south, it could be a country on its own. We enjoyed the drive up to the desert, choosing to leave the I84 which led to Idaho and instead taking the 395 route through cowboy country and the Malheur National Forest where, in early 2016, the Bundy brothers and a group of armed militias would seize the headquarters of the Malheur National Wildlife Refuge to protest the BLM and the federal government control of public land. We camped at a National Forest campsite where a hunter strung a deer from a tree and butchered it while we grilled chicken over a fire.

In Portland, hipsters wear tweed and have huge beards and ride retro bicycles, while in Burns good old boys drive pickup trucks and don't have time for bullshit. Burns is flat, dry and stuck in 1978, the only visible sign of progress the ubiquitous Walmart. If your town is too shit to even have a Walmart, you aint got shit, pack the RV, burn the house down and move on, sunshine. We are the people of Walmart and we joined our brethren for a quick shop, stocking up on water, beer, fruit and sandwich filler before we headed out to the desert. While filling the Landy with gas, a glamorous old woman, driving a white Cadillac pulled up next to the Landy for a chat. Her makeup was impeccable and her clothing expensive. She too was living in the '70s and loving it, thank you very much. "Where are you all from?", "South Africa ma'am". "Africa? I think you might have taken a wrong turn, sonny. What brings you to Burns?". "Ah, we are heading to the desert ma'am. Going to meet some friends. I love your car". "Thank you, I like your Jeep, is that from Africa too?". "Yes, ma'am, we shipped it to Uruguay in 2012 then drove it up here, we have two kids in there as well". "No kidding, times must be good in Africa. I used to go to Mexico for my holidays and spent some time in Europe, but since my husband passed, I don't get to go anymore". "You should take a drive down there in your Cadillac ma'am, you have plenty of space for camping gear or could stay in hotels". "I haven't camped since I was a kid, no I am an indoor kinda gal. Well, it was really nice to meet some real Africans. Enjoy America". "We are, thank you, ma'am".

The old lady flashed a perfect smile and drove away back down the big, empty street. Leaving Burns, I felt like I was driving through Endora, Iowa, the fictitious town where Gilbert Grape was eaten. That movie, "What's Eating Gilbert Grape", had been one of my favourites when I was a young adult, I identified with Gilbert, I too lived in a small, dry town, my family was dysfunctional, I too had no future, but I lived halfway across the planet, in Africa. I like to think that young me would be quite happy with old me, he would not be too impressed that I was fat, but he might be amazed by what I had achieved. In many ways I think it was movies like Gilbert Grape which motivated me to try and live a life less ordinary, to break the shackles of a little life, to be spontaneous and adventurous and independent. We all have the ability to change who we are and where we are, in a parallel universe I could have been an even fatter couch potato, accepting that I had no future, resigned to a dull existence of routine and compromise.

The Alvord Desert is 170 kilometres from Burns, a long, dry drive past homesteads surrounded by dry grass and nothingness and ghost towns which could not keep up with progress. We turned left at one of these ghost towns and found ourselves in Namibia, long corrugated dirt roads leading towards mountains. Our navigation system was playing up and we missed our turn onto the desert, which is essentially a dry lake bed which resembles a salt flat but is not salty. In the dry season, the lake bed is perfect for camping and high-speed records, photography and land yachts. We followed a bumpy road of dirt sand, tracks heading off in various directions and it was only by following the freshest tyre tracks that we eventually made our way onto the pale white "desert". The sun was setting as we drove out, not sure of where we were going but confident that we would eventually find Carl and his tribe, which we did. Some vehicles had already arrived and were arranged in a circular laager, a large pile of firewood in the middle. We drove into the laager and headed towards the firewood pile so that we could offload our own huge pile which lay piled on the roof of the Landy, between the jerry cans and roof tent. We could tell immediately that this was going to be an incredible weekend. The Steens Mountains shadowed us to the north and the stars began to twinkle in the sky as we greeted Carl and were introduced to the group, most of whom were from Portland or Seattle. With the Land Rover parked and the tent open, we arranged our chairs around the fire and got to know our fellow Defender enthusiasts, a mixed crowd of professionals. There are those who travel long distances and go to far-flung places across foreign borders and there are those who travel long distances and go to far-flung places but do not cross borders. With fellow international overlanders, our conversations about various countries are anecdotal and fun, but with overlanders who do not travel internationally, we sound boastful and, perhaps, condescending. And we diminish the stories of others, completely unintentionally. Someone who has driven to 28 states in the USA cannot boast when in the presence of someone who has driven to 28 different countries. Our stories are sometimes unwelcome and we have learned when it is best to just sit back and let the conversation stay local, lest we unwittingly outshine the storytellers, I hope I don't come across as boastful or superior, this is just the way we talk! Luckily, there was one of our people in the crowd and his name was Steve, soon to be renamed and forever known as Good Guy Steve.

Good Guy Steve was a tall, handsome and athletic rock climber who also rebuilt Defenders in his spare time, was a professor who ran the children's cancer research department at Berkeley University in San Francisco and had driven a Defender from the US to Argentina. It would be very easy to dislike Steve, but he was just such a great guy and he had the cutest dog you have ever seen, he had rescued the dog from certain death in Baja, California. The dog was the perfect travel dog, small, did not shed, was as relaxed as Good Guy Steve and charmed the locals. Good Guy Steve took us on a tour of his Defender which he had converted from a pick up into a camper using the Marshalls ambulance body from a 109 Series 3 and adjusting it to fit the Defender 110 chassis. Immediately light bulbs went off inside my head. He could sleep and cook inside the vehicle and because it was insulated, it was always a comfortable temperature inside, not too hot and not too cold. He had a bed which could be converted into a double bed and a counter for cooking, cupboards for storage and there was open access from the front of the vehicle to the rear. This was almost exactly the set-up we needed! I made sure that I drove with Good Guy Steve the next day when we went looking for trails, eager to see how his Defender camper performed off-road.

LA LUCHA

We headed out across the pan the next morning, a small convoy of hungover Defenders headed towards the hills which surrounded us, trails of white dust, like benevolent chemtrails, flowing behind us. Carl had been studying the maps of the area for a while and had found a few tracks which might or might not cross some private land. I sat next to Steve in his 110 accompanied by a wonderful man with a wonderful beard and equally interesting sense of humour, his name was Matthew and he was designated in charge of moral. We crossed the dirt road we had entered on and after drive for a few minutes, followed Carl and the rest of the convoy onto a track which led up into the hills. Good Guy Steve proved to be an excellent driver, damn him, and his 110 tackled the rough road with ease. We stopped at an old abandoned cottage and had a beer while Carl tried to figure out which road to follow before opening a gate and leading us further into the hills. There were a few steep inclines and a muddy stream to cross before we reached another gate, then another, then another. A few of those gates may or may not have had private property signs. Good Guy Steve's 110 handled everything the others did with the absolute minimum of fuss and I enjoyed letting someone else do the driving for a change. We crossed a large field, searching for a road which would lead us back down to the Alvord, found the gate eventually and drove past a hunter's camp, bottles of alcohol on a table but no people in sight, a good thing I suppose. It was dusk by the time that we eventually returned to our camp, tired, hot and thirsty.

The wind began to blow as the sunset and increased in ferocity as the sky darkened. The gust of wind would occasionally whip through the camp, ripping at the ground tents and our roof tent (which had seen much worse having survived a hurricane during our very first-weekend camping in Uruguay all those years ago). Carl had, very thoughtfully, brought a porta-potty on a trailer and it stood out there, alone in the dark, being assaulted by the wind. No-one dared use the toilet in case it was pushed over by the wind, covering the occupant with shit and blue disinfectant. We made bets how long the poor green receptacle would last. Some people hid behind their vehicles and tried to ignore the wind and biting sand, the dust blowing into everything.

Meanwhile, in Good Guy Steve's 110 camper, he was hosting a party. I sat on the bench surrounded by people, at least eight who were crowded in there at any one time. Good Guy Steve had parked facing the wind and the vehicle did not rock at all, you could hardly hear the wind despite the two large rear doors being open. Occasionally a small sandstorm would gust around the corner and fill the camper with dust, but we were otherwise extremely comfortable. We moved our Defender to face the wind and secured the rain cover, to prevent it from flapping all night. Of all the campers only Good Guy Steve and my family slept well, he because his camper was so well insulated and us because we had been on the road so long that we could sleep through almost anything. In the morning, the wind died down and the camp was full of dusty Defenders, unhappy campers and us happy campers. Miraculously the porta-potty had survived the night, very good news, particularly, for the ladies in the group. By mid-morning, we packed and drove out towards the trails and the Mickey hot spring stopping first at the Fields station, the only gas station and restaurant for many, many miles. The owner's young son had been voted "mayor" of the "town" and they served "the best burgers and shakes in America". Tina Turner made a billion dollars in the USA with that tepid song, Simply the Best, like every restaurant, plumber, corporation, hot dog stand, hairdresser and gynaecologist is "the best". Carl treated us to a shake and, I must admit, they were pretty good, especially with a desert-dry throat and the second day in a row hangover. The hot springs were hot and slimy and peaceful, we joked a bit, roasted in the sun, then headed out with our 130, Good Guy Steve and another 110 to find some tracks which would lead back to the desert. Carl and another group headed off in another direction. The track was mostly easy driving and scenic, an eagle swooped down in a dry field and caught a snake before flying in front of the Defender, the snake writhing in panic. When we descended back into the desert the track became a mix of hard dirt and fesh-fesh bull dust which erupted in massive plumes as we drove through it. I would purposely drive fast through the fesh-fesh while Luisa hung out the window taking photos of the eruptions, becoming covered in dust in the process. The day ended with a long, dusty drive across the desert to return to our camp.

In the morning, we did a presentation for the group but, because one of the campers was trying to stuff his products down people's throats, only two people bought books. They did not want to turn the meet up into a commercial event and we found ourselves boycotted. I could respect that, even though it pissed me off after I had been standing in the sun for two hours working my ass off and answering all their questions. This is our bread and butter and it is a bloody good book, we are not trying to sell you a bloody space pencil which can write underwater. The boycott stung as we had spent good money to go to the event and left with a deficit. Had I known of the boycott, I would probably still have attended the event, and I still would have gladly done a presentation and Q&A, I am a Land Rover man first and foremost, but I would have adjusted my expectations. The upside was that we were able to take some amazing photos (one of which would become the lower half of the Travel the Planet Overland cover), had met some amazing people and were able to hang out with our friend Carl. Before breaking camp, we said goodbye to our new friends, promised Good Guy Steve that we would visit him in San Francisco and took a few more photos. Carl hooked up the porta-potty and we drove to a small town to deliver their wind-battered poo can and then headed towards the Steens mountains. We stopped at a convenience store to buy beer and water and an extremely large woman looked at me like I was a bug, perhaps I was being too friendly, maybe she was pissed that we did not buy any over-priced curios, maybe I, as always, smelled like a homeless man and maybe it was coz I spoke funny. Maybe she looked at everyone that way. I should have asked for a cuddle. We drove up into the Steens mountain, I drove with Carl and Keelan took over the driving of the 130. This was the first time that Keelan had driven on public roads in the USA for any decent distance, but we had seen so little traffic that we doubted there would be any cops up there to catch him driving without a license. He drove a little fast for his mom's liking, but once he slowed down she relaxed. The Steens overlook the Alvord and we were able to see where we had camped an ivory expanse. The Steens mountain is a standalone mountain with an elevation of 2968 meters.

I suggest you visit it some time. Close to the summit, there is an AT&T tower, what a great photo that would have been for the campaign? Joseph Gordon-Levitt would never take this photo, his lips might crack from the dry air, he might sweat, smudging his mascara. I posed ironically for a few pouty face photos, let's do this guys! Yeah! Bring me my drums, bitch. There is even a lake up there called, Wildhorse Lake. I could have drowned JGL, as his friends call him, in that cold, beautiful lake. I must grow up; write that on the board a hundred times.

We camped at the South Steens campground and I decided to wash in the lake. I jumped in and immediately went into shock, I could stand up, but my heart was beating so hard that I froze, a massive pain in my chest, I could not speak for about ten seconds. Carl lectured me about being fat. He did not eat sugar, I should not eat sugar. Hey, Carl, I am dying here, can it wait? If there were any clots in my blood, I would have had a stroke, lucky I am perfectly healthy despite being slightly round. We made a fire, drank a few drinks and tried to solve the world's problems, but there were too many and Luisa and Carl launched into a debate which I left them to have, Carl, won, but only because I agree with him and Luisa uses dirty tactics. The next day we drove in the direction of Crater Lake, Carl would accompany us until we reached the lake and then he would split off to return to Portland. We drove all day after visiting a wild horse sanctuary (most of the beautiful horses were culled in 2016) until we found a shitty campsite, made a fire and ate meat, Carl was missing his sons and I was trying to find out where he hid the whisky in his perfect Defender 90. A hot shower made us all feel human again.

The next day we drove to Crater Lake, arriving late and immediately setting off for a hike during which Luisa and I had a rare blowout. We were tired after a week of socialising, Luisa was being stubborn, and I was being impetuous. We blew the birds out of the trees with a quick and emotional argument before kissing and making up down by the lakeside. Carl ran down to the lake and ran back up again, being fit ruins a perfectly good walk, if you ask me. Crater Lake is a caldera lake formed almost 8000 years ago by the collapse of the volcano Mount Mazama, a collapse which left a beautiful 655-metre-deep hole in the ground. No rivers are running into or out of the lake which has resulted in incredibly cool and clear water, the water provided exclusively by rain and snowfall. At 594 meters deep it is the deepest lake in the USA and a beautiful nightmare for anyone, like me, who is petrified of deep water. If we had a kayak, we could have taken a paddle to one or both of the lakes islands and, if it wasn't freezing cold, we could have had a swim. Officially the park was closed, there were fires nearby and it was the beginning of winter and the campsites were all closed. Like the sunset, our Defenders drove along the rim road which surrounds the lake, searching for a decent place to camp. At the end of an isolated road, we found the Pinnacle Valley trail parking. As the sunset we made the decision to camp in the sloped parking lot and, as there was no wind, to make a little campfire in our stand-alone braai, far from anything flammable.

Carl instructed the sad harp girl to sing for us again and I was wishing he was a Metallica fan, Luisa prepared the food and together we solved the world's problems, again. You would think that after all these years we would have reached a conclusion other than, "we are all screwed". We agreed that overpopulation is the greatest threat to human survival, that regressive and oppressive religions are the greatest threat to our progress and that education is the future. We agreed on so much that there was very little left to discuss. Instead, we synched via ancient Bluetooth and sat studying the patterns of the fire, engaging in an activity which almost all men enjoy. Before we went to sleep we killed the fire with water and packed up, we were going to hike the trail in the morning and wanted to get an early start. The hike was relatively short and enjoyable and by mid-morning, we were ready to head out. Driving with Carl in his 90 you could hear crickets chirp outside, Luisa and I had both driven with Carl and we had both been amazed by the very long silences, it is as if the man has a mute button which engages when the engine turns on. All attempts at conversation were met with a wall of silence and that silence is unnerving. We drove to Umpqua, a small town where days earlier, on 1st October, a disturbed young man armed with many guns had attacked students and faculty at the Umpqua Community College, killing nine and injuring nine. It was a sombre end to an eventful week, Carl quietly said goodbye and disappeared in the direction of Portland. It was only later that I realised how terribly he was missing his children.

Remember Good Guy Steve? Well, he had invited us to visit him in San Francisco and we took the opportunity to head to the coast and drive down the coast to California. The Alvord Defender International Overlander Boycott of 2015 had left us low on travel cash and we were fortunate to meet great people as we drove, generous, friendly people who happily purchased our book, we were averaging three sales a day. Luisa found us a campsite along the Oregon Pacific coast (there is no other) and we drove almost all day to reach the camp which had a small recreation room and decent WIFI. We immediately invaded the rec room and set up a base for the next few days, working, watching TV and relaxing. The owner of the camp, a very friendly bearded man, named Mike, was sure that he could replace the butane in our gas can with LPG, we were unable to cook normal food and were having to braai every night, a situation which I secretly relished. Mike removed all the butane from the can and struggled for the next twenty minutes to convince some LPG to relocate into our tank. Eventually, he gave up and offered the use of his own camping stove, an offer Luisa gladly accepted and within half an hour was boiling horrible vegetables.

Luisa had plotted a course from Oregon down to San Francisco and we were amazed by the Pacific coastline which is incredibly rugged and beautiful. As we travelled south, we tried to hike at least once a day and often had remote areas to ourselves.

As outsiders, we were in a position to observe the American political process. Having paid attention to American politics for many years, I had formed an opinion, which you may or may not agree with but could, perhaps, consider.

The drama of the US presidential election was ramping up. It seemed that Donald Trump had created a movement amongst angry Americans and a loyal fan base was growing behind him. The mainstream media ridiculed Trump at every opportunity. CNN USA is a completely different animal to CNN International - CNN USA is not impartial and their journalism often drifts intentionally into the realm of propaganda. The liberal media, which includes CNN, The Washington Post, The New York Times and The Huffington Post, had ridiculed Trump from the beginning, mocked him for his lack of vocabulary, his fake comb-over hair, his weight, his orange tan and, of course, the things he said in public. CNN, when covering the Trump campaign speeches, used circus music and unflattering images. What the Liberal media soon learned is that they were preaching to the converted, that there is a huge proportion of Americans who have learned to despise the liberal media for many reasons and who refused to watch CNN with gay Anderson Cooper and the pro-Democratic party, pro-Obama rhetoric.

Traditionally, Fox News was the mouthpiece of the Right, but there were many sources of conservative opinion which were listener-funded and who did not have to practice the restraint that mainstream media employs.

We visited the home of a friendly, kind and generous man in Seattle. He welcomed us into his home, offered a cold beer and a meal. He then gave us a tour of his home. The gun collection, which included AR 15 assault rifles he had built from parts bought on the internet (legally, without serial numbers) was impressive. He had a garage full of motorbikes, American muscle cars and Sarah Palin posters. He had a sticker of Barrack Obamas face on his guest bathrooms toilet seat. When I asked about his views of the Obama presidency, the nice, friendly man disappeared and an angry and bitter man took his place. He hated Obama and the Democrats and everything that they stood for. The Dems had destroyed America and the government, in general, had been dragging the country down the tubes for years, trying to create a multicultural, nanny state where those who had worked their fingers to the bone for decades were now expected to pay the bill for those who were too lazy or stupid to take care of themselves.

The right-wing conservatives had, in the last few decades, always voted Republican but the Republican party had wandered off course and could not present a leader who represented their traditional core values or the marginalised base.

My observation was that the Right of the political centre in the USA was populated near the centre by traditional conservatives, Republicans who voted George W Bush and were aware that the economic crash in 2008 happened during W's tenure and understood Obama had been handed a country on its knees and this demographic makes up the majority. But, the further to the right of the political spectrum you travel, the more you will encounter people with very specific and passionate opinions. The Christian right is the meat and bones of the Republican party and they are pro-life and pro-Israel and conservative. If you continue travelling to the Right, you will begin to encounter the Individualists. An Individualist does not want big, federal government controlling his life, he defends his right to bear arms and loathes paying taxes which are destined to be squandered. The individualist may be an anarchist (something he had only realised recently and a term he used to hate) who does not give a flying fiddle if Arthur marries Arthur or if you are black, white, pink or purple, you just have to leave him the hell alone. The individualist may or may not believe that the Illuminati is a cabal which controls the Federal Reserve and therefore controls the government, that the Protocols of the Elders of Zion is an accurate historical document, that the Waco, Texas Branch Davidian massacre in the '90s was the beginning of massive government overreach, that Timothy McVie was a patriot and that the 9-11 attacks were false flag, orchestrated in order to terrorize the American public who, for the sake of security, would not oppose the Patriot Act, which gave the federal-state massive powers of surveillance and interrogation and the right to suspend civil rights without warrant or oppose the Middle East wars which were to follow. And to the right of the Individualist, you will bump into the white supremacist and, having grown up in Apartheid South Africa, I know a few things about White supremacists, believe me. The White supremacist may or may not be a Nazi, but chances are very good that he will eventually embrace the doctrines of the National Socialist movement even though he hates the word, socialist, but is not entirely sure why he hates that word. He calls himself Alt-Right and he will eventually be convinced by the internet and a frog called Pepe that there was no, large scale, Holocaust, that history is written by the victor and that Hitler was an all right guy. He will believe that what is rightfully his, is being stolen from him, that the Jews control the World Bank and the IMF and the Federal Reserve and are trying to destroy the White race, a race so perfect that progress is unnecessary.

The Right considers the Left naïve and, from the centre to the fringe, the Right loves America, but not what she has become. America first.

To the Left of the centre, you will find the Liberal. He, or she, was swept away by the optimistic Obama campaign and embraced the first Black president. The Liberal tends to live in a city and usually has some form of higher education, has travelled out of the USA once or twice or at very least plans to travel in the near future. The Liberal has friends of many ethnicities, or would really like to, and listens to NPR radio, because, science and progress, duh. As we wander left of the centre, we find people who have watched the Michael Moore productions with a great embarrassment and believes America's oil addiction is her single largest problem. Then we meet the Snowflake. The Snowflake believes we are the world, we are the children, she, or a feminine he, wants the world to hold hands and sing Kumbaya, but maybe not because that might be a Christian song and might offend someone. The Snowflake wants to take all the world's poor, hungry and displaced and cuddle them, give them a warm blanket or a big piece of chocolate cake, unless of course the poor person can't eat chocolate cake for cultural or religious reasons in which case the Snowflake will bow and beg forgiveness before cooking their twenty new house guests something more culturally appropriate while wearing a Burka, so as not to offend. Snowflakes usually do not have children but do have small dogs. Then we meet the Internationalist, a Liberal who insists that Martha should have the right to marry Martha and who thinks Michael Moore chickened out when he produced Fahrenheit 9/11. The Internationalist may or may not believe that the Illuminati is a cabal which controls the Federal Reserve and therefore controls the government, that the Waco, Texas Branch Davidian massacre in the '90s was the beginning of massive government overreach and that the 9-11 attacks were false flag orchestrated to terrorize the American public who, for the sake of security, would not oppose the Patriot Act which gave the state massive powers of surveillance and interrogation and the right to suspend civil rights without warrant or would not oppose the Middle East wars to follow. The internationalist may be an anarchist, is almost certainly not religious, hates paying taxes (but would gladly do so to fund universal medical care), owns a AR 15 and believes that state and church and corporation are entities which should never influence one another.

The Left considers the Right ignorant and, from the centre to the fringe, the Left loves America, but not what she used to be. They believe that as the most powerful country on the planet, America has international responsibilities.

It is into this mayhem that Trump stumbled, advised by people who know exactly where they stand on the Right. "Mexicans are rapists!". To the ears of the civilised world, and anyone who has spent some time in Mexico, these words are a shock, a racist declaration which should never be permitted in polite society. But, to millions of Americans, these words were a catalyst. Despite the fact that American appetite for drugs had created the War on Drugs which ripped apart Mexican society and that Mexicans do the work White America does not want to do. Many blame Mexicans and Mexican Americans and foreigners and illegal immigrants for their problems and rally behind the slogan Make America Great Again. The mainstream media, including Fox News, mocked and derided Donald Trump but that criticism only served to strengthen Trump's base, a base which would not trust CNN to tell them the weather, a base which gets their news and opinions from the podcast and social media. Fox News found themselves on the wrong side of the right and labelled fake news, while conservative podcasts dithered, not wanting to commit to backing Trump. Trump, whose campaign was self-financed, did not have any political or corporate masters to answer to and knew that the more controversial his statements were, the more the media would be forced to cover his rallies and the more people will become convinced by his rhetoric. He had nothing to lose, the "free" publicity was excellent for his golden cock brand and, win or lose, he wins. Eventually, public opinion forced the conservative independent media to choose a side but there was no-one else but Trump they could support. The Republican party, who hated Trump more than they did Bernie Sanders, fielded a bunch of limp-wristed plutocrats. Ben Carson is Black but can't get the Black or White vote, Ted Cruz is liver lipped, reptilian and has a Hispanic surname, Marco Rubio is impish, boring and Latino and Jeb Bush still cry himself to sleep at night, cowering in the shadow of W and HW. Slowly but surely Trump gains support and confidence, telling the GOP to get behind him or he will run as an independent.

President Trump, believe it or not, is the result of democracy, the people won, right or wrong. And his election was the American equivalent of the Arab Spring - internet-driven, optimistic, populist and dangerous.
In 2015 the only candidate who could stop Trump was Bernie Sanders. Hillary Clinton was despised by everyone, including Democrats. She was a cold fish and had allowed Americans to be slaughtered at Benghazi, Libya and had been irresponsible by communicating government information via her private email. She was part of the political establishment and, under her leadership, it would be business as usual. More Middle East turmoil, more Wall Street corruption, more big government. Hillary cared about the American public less than she cared about the colour of her shoes, whereas Bernie, the old Marxist, loved the American people. He was going to clean house, get those corporations back in line, expand Obamacare, raise the minimum wage, legalise abortion, marijuana, same-sex marriage and transsexual public bathroom access, significantly reduce college fees and student debt, increase welfare spending, increase corporate tax, cut military spending, withdraw from the Middle East, befriend North Korea and cuddle a Panda bear. Good old Uncle Bernie would have won had the cold fish not been a shark.

11

California Dreamin'

The drive down to San Francisco from Oregon was wild. There are a few beautiful towns (mainly coastal) and there are a few towns which have not had a functioning municipality in at least a decade. We had heard a rumour that it was possible to earn a few hundred dollars a day trimming marijuana in California and with our dismal financial situation, a few hundred bucks a day would go a long way though, Lord knows, we would probably waste every cent overlanding. The Redwoods forest is an amazing place and we often stopped to hike and enjoy the massive trees which had been saved from logging companies, thanks to the foresight of an intelligent governor. In the middle of the dank forest, where the sun never shines, we drove towards a compound of some sort. Old cars littered the side of the road and high walls surrounded a mixture of nailed together structures, tents, RV's and more junkyard material. I could not resist and stopped the Landy to take a few photos and a look over the wall. As I peeked over the wall a tall, skinny and luminescent man exited one of the buildings wearing only a pair of old brown, saggy corduroys. His back hunched, long hair grew over his ears but not on top of his pale skull. He stopped loping, staring at the ground, turned and looked directly at me as if he had a sixth sense or could smell an intruder. I was back in the Landy and halfway down the road before he could take a step in my direction. We were perplexed how a junkyard could be allowed to exist in the middle of a pristine National Forest and could only assume that the junk had been there for almost as long as the forest had. Again, we were not only astounded by the natural beauty of the country but also by the extremes in the people we met as we moved down that incredible coastline. Most of the people exploring the hiking trails were fit and healthy, young families with zero body fat happily chatting and hiking, middle-age couples dressed comfortably marched confidently up and around the Tolstein landscape. They drove nice cars and RV's, was polite and knowledgeable and friendly. And then some people had obviously made very different lifestyle choices. In a few of the towns we came across herds of "on a pilgrimage, looks homeless but just being cool", new-age hippy traveller kids who were hanging around the QFC trying to bum a lift or a cigarette or some change. We had seen members of this tribe in Boulder, toothless girls, no bras, puppies on a leash, asking us where we were from and telling us we were cool. They reminded me of the "on a pilgrimage, looks homeless but just being cool, new-age hippy traveller kids", which originated in Argentina and who wore zombie apocalypse clothing and juggled swords at traffic lights. They were of one tribe but on either end of a large and impressive landmass. Perhaps we should introduce them but, without means or technology, they would never communicate. The American tribe seemed to be on a Jack Kerouac/The Doors inspired journey, many Alexander Supertramp's each writing their own books, turning their backs on the hedonism of modern society and seeking hedonism of another sort, their grandparents had been hippies, their parent's accountants and engineers and estate agents and bank clerks. These young people were the young person I was, once a long time ago.

When I was younger, I worked as a barman for a few years after school. I had no contemporaries in the little town where I lived, other than the misfits and druggies who too did not fit in with the normal crowd. I drank myself into a coma after work almost every night, desperate for escape and eventually, after saving for many months pouring drinks, buying and selling old cars, I had managed to save enough to be able to afford a flight to Israel, where the Kibbutz volunteer program was popular with the work and travel crowd. Within six months of living in Israel. I found myself spending my days washing dishes and my nights banging a tambuka with my new British friends on the Tel Aviv beach. They, my British friends, were all younger than me by at least two years, it felt then that they were a decade younger but a century wiser. Kelly, Steve, Adam, Simon and I were always on the hunt for weed and they introduced me to LSD (I had tried it before in South Africa in a club called The Doors, but little Goth girls freaked me out) and we occasionally sat together on the beach and shared inter-galactical experiences. They were my tribe. When they returned to the UK I was left lonely but managed to continue the party in their absence. I returned to South Africa after exactly one year a tanned, long-haired stoner, dressed in post-apocalyptic clothing and a strange attitude. I discovered, once back in my horrid little home, that I had taken my little tribe for granted and the tribe did not exist in Krugersdorp. I was as lonely as a person could possibly be, but I had convinced myself that I preferred to be alone. I met Luisa and she motivated me to forget the tribe and to work. Almost twenty years later, in Argentina and again in California, I looked at the tribe I used to belong to and wonder what I would have become if I had followed an alternative path, had not returned to South Africa, had continued smoking marijuana, religiously, daily. I now am a professional, admired by the tribe, outside of the tribe and not sure that I want to return to the tribe. Besides, Fat Albert kicked my ass, there is no way I could go back to being "enlightened".

Heading south, we eventually found a gas company which would fill our gas can and, after a stop at our friend Walmart, we headed to the coast to look for a place to free camp. At every parking area along the coast, we found only wind and "no overnight parking" signs. Almost defeated we headed towards the town and drove along the coastline, looking for a secret spot. Luisa noticed a slip road which heads down past a small cliff to a secluded parking area. We drove down and found no "no overnight parking" signs. This could be it. A couple houses overlooked the parking lot which was surrounded by a stone beach and large rocks, the houses appeared to be unoccupied holiday homes and we decided to wait until dark before opening the tent. About 20 meters from our parked Land Rover a firepit sat surrounded by tree trunks, a place to hang out with your friends and chill. A man and two children appeared not long after we arrived and started a fire in the fire pit, we had gas in the can but wanted to grill some meat over a fire, so I approached the man and asked if it was possible to light a fire anywhere on the stone beach. The man's name was Mike and he invited us to join him, he had spent the day fishing with some friends but was not making the fire for grilling. Mike seemed like a good guy and his kids seemed happy, so I agreed to join him, I grabbed a cold beer and answered his questions.

"South African huh, wow?". He left to fetch his friends and returned five minutes later with three inebriated women, one of whom was African American, and she looked at Luisa and me as if we were cockroaches. At first, I could not figure out why the lady was being hostile. We had introduced ourselves politely to everyone and offered our food. A while later we were answering the common, "how can you afford to travel the world?", question and I told the story of how the South African government had incorrectly seized all our cash in Ecuador and how our African money had lost half of its value. "That's racist", the African American woman commented dryly. Shocked, I asked, "what is racist?". "You said 'African money', that's racist". Her thirsty friends gave us a disgusted look. "No, it is not. We are from South Africa, we might be white, but we are also African, it is implied in the name, South 'African'". "Yes, but why did you say 'African' money?". "Would it be racist if I say 'American' money?". I was not going to convince anyone of anything that night, the three women had been drinking all day and had made up their minds that they did not like us even before they had met us. Mike just laughed it off and did his best to lighten the mood, but there was no saving the ambience of the evening, being called a racist is difficult to ignore or brush off. We quickly cooked our chicken, thanked Mike for his hospitality and returned to our Landy to feed the little birds waiting up in their canvas tent. Mike drove down a little while later and gave us a large salmon he had caught earlier that day. He had cleaned and gutted it and it was ready for cooking. He apologised on behalf of his friends, but he did not need to, I had liked Mike from the moment I had met him and I knew that he was the kind of guy I would happily call a friend.

Rolling into San Francisco was a massive event for us. How many movies have you seen with the Golden Gate Bridge and Alcatraz, Berkley University, street trams and China Town? A thousand. Good Guy Steve had invited us to crash at his home near Berkeley and we found his house by looking for Land Rovers. Good Guy Steve has a herd of Landy's and a collection of parts huddle in the corners of his yard, including Series 1 wheels and a bonnet. My China, Greg, lived in the city and he invited us for a tour. We left GGS's house early on a beautiful Wednesday morning and headed towards the Bay Area Rapid Transport (BART) train station. This was to be our first-ever subway ride and we were excited. BART, however, was not very impressive and stepping into one of the ancient trains felt like a step back in time, to the seventies, perhaps. The windows of the train were green with age, the carriages rickety aluminium. Our fellow passengers stared at their phones, listened to their headphones, avoided eye contact or stared. Tiktatukatikatikatukatikatuka. We emerged from a subterranean system into the brightness of day, running parallel to the highway leading into the city. Occasionally the train would stop to absorb or dispense unsmiling faces. We passed neighbourhoods and businesses and grey, graffiti walls beneath deep blue skies before sliding back underground to ride an ageing network of rails, beneath the ocean and disembarked into the bowels of the city above. We rode the escalator and climbed stairs, dressed in overlander clothing, old khaki shorts, crumpled shirts, flip flops, eventually breaking through the crust and emerging into the cool daylight of a beautiful city. Beautiful people dressed in designer clothing and critically low body fat swarmed about us. We stood in awe, an island in the flow. A homeless man asked me if he could help us. I was not accustomed to being offered assistance by the dejected, I looked at my family and then at myself in the mirror of a skyscraper. There were two types of people on the streets; the rich and the poor. We did not look like either and we did not look like tourists. Sunburned and dusty (our default appearance) we looked like we had just stepped out of a Land Rover from a journey around the world. City people act aloof but are incredibly curious, they look for the new, the interesting, the inaccessible, the impossible and the strange. We represented these things and we could feel the city taking an interest in us. A man walked past swiftly, a slim-fitting, bespoke blue suit competing with his fresh haircut and expensive scent. He wore no socks beneath handmade Italian shoes, an outfit which cost as much as my family's annual grocery bill. We waited for Gregory to arrive and soaked up the sights. The more we watched, the more we realised that San Francisco is shared, unevenly, between the rich and poor. Homeless people dotted the streets and they owned the streets. Three homeless men sat in the middle of the sidewalk, as casually as if they were having a picnic on a green lawn overlooking a beautiful bay. They stretched out and had a conversation, forcing the glistening people to step around them, queueing at the bottlenecks created by the odorous, lounging dropouts who shouted obscenities at anyone foolish enough to walk through their rush hour roadblock picnic.

Gregory arrived and immediately took us for the first of many meals that day. We ate Chinese food in the basement of an extremely popular restaurant which smelled like food and disinfectant, the standard odour of a Chinese restaurant. The portions were massive and delicious, and we offered our leftovers to a homeless man who sat on the street outside. He looked in the bag of Styrofoam containers and spotted a noodle. "Nah, I am sick of Chinese". Oh, I am sorry, would you like a steak? Gregory shared the history of the city as we walked towards the underground parking area where he kept his matte black Nissan. We cruised the city visiting the cemetery and Golden Gate Bridge before driving across the bridge to join tourists and gape at the beautiful city below us.

The mist rolled in from the ocean and covered a portion of the city where rents were cheap and homes moist and grey. We drove back into the city and visited Chinatown which is transplanted from Asia. We were disgusted to find shops selling shark fins for soup and enjoyed the dim sum at the oldest little restaurant in the area. Old men sat beside scruffy parks and played board games, admonishing us as outsiders. Driving back into the city, we explored the rolling hills where some of my favourite movies had been shot and enjoyed Gregory's insightful tour. He knew so much about the cities past and culture and his love for the city was infectious. We were reminded of our own beautiful Cape Town and we too were in love with the city before the sun began to set. It would be impossible for us to ever live in the city though, property prices were so astronomically high that even well-paid professionals struggled to find a home and those who had affordable apartments had no intention of ever leaving. GGS had introduced us to a friend of his, a beautiful, motorcycle riding, rock climbing, engineer who lived in a tent on the roof of an apartment building in the city. Her friends owned an apartment in the building and she paid them a large sum each month to be able to use the kitchen, living areas and bathroom. At night, she would have to climb a precarious fire escape to reach the tent where she camped. She had a full time, well-paid job as a fully qualified professional.

Back in the CBD we walked the streets, surrounded again by the well-heeled and unloved. Crossing a street, a group of three professionals chatted, a benign activity in which a fat homeless woman found offensive. She targeted the male in the group and followed them across the road, shouting. "Fuck you, sir! You think you are so clever, but you are a stupid bitch. Pussy.

Why don't you just fuck yourself? Stupid asshole!". The group ignored the insult completely and continued their conversation without missing a beat, which enraged the fat, dirty woman further, she continued to follow them, assaulting them with verbal abuse until they sought refuge inside a restaurant. That night we walked with Greg to a corner store to buy a six-pack and passed a pitch-black woman wrapped in pure white sheets. The stench of urine attacked us as we passed the woman who had fixed a dead, zombie stare at us. She began to lope forwards, her white sheets trailing, and she followed us as we walked, now with purpose. Other homeless people had begun to build a cardboard village on the sidewalk and were completely unmolested by anyone wearing a uniform. Back at Gregory's apartment building, we stood on the rooftop and sipped cold Pabst Blue Ribbon beer and gazed upon the beautiful city lights. Gregory and his wife Abbey, who worked as the concierge at the local Hilton, had bought a comfortable apartment in the centre of the city as an investment. It simply does not make sense to pay a massive amount of rent when a mortgage repayment would not be that much more. I gave Gregory financial advice as we sat on the roof, he patiently listened and bit his tongue, I was broke, he was not. Abbey joined us after work and took us to a restaurant for our fifth delicious meal of the day. She rubs shoulders with the likes of Kim Kardashian on a daily basis and recommends restaurants to her guests, the restaurants know this, and though the waiter was surprised to see Abbey hanging out with strange-sounding vagabonds, we were still treated like royalty. We ate pizza, scallops and more while drinking delicious wine and had a wonderful evening before saying a grateful goodbye to our hosts and heading back to the BART for a sad ride home.

Waiting for the train, late at night, we pondered the suicide hotline posters which covered the walls, overlooking the rails. "It's not worth it". Golden Gate bridge was another popular suicide location in the city, and I had to wonder how often the suicidal had contemplated their options. A quick but extremely violent death at the nose of a grungy old train or a long, terrifying and scenic fall into icy, shark-infested waters. If you jump in front of a train, there is a small chance of survival, but there would be tens of thousands of people who would instantly hate you and condemn you to hell as they had to wait hours for the forensic teams to clean your depressed remains off the tracks. Jumping off the bridge would be horrific, and there was the chance that you might land on your back and float, paralysed out to sea while marine creatures treat you like a floating buffet. In 2010, a sad boy jumped from the bridge but did not die on impact, instead, he lay there, unable to move while a sea lion kept bumping his body up to the surface until a coast guard boat arrived to rescue him. Predictably, the sad boy is now a motivational speaker, true story. An hour on the BART was enough to make me contemplate my options*9+. We almost missed our station, people stared. We joked and laughed, "sjoe, that was close", people stared. We escaped the Zombies of the BART and promised to return to San Francisco one day, but never to BART. We stayed at Good Guy Steve for a few days, much of that time was spent looking at his Marshall ambulance and discussing ways that we could convert our Landy into something similar. Good Guy Steve had sold the back of his Landy for good money and had bought the ambulance box for a lot less. He had actually turned a profit which gave us a few fresh ideas for converting our Landy. Gregory and Abbey joined us at Good Guy Steve's home for a South American style Asado and a few beers.

Good Guy Steve's house was situated on a street with other homes which were well-loved and filled with intelligent, friendly people. Except for the house on the corner. That house was overgrown with weeds and a myriad of plants but, there seemed to be a path cleared to the front door where a dusty light bulb hung from the veranda and no post littered the stoop. Walking along the pavement (sidewalk) you did not notice the spooky house until it was too late and you were enveloped in the Narnia darkness which surrounded the little grey house. I had seen it first during one of my early morning pre-sunrise walks and, before the sunset on the day of the Asado, I took Abbey, Keelan and Jessica to see the house. We walked around the house, emboldened by daylight, peered through the back-yard fence only to find an overgrown mess and peeked into the garage where an old VW Beetle stood, dusty. "Do you think anyone lives there?" "I dunno?'. Good Guy Steve knew nothing about the house, he had not looked at it in years and I became more curious. Surely some brave estate agent had attempted to gain access to the home, cleaned up it would be worth at least half as much as God's favourite palace. After the sunset, we decided to return to the house which now sat in complete darkness. "Knock on the door Abbey". She wouldn't. "Jessica, knock on the door". She wouldn't either. Something bumped inside the house and the girls ran away while I walked back calmly, nonchalantly. Luisa returned with us, marched up to the door and knocked. Pffffft. Killjoy. Nobody was home, the game was over.

The next day we left and headed to Sacramento. Good Guy Steve had a friend called Jeff who lived there and had offered us their little cottage for a week. Since returning from Alaska, we had been a bit listless. We had achieved both a circumnavigation of South America and our initial Argentina to Alaska plan, but now we were up a creek without a paddle. Of course, we would have loved to ship the Landy across to Europe and drive to Asia, but to do that, we would need some kind of miracle. The AT&T project would have been our ticket, but we were not at all optimistic that that campaign would ever see the light of day. While staying at Jeff's we had to do some maintenance of the Landy and a major clean. We unpacked the entire Landy, not thinking that this would cause Jeff's wife to have a minor heart attack, "OMG, I think they are moving in!". Jeff received an urgent call and had to leave on a week-long business trip and his poor wife and lovely kids were stuck with these weird Africans who had just moved, lock, stock and barrel into the guest cottage. We assured them that we would be out in a week but did not really have a clue where we were headed. Luisa had sent out a few applications for house sitting assignments and after a few days received a few responses. One of the house-sitting gigs, in particular, had caught my eye.

The advert described the house as a homestead high in the San Pedro de Martir mountains in Baja, California, Mexico. The house was large and modern but completely off-grid with water supplied from a stream, solar power, chickens, a couple dogs, a large and productive vegetable garden, fruit trees, no neighbours for miles and the assignment was for six months. This was almost exactly what I had been dreaming of for all those thousands of kilometres up to Alaska and back down. We would be almost completely self-sufficient! Luisa contacted the owners and waited for their response. "No, sorry, we have already found someone to take care of the farm, goodbye". Oh, well, what can you do. They responded the next day again. "Something has come up, are you still available?". Hell yes!

We packed and left Jeff's house within a few days, much to his wife's relief. We were very grateful to Jeff and his wonderful family, the time spent in their cottage had allowed us to regroup our thoughts and come up with a plan for the foreseeable future. Heading south, we set our sights on LA and then Baja. Between lay the famous coastal highway and some of the most beautiful scenery in the world, we were sure to have a good trip and had the comfort of a destination. We made our way to a town called Hollister Hills where we found the Hollister Hills State Vehicular Recreation Area which was essentially a state park with dedicated 4x4, quad bike and dirt bike trails and camping areas. At $10 the campsite was well within our budget and had a large fire pit at the site and clean bathrooms. Luckily, we arrived on a Tuesday and there were not many people around, this was the kind of place people would really get their party on over the weekend.

The next morning, we returned to Hollister to catch up on emails and buy some groceries and while we were parked, we noticed a man taking many photos of the Land Rover. Once inside, we passed the man in the dairy aisle and handed him one of our business cards, he had a look at it for a while and then asked me if we needed a place to camp. He had a ranch nearby which had an Old West town and an Indian village and we were welcome to camp there. At first, I said no thank you, but once Luisa heard of the offer she made me go and ask the man if the offer still stood. He said sure and gave us the security code for the gate, telling me to make myself at home. This blew me away. The man's name was Luc and he told us that we could stay as long as we wanted to. As it turned out Luc was a French-born property developer from LA and the ranch was his country getaway. The Old West town was built to cater for large events like weddings and had a jail, a saloon, a conference area, a huge BBQ area and the largest tarantulas we had seen since South America. We played hide and seek with the kids, had gunfights and locked Luisa in the jail. At night the coyotes howled, and we slept well, dreaming of being cowboys and cowboys, overlanders on horseback, fighting Injuns and hunting bad guys.

In the morning Luc gave us a tour of his toy shed, a large warehouse which contained a variety of novelty and off-road vehicles but the feather in the cap of the collection was an Alaskan bush plane which could take off and land where other aeroplanes simply could not. The small two-seater plane had very large, soft tyres and massive shock absorbers which allowed the plane to handle rough terrain. His son gave us a demonstration, taking off and landing on the purpose-built runway. To thank Luc for his hospitality, we gave him a copy of We Will Be Free, then said goodbye. (A few weeks later we received an email thanking us for the visit and for the book which he described as art, well written and inspiring).

LA LUCHA

We had a late start and camped in a small town before heading onto the Big Sur road which was notorious for having very expensive campsites and zero options for free camping. We received a message from the owners of the ranch in Mexico, "Something has come up, the ranch may not be available, we will let you know asap". These guys were jerking our chain. The campsite was clean and tidy despite being located next to the train tracks. The local residents took an interest in Jessica and us befriended a woman named Anna, who soon became our friend. Anna was from the south, was Black and in her sixties. She sang spoke the blues, every sentence ending with a musical "mmmm hmm" and an interesting sentence ended with "mmmm hmm, alright". Anna invited us into her trailer and we spent some time with her drinking tea and shooting the breeze. She had had her fair share of heartbreak and hardship but had married a White man named Tim, a large and kind man who managed a local hotel. We stayed at the camp for three nights, waiting for the owners of the ranch in Mexico to give us a final answer, the kids catching up on schooling and Luisa and I working on a few ideas for the future. It was while camped next to the tracks that we discovered, first hand, why America is the land of the motor vehicle. The nearest supermarket was a kilometre walk along the main road and over a bridge. A sidewalk bordered the road until just after the bridge and after that we had to walk on the verge of a field. People would stare at us as we walked, and the police took an interest in us. Even the poorest person has a car of some sort and two people walking along the road was a strange sight. Perhaps if we had been dressed in lycra exercise clothing and walking briskly, we would not have attracted so much attention. At night Anna and Tim would join us at our picnic table and we would have a few drinks and solve the world's problems. Anna had grown very fond of us and was worried about us. We told her not to worry. We knew by now that we could sell the Landy for parts if we had to, and still, earn more than what we had paid for her. That was our insurance, our very last ace up our sleeve when and if we had played our last hand. Anna bought a couple of books and sent us on our way with a huge hug. For days after meeting her, we spoke with a southern lilt. "Mmmm hmm, alright".

The coastal road to LA was called The Big Sur and was every bit as beautiful and expensive as we were told it would be. This was the land of the San Andreas Fault and the tumultuous sea and dramatic cliffs bore testament to the volatility of the landscape. We drove slowly, often stopping to take short hikes and walks along tourist paths. Finding camping was difficult as all the camps were full and we were being quoted ridiculous amounts for campsites with no electricity or facilities. $60 for a night was unthinkable and we were lucky to find a state park where the volunteer camp hosts charged us $20 to camp next to a dumpster. We had no choice but to pick up the pace and get down to Santa Barbara where Luisa had found camping next to the ocean for a reasonable $25. The campsite was a parking area alongside the busy road and we parked between large RV's which ran generators to power their numerous gizmos. A pretty blonde lady with two dogs occupied the RV to our left and after a short conversation, Holly invited us to make a fire between the rocks in front of her RV and enjoy a glass of wine. We grilled some meat and enjoyed a beautiful sunset and a relaxing conversation before going to sleep to the sound of waves crashing, generators rumbling and vehicle passing by. It was near Santa Barbara that we enjoyed our first In-N-Out Burger experience, triple-decker cheeseburgers, crispy fries, sweet, smooth shakes and the atmosphere of good old America, the America of the Beach Boys, Cadillac's, pretty girls and happy families. It was here that the Baja ranch owners eventually committed, "All is good, you can come through". This exchange bothered me, but we were excited to have good news and tried to put our concerns to rest.

Driving into LA was not what we expected. Malibu was dry and crowded with mansions and everyone drove a black Range Rover. We squinted to see the drivers and passengers through the dark, tinted glass and I was able to spot a whole host of celebrities. I saw Danny De Vito, Eddie Murphy, Brad Pitt and Angelina, Robert de Niro, Robin Williams (who had committed suicide the year before) Ryan Reynolds, Pamela Anderson and Charlie Sheen. Nobody believed me, but I think they were just jealous. We pulled into the Santa Monica pier carpark and waited to be reunited with our Pan America friends, Toby and Chloe. We had not seen each other since Argentina and we enjoyed an evening of healthy food and conversation, celebrating Luisa's birthday the following day. Both Toby and Chloe had worked in the film industry and they knew the ins and outs of Hollywood better than anyone else we might have hoped to meet. The evening was surprisingly sober and we were all very well behaved and too soon it was time for us to leave. The ranch owners had asked us to be in the mountains within the next few days and we had to be sure to get through the border and into Mexico with a few days to spare. There would be no time for sight-seeing in LA, but I promised the girls that we would return after our stint in Mexico and we would do all those horrible tourists things they wanted to.

GRAEME BELL

LA LUCHA

Our route through Mexico

12

Ola Mexico

We arrived at the Tecate border crossing that night after doing some grocery shopping and grabbing a burger at In 'n Out. It was Luisa's fortieth birthday and I felt like a bastard that she had to celebrate it with a cheeseburger and a border crossing. "Look, honey, I am taking you to Mexico for your birthday!". She was not amused and again, I had to promise that I would make it up to her when we returned to the USA. However, since we had been on the road, Luisa and I found we no longer needed to lavish each other with gifts and expensive treats on our birthdays. The kids were still spoilt rotten on their birthdays but us adults were doing what we loved, living a life less ordinary. Luisa will never forget turning 40, crossing into Mexico and having a simple, quiet evening with me doting on her, making her feel like a princess. Would you choose a diamond necklace, Swiss watch or true love and a life of adventure?

We had chosen the Tecate border crossing because it was much smaller than Tijuana and we hoped that we would be treated better than at a border which processes thousands of people every day. As we reached the border and drove into the inspection area, one of us let out an enormous fart, I won't tell you who. As we jumped out of the Landy, the Mexican border officials came over to inspect the vehicle. We knew we had way too much food and groceries and were worried that they would confiscate our illegal pork ribs. The official reached the Landy and poked their heads inside only to recoil in horror. Dios Mio! "It is ok, we don't want to inspect anymore". We were embarrassed but relieved. The stench had driven away the officials and had saved our food stash which, thankfully, was stored in the back of the vehicle, far away from the chemical warfare. The immigration official took our passports and reacted with a pleasant surprise when we spoke to her in Spanish. While she issued the visas, I took a walk into the town to draw some cash for the visas and returned later to find the family and the official had become close friends, they were making plans to get together someday and our new friend would take us on a tour of the town and show us the best restaurants and bakeries. With our passports retrieved and our stinking Land Rover back on Mexican soil, we drove to a campsite outside of town and had a glass of wine to celebrate both Luisa's birthday and being allowed to return to Mexico (we had also made sure that we walked back to the Americans and handed in our white tourist card). It was simply incredible that we were back in the third world, a line in the sand (and a wall and helicopters and sniffer dogs and border patrol and infrared technology and a few trillion dollars) made all the difference from one country to the next.

Baja, California is a dry peninsula bordered by the USA to the north, the Pacific Ocean to the west and the Sea of Cortez to the east and is known for its beaches, fishing and surfing. It is not known for its mountains and of course, us being us, we had to do the opposite of what everyone else does and we headed for the mountains after stocking up with supplies in Ensenada. We drove south, following the coast and after three hours came to a small dusty town called San Quintin and a sign which read "San Pedro de Martir – 100 km". The ranch we were heading to was called Rancho Misconcepcion and the entrance was opposite the 67-kilometre mile marker. At first, the road ran flat and winding through a valley past poor villages, but after 30 kilometres the road began to climb. We could see high grey mountains in the distance and over the next 37 kilometres climbed from just above sea level to about 2500m above sea level. We had driven all day from Tecate and as we drove the sun began to set rapidly. I engaged low range for some of the steeper sections of the road which had been built and paved to service an observatory at the top of the mountain. For many years this had been a dirt trail and I imagine that only Land Rovers and helicopters would be able to make it to the top. In the darkness, we reached the 67-kilometre mile marker and spotted an open gate further up the road. Behind the gate lay a steep track littered with rocks and gouged by water. I engaged low range again and drove onto the track, a sign behind us bore the name "Baja Blue Skies", the name of the bed and breakfast which the owners had been running for the last six or seven years. Mafuta, the faithful Defender, climbed the hill and turned ninety degrees to the right and climbed for a few hundred meters until we reached a crest and began to head downhill, still in low range and using engine braking. Down we went, around a few bends and over sections of road which had essentially been washed away, deep gouges in the surface at least half a meter deep in places for the Landy to exercise her full articulation, loose rocks impeding our downward progress. We descended into a valley and drove parallel to a river bed until we spotted a campfire.

We were expecting a friendly greeting, but the Gauchos (cowboys) sat still and shone their torches in our eyes, blinding us. "Rancho Misconcepcion?" I asked. "Ariba", (up) came the answer. "Gracias!". We drove into the river bed and up the other end, the Land Rovers left rear wheel spinning as the vehicle articulated. Up we climbed and were faced with four hairpin bends, the second of which was badly gouged and difficult to cross, the heavily loaded Land Rover rocked as her tyres fell into the deep scars in the trail, in low range second gear and with the diff lock engaged I feathered the throttle and the mud terrain tyres gripped, propelling us gently forward. After the fourth hairpin, the road straightened and we came to a locked gate, Luisa had the lock code but had to try repeatedly to unlock the large combination lock which secured the white gate. I drove through and Luisa locked the gate, I was tempted to drive off and leave her screaming in the dark, but that prank would end with my death.

Up we climbed, around a corner, scraping under some trees, around another corner over a section of road "paved" with rocks, large and sharp, round and small, up another large scarred incline, the Landy at an angle, the tyres spinning and grabbing, spraying rocks and sand. The track to the farm was just over six kilometres but it felt like sixty and took nearly an hour for us to reach a plateau where willows hung across the road and a concrete pipe bridge led us over a wash, down to a stream and up a steep incline which led to a branch fence and a rope gate. The air was cold as we drove towards the large farmhouse where two dogs and two humans waited to greet us and lead us inside. The female was called Bruce. She had a wide face, cauliflower nose, tiny eyes and an eight-year-old girl's blonde hairdo, a ponytail and a wide fringe (or bangs as the Americans call them) which formed a thatch roof over her face which sat atop a stocky body. She grabbed my butt within ten minutes of meeting. The male, Penelope, wore the grey hair helmet of a precarious child of the seventies, his pixie features magnified by the reluctance of his body to retain any form of muscle. His shoulders sloped down from his little neck at a 45-degree angle and were draped in a tie-dye shirt which hung down, almost to his knees.

Bruce wasted no time impressing us with the story of her childhood. She had been raised sailing the ocean with her insane trust fund mother and younger brother. The house was beautiful, built of adobe sourced from the soil of the ranch, it had a large main bedroom with triple pane windows and a large bathroom, a smaller guest bedroom with en-suite bathroom and a very large room, empty except for a double bed, which used to be Penelope's media room. We chatted for a while, Penelope showed me how to use the fireplace efficiently, we unpacked the Land Rover and then went to sleep, Luisa and I in the guest room and the kids in the media room. We were excited to see the ranch in the daylight and could not wait to see the vegetable gardens and the trees hanging heavy with fruit. Bruce and Penelope would be leaving the next day and we looked forward to being alone with the dogs, exploring the ranch and working on a project which Luisa had recently suggested. In the morning we made breakfast while Bruce told us more about herself and then stepped outside to greet the dogs, Pepita and Wags, Australian Blue Heelers which Penelope kicked if they went near the front door scared that the dogs would kill their babies, three old, skinny ginger cats which meowed constantly. We had been told that the ranch had abundant vegetables and fruit and that we could be self-sufficient, but we found, to our despair, that the vegetable garden was dead and full of weeds. A few rotting pumpkins sat in a corner surrounded by dry dirt and stones. The fruit trees were bare. Bruce shrugged, oh well, in summer you may get some tomatoes. The chicken coop housed two cocks and three young chickens which were too young to produce eggs. We followed Bruce as she stomped around the property, showing us the solar system which had was missing half the solar panels, a generator too small to run an iPad, the water system which relied on a tiny submerged pump to deliver a trickle of water to a large tank which sat on the top of a rocky hill overlooking the ranch. We were shown how to use the tractor and the push lawn mower which I would be using to cut the acre of grass every weekend and which was housed in a large empty building which had a complicated sliding roof, and which had served as an observatory. Two fat horses waited to be relocated to a farm in Canada where Bruce and Penelope were originally spawned.

We helped them to load their belongings into a black Toyota and happily watched them leave. Despite being lied to about the produce on the farm, we were delighted with the house and had noted that there was a large outdoor braai where I could spend my evenings sipping a Tecate beer, counting the stars. After cleaning the house and moving into our separate bedrooms, we started a fire in the braai and had a good talk. We had been talking about writing a "how-to" overlanding book and Luisa suggested that we should launch the book through a Kickstarter campaign. I did not know much about crowdfunding and I regarded Kickstarter campaigns with the same disdain with which I regarded Go Fund Me projects. I hated the idea of putting my hand out, asking for help. Luisa explained that the Kickstarter campaign was all about pre-sales, that we set a target and if we achieved the target, we would then be able to print the books and deliver them internationally. The sales of We Will Be Free were growing every month but were not enough to cover our expenses, let alone fund our future. I agreed with Luisa, she made an excellent case for the campaign and set my mind to writing the book which was yet untitled.

We had agreed to take care of the ranch, which Bruce and little Penelope had put on the market for a huge sum of money, for a period of six months. Before leaving, they had warned us that the local farmers had been a source of conflict and that they did not have a good relationship. The track which led to the ranch continued over the mountains and connected with other ranches and a guest farm called Mikes Sky Ranch. Off-roaders enjoyed driving the tracks but Bruce, in particular, did not like visitors. After a few altercations with the local ranchers and off-roaders (including Bruce smashing the windscreen of one 4x4 with a tyre iron) she had decided to build locked gates across the road, three separate gates, the first the white gate we had passed on the way to the ranch, the second next to a small cottage 100 metres from the ranch house and the third a couple kilometres away where the road entered a dry river bed. They had promised a local conservation group, which might be interested in buying the property, that they could have their Christmas party at the ranch the following weekend, so we would have to host and accommodate these people. We had no problem with that other than that they would use our renewable resources of energy and water and we asked only that they bring their own food, toilet paper and bottled water.

My first priority was to explore the ranch and the surrounding hills and tracks. The ranch sat at the centre of the plateau, to the east the owners had built a tin shack observatory with a sliding roof and from here you could see the coastline, a three-hour drive away, and a rough path to the closest ranch. To the north lay more mountains and, eventually, the USA, to the south, in a deep gulley which bore testament to the power of flash floods, lay the stream which supplied our drinking water and above that the face of a mountain which channelled air from the ocean and which formed a massive natural wall beyond which you could see only blue sky. To the west lay more mountains, Mikes Sky Ranch and a path to the Sea of Cortez. We were completely alone, the nearest ranch six kilometres away. I stripped the Landy of all unnecessary overlanding gear, repurposed for farm work and drove her up along a track which ran parallel to the stream and ran out of track in a large field. The trees were mostly pine and oak and I could see tracks and dung pats, proof of a wild herd of cattle which would apparently raid the ranch garden if given the chance. Keelan and I left the Land Rover and continued to explore on foot, crossing the gulley and eventually reaching the ruin of an old farmhouse which had apparently been occupied by an old Indian woman until she was run off the land by the local gauchos. The old farmhouse was small, merely a stone cottage with an outhouse and the roof and front walls had been torn down. A few barren fruit trees and a vineyard stood silent witness in the yard, an old steel box, emptied of its contents sat rusting under the shade of an enormous oak tree. We explored the area for a while, looking for wild crops, fruit-bearing trees and signs of wildlife. Keelan had his pellet gun and we were considering the possibility of hunting wild rabbit for the pot, I had even come up with a plan for hunting the wild cattle using a trap and homemade spears. Don't forget, I had spent months dreaming about living off the grid and this was my opportunity to see if I could do it, without the investment of building a home with my own hands. Down in the gulley, the stream ran cold and clear, surrounded by greenery which stood in stark contrast to the dry arid landscape which surrounded us. We located the mouth of the large, partially submerged, black pipe which was the source of our "agriculture" water, a separate water system from our "house" water which relied on water pumped to the tank on the hill above the house. The agricultural water system relied on gravity and a system of large black pipes which lay in the stream and meandered towards the house. These black pipes were old and often trod on by the cattle and would need regular maintenance. The house water was sourced from a little dam which fed two black tanks, it was from the second of these black tanks that the water was pumped up the hill by a submerged pump which was powered by a solar panel and which needed to be turned on and off daily, as water was needed. We hiked back up to the Landy and drove back down to the farmhouse where Luisa and Jessica were working to clear the vegetable garden. Keelan and I joined in the labour and by the end of the day, we had managed to clear out most of the debris and dead plants. In terms of edible haul, there were only a couple of pumpkins and a few herbs! Bastards, why lie? The entire theme of the description of the ranch was that you were extremely remote, but, don't worry, you have everything you need. Our next surprise was the weakness of the solar system which Penelope had boasted was the best that money could buy. I am sure it was until they removed half of the solar panels and half of the bank of batteries. At night we had to carefully measure the amount of power that we were using and even though we used almost no electricity, the system would shut off completely by three in the morning and would only reboot once the batteries had achieved 85% charge. Admittedly Luisa would try and run the vacuum cleaner and the washing machine at the same time during the day, but we soon learned that we had to sweep the house, which seemed to shed, and vacuum only the hard to reach areas. The internet was also extremely slow and very expensive at $100 a month, but we had no choice but to pay.

13

Ranch Life

Keelan and Jessica focussed on their schooling during the week while Luisa and I worked on the Kickstarter campaign. We had decided that we would live a structured lifestyle of Monday to Friday indoor work, Saturday outdoor work and a braai and Sundays for exploration and relaxation. I would take a walk every morning to check on the ranch and had to dedicate a couple of hours every afternoon to cut the lawn. I also had to water the garden which surrounded the house and set about trying to grow a lawn which was not 80% weeds, at least in the area around the braai. Within a few days, we were settled in and were being extremely productive but had to leave the ranch within a week to buy groceries as we had brought almost no fresh vegetables, fruit or herbs. Wags and Pepita were incredible animals, friendly and as tough as nails, we did not have to worry about leaving them alone for a few days. Bruce and Penelope had moved into a new RV by the coast in Ensenada and they suggested that we camp near them for a night. We locked up the farm and drove out, seeing the road we had driven in on, in the light of day for the first time, it was a lot easier to drive down than it was to drive up and we were amazed by the state of the road which had been carved out of the mountains over many years. With less load, the Landy was able to really stretch her legs and we had a good time driving her back to the paved road which dropped down dramatically from the cool peaks to sea level. It took us almost six hours to drive to Ensenada, which was the most modern city on the peninsula and which boasted a Costco, where Luisa could stock up on a case of wine and large quantities of frozen fruit and vegetable. Ensenada has all the charm of a third world city and is a mix of rich and very poor. We drove through the dusty back streets trying to find a route to the campsite where Bruce and Penelope were watching Star Trek. They invited us into the RV and while Bruce threw back one whiskey after another, they suggested that we could rent out the cottage next to the ranch house if we wanted to make some extra money. We were extremely grateful for the offer but, being suspicious by nature, I believed the offer was too good to be true. Only much later did I realise that they had grown to hate the ranch and knew that it would take a very long time to sell it. They were encouraging us to stay for as long as it took to sell the ranch, an offer which, at one time, I might have been tempted to accept.

The next morning, we said our goodbyes and headed back towards the Costco which sat in the heart of Ensenada. The camp security guard warned us that there was a roadblock which was causing severe traffic congestion, but there was no way around the military base which stood between us and the city. Reluctantly we joined the snarled traffic and inched forward. It took an hour to travel a few kilometres and when we eventually reached the source of the congestion we were amazed. The Ensenada bus drivers were protesting Uber or a fuel hike or a tax or something similar and had shut down the city by parking their buses across all lanes except one. This is the Latin Americans greatest form of protest, he shuts down the city when he has a grievance and each group or organisation takes turns pissing on the local economy. Next week it will be a teacher's strike or a municipal workers strike (who take it to the next level, covering the city in the trash they have not collected and will later have to), or a general protest over a 1% tax hike. I wrote about this phenomenon in We Will Be Free and was amazed to see that Antifa was trying to do the same on the highways of the Pacific

Northwest in 2017, I hope they did not get the idea from me and, if they did, I apologise (Antifa soon learned that Americans will not tolerate having their highways illegally blocked and will not hesitate to keep on going). When we eventually arrived at the Costco, Luisa had the bright idea that she wanted to drive to every supermarket in town to find the best prices and we spent the day doing just that and eventually left the city by late afternoon. The 160-km drive along winding single-lane roads again took three hours before we reached San Quintin and, again, we drove up to the ranch in darkness. Arriving late, the dogs greeted us warmly and we settled in after unpacking the groceries and parking the Landy in her new spot under a large pine tree.

By now it was mid-December and the nights were cold. We were burning quickly through the firewood which was stacked against the houses south wall and it was decided that Keelan and I would have to start cutting down trees to ensure that we did not run out of dry wood. On the path to the little dam, there was a thick-trunked tree which had been struck by lightning and which lay across the path. This tree was the first choice for firewood as we preferred to use deadwood before cutting down live trees. We had never used a tractor or a chainsaw before and we soon realised that the tractor was too large and the chainsaw too small, with a blade of approximately 40cm. In preparation for a day of cutting, we dressed in thick work clothing, sharpened the chainsaw blades, checked the oil and fuel in the tractor, the chainsaw and the splitter and sharpened our machetes. We used the machetes to hack away small branches and clean the trunk, we then measured the size of the logs we wanted and hacked a mark into the trunk, trying to avoid elbows and knots in the wood. Keelan and I then took turns with the small chainsaw, slowly cutting through the thick trunk before loading the cut sections into the scoop of the tractor. We then drove the tractor back to the splitter which sat below the shade of a large oak tree. The splitter worked by pneumatic action, a Honda engine drove a metal wedge forward and pinned the stump between itself and a metal backplate, the wedge would then split the stump in half and, being careful not to lose fingers, we would shift the stump until the stump was reduced from half to quarters to eighths or more, depending on the thickness of the stump. The splitter was not working as it should, spluttering and dying when under load. We had to use a splitting maul to split the wood; instead, a job I usually enjoyed but this wood was badly knotted and the stump large, which made the work difficult. I swung the maul and chopped the stump while Keelan placed the wood for me and carried the cut logs and placed them in the tractor scoop. Once the scoop was full we would drive the tractor to the south wall and stack the wood against the wall to dry. I enjoyed working the wood but would have to get the splitter fixed, it had fuel and oil, and I guessed that the spark plug was the problem. A little ancient caravan full of rats and old tools served as the workshop for the ranch. The caravan contained all manner of pipes, including copper pipes, garden tools and no spark plugs, I would have to purchase a new one when we next drove down to town in two weeks. A twelve-hour drive to buy groceries cost a couple of tanks of fuel and it was decided that we would visit the town of San Quintin when next we needed supplies.

After a hard day working cutting wood, it was great to make a fire in the brick braai and watch the sunset with a cold beer in hand, petting Wags and Pepita. It was so quiet out there, no sound at all except for the chirping of birds and sometimes you could hear the stream gurgling 300 meters away. We had heard that there were condors in the area and we watched the sky for them. A hawk owned the mountain which shadowed over us and he would watch me watching him as he circled above, looking for rabbits and field mice. Luisa would join me for the sunset and we would stand and chat as the fire died down to coals, we would lower the grid and grill some chicken and American spare ribs. Life was good. We had time and space and adventure on tap, we could go hiking every day and it would take us months to explore the surrounding mountains. We were confident that we would enjoy a decent amount of exposure and that we would be able to be highly productive in the absence of the distractions of modern life.

That evening, as the sun began to set, I noticed a storm moving slowly up from the ocean and by ten that evening it hit us. At first, it began to drizzle, thunder and lightning ripping at the sky. The drizzle became rain, the rain became hail and the hail became snow. It snowed for a few hours and the temperature plummeted outside (the house had a weather station which showed inside and outside temperatures, humidity and wind strength), but inside the house we were warm and comfortable, the fireplace doing a great job of heating the large house. In the morning we awoke to blue skies and a few inches of snow on the ground. You probably won't believe this, but even though we had travelled the length of the Americas and much of Africa, we have had very little experience with snow, the most we had ever seen had been in the Rockies. The children built snowmen and had snowball fights, while I cleaned the solar panels which were covered by a thick layer of snow. As the day progressed the snow began to melt and slid off the roof in large sheets much to our amusement. Keelan and I went for a long walk in the snow, following the road back towards the gate, and we found that the snow had only fallen within a kilometre below the ranch. We found the tracks of deer, rabbit and many species of bird. Luisa was not happy with the little kennels which the dogs had to live in and we set about building new kennels from old building materials which we had found lying around near the old caravan. The dogs had disappeared early in the morning and only returned two days later when all the snow had melted and they returned to find that Luisa had built them a warm new home.

A few more storms hit us over the following weeks but not all brought snow, some only brought rain and clouds, clouds which blocked out the sun and killed our solar power. The generator was noisy, the dogs hated it, and it only provided enough power to keep the fridge going. When the ranch was cold, wet and dark it was not a great place to be, but we kept ourselves busy, sitting by the fire, reading or writing or repairing our clothing and broken electronics. Christmas was warm and cosy. Keelan and I had searched the ranch for a young pine which could be sacrificed as a Christmas tree, Luisa made a wonderful Christmas dinner and we relaxed for the day, doing no work at all, just spending the day together. On the 29th December, I woke to find that I was 41 and that it had snowed during the night, the sky was perfectly blue and the ground pure white.

We had decided on a title for the book project, our new baby was to be called, Travel the Planet Overland. We chose the word "Planet" and not the word "World" for a few reasons. Firstly, calling the book Travel the World Overland might imply that we had travelled the whole world overland, which was not the case and we owed respect to those who had driven around the world, we do not inflate our achievements. Secondly, even if you are overlanding in your own country you are overlanding the planet, there is no implication that you need to be crossing multiple borders. I also like to remind people that we live on a planet, a beautiful orb which is merely an impressive speck of dust relative to the known Universe. Hopefully one day, one of my descendants will write the book, Travel the Universe (Overland) once intergalactic travel becomes a reality and IF we do not manage to destroy this planet and humanity before then. We wanted the book to be beautiful and well made in a large, hardcover, full-colour format. Essentially the book would contain all the secrets we had learned after being on the road for so long and I intended it to be a fun read, not a dour academic journal. Luisa worked night and day on the Kickstarter campaign, she had done her research and knew that we had to make an introductory video and design a campaign which was simple and to the point. There were a million tasks which needed to be done very well and most required an excellent internet connection. We had an absolutely awful internet connection, it took a week of Luisa staying up all night (when the internet connection was at it's strongest) uploading the video which would load 79% and the connection would be lost, meaning she had to start all over again. La Lucha!

From December to March, it continued to snow once a week on the ranch and there were long periods where we saw no sun for days. We ran the generator most of the day, either to power the fridge or our laptops so that we could continue to work. I was realising slowly that an off the grid lifestyle can be intensely boring once the novelty wears off. When not writing, I would explore the ranch, walking as far as I could in a day, in either direction. Wags and Pepita were my constant companions and they proved to be incredibly tough and loyal animals. Pepita would walk directly behind me and would not leave me, no matter where I went, whether there was a track or not. Wags preferred to run in the bush, parallel to the road and would often disappear for long periods. At first, he had tried to get me to follow him into the bush, the poor boy did not realize that I was massive compared to him but, if I could of, I would have followed him through the small tunnels in the undergrowth. I can only imagine the amazing things he would have shown me. I worried about the dogs all the time, there were packs of coyotes who would love nothing better than to eat the dogs and there were nights when the predators surrounded the farm and terrorised the dogs. We would turn the lights on and step outside, armed with the pellet gun, but the coyotes would run and hide, only to return once we went back to bed. I sometimes suffered from insomnia and many quiet nights I would lie awake and listen to the darkness which surrounded us. The night buzzed. A constant low drone which only I could hear, evidence that we were far away from civilisation.

Once every two weeks, we would lock up the ranch and drive down to the coast, usually on a Saturday. The drive to Ensenada required a sleepover and any Costco savings were lost to the fuel bill. Instead, we had scouted the local coastal towns and had found a Calimax supermarket, a wholesaler called Bodega and a butchery in a dusty little San Quintin. We stuck out like a sore thumb driving around the town, but we never felt unsafe. At the Bodega, we would buy milk, snack biscuits, pasta sauce, canned goods, beer, and other bulk products. At the Calimax, we would buy some meat, wine and fresh produce. Luisa had a crush on the butcher who worked at a little family butchery on the main strip. His name was Alex and he dressed for the runway, not for butchery. Luisa liked his little butt and would endlessly send him back to the cutting table to prepare cuts for her. She had found a recipe for boerewors (a large South African sausage made with a mix of beef and pork mince, fat, crushed coriander seeds, herbs and spices encased in a sheep intestine) and after much trial and error had found that the fat from a pig's cheek should make up 50% of the sausage. We often bought in excess of a thousand pesos worth of meat on each trip to the butchery, but we soon learned that none of the meat was really any good. Baja is dry and dusty and the cattle live on a diet of dirt and plastic bags. In Uruguay, the cattle live on a diet of sweet, green grass, which is why they taste so good and a one-inch steak is as tender and juicy as veal. In Mexico, the meat is sliced thin for the BBQ because the meat is tough and cannot be eaten as a traditional steak. Obviously, you can find very good beef in Baja, but you won't find it at the mom'n pop butchery next to the road, the good meat is almost always imported from the USA, though mainland Mexico does have good beef in certain regions. In Baja you should not eat meat, there the staple meal is the fish taco which is most often made of marlin or shark. All our American friends rave about the $1 fish taco which is served with sliced lettuce, raw onion, diced tomato, guacamole and a hot sauce. We could easily eat three each. A pair of little street girls would greet us every time we went to the Calimax supermarket, selling chewing gum and small woven bracelets. We would buy a couple bracelets form them every time we saw them and would also buy them a bag of fruit and vegetables. This kindness was rewarded later in the year when the girls followed us into the store and tried to steal the wallet out of my pocket, as I walked past the one little girl who I had nicknamed Cheeky Monkey and who had been following me around the store, smiling and laughing as if we had been playing a game. She almost managed to steal the wallet, the pocket of my old shorts was large, and the wallet sat loosely in the pocket, highly visible, a mistake on my part. At first, I was angry and considered calling the police. Had she succeeded in stealing the wallet, I would have called the cops. But, I knew that it was not her choice to beg or live on the street or become a thief. She was forced to do these things by the dirty parents who sat on the pavement outside and made the girls beg and steal. These girls had a dark future ahead of them, they must have been eight years old when we met them, but soon they would be pubescent and a poor street girl has one asset for which some men will pay well. Tijuana is one of the worst places on earth for child prostitution and human trafficking. Children are sold into sexual slavery for as little as $200. Prostitution is essentially legal in Mexico and government officials, policemen and NGO's have been found to be complicit in the sex industry, frequenting or operating brothels and, sometimes, engaging in human trafficking themselves. Cheeky Monkey needed a miracle to save her from a future of prostitution and abuse. 200 kilometres to the north that existence seems almost impossible. A poor family could spare their children by finding a way to sneak over the border into America, where they would pick crops and work as seasonal workers, own a car and rent a house in an area far safer and prosperous than the litter-strewn slum where the poor eke out an existence in Baja.

Much of the writing I was doing was not just for the new book but also for a few online adventure and overlanding sites. While sweltering under the sun at the North West Overland Rally earlier that year, we had been introduced to a tall, slim and friendly man by the name of Christophe Noel. Christophe worked for Overland International and was an editor of both the Overland Journal and Expedition Portal. He had heard about our journey and had read We Will Be Free and invited me to write articles for Expedition Portal, he would pay a fair rate. Over the first few months of 2016, I wrote a few articles for Christophe, who patiently coached me on how to become at least a half-decent photojournalist and who always paid in full and on time. With the experience learned from writing for Christophe, I was able to begin contributing to other online journals and magazines and soon was able to cover most of our monthly expenses with the income from those articles.

It was decided that we would ask Bruce and Penelope if they wanted us to house-sit the ranch until October. This would allow us to finish Travel the Planet Overland and prepare ourselves for the next phase of the journey across the USA and over to Europe. We would have to leave the ranch for a month to attend the Overland Expo in Flagstaff, sure that we would be able to sell books and finally have a media breakthrough. Bruce was happy to have us stay on for the rest of the year, I believed that she had grown to despise the ranch, but was not at all happy that we would have to leave for the month between. We had no option really, we had to promote our book projects and earn enough to be able to continue our voyage across the planet. Ranch life was incredibly interesting but was also quite frustrating, we were so isolated and at the mercy of the elements and a journey back into the USA was exactly what we needed after almost five months up in the dry mountains.

Bruce organised that their regular ranch hand, Chavez would come up to the ranch and take care of it while we were gone, he would stay in the old fifth-wheel trailer which was parked next to the maintenance caravan and he would do some work clearing the fields and maintaining the garden, which we had lovingly brought back to life after the coldest winter months had passed. The ranch house was now surrounded by green lawn, grapes were growing on the vines and flowers filled the beds which we had cleaned and fertilised. The vegetable garden, which had been barren and dry, had also been nurtured back to life and an abundance of vegetables and herbs now grew, providing for much of our daily intake. Yes, we had had to kill the cocks but without their drama, the chickens had relaxed and were now producing at least three eggs a day. Although it was not our property, we had cared for it as if it was our own, even though the maintenance of the grounds was back-breaking work. We were all looking forward to a change of scenery and the Landy was packed and ready for the return to the USA two days before we were scheduled to leave. Luisa has an incredibly annoying but effective habit of packing a week in advance, even if just for a weekend trip, often I would have to retrieve half of our possessions from the Landy because she was so thorough in her packing. Chavez arrived at the ranch the morning we were to depart and we spent some time showing him the work which needed to be done. Chavez, a tough little man, who had been hardened by decades of manual labour, quickly got to work setting up his base for the next few weeks. He drove an old white pickup which he kept in excellent condition and he wore a thick, equally cared for, moustache. Bruce would not allow Chavez to use the solar system at all but instead advised us that he may use the generator and should have cold showers in the guest cottage. Chavez smiled and nodded, we could tell him to stand on his head for a month and he would smile and nod, as soon as we left the ranch, he would do whatever pleased him. We knew this, Bruce knew this, but we hoped that he would not do any permanent damage to the infrastructure.

We hugged the dogs and left the ranch, happy to be heading out for a new adventure. A couple from Ensenada had come to visit the ranch and see the snow a few months earlier and we had become friends over a few cold Tecate beers. Aaron and Marianne were both marine biologists and incredibly warm and funny people. They had invited us to stay at their home near the beach in Ensenada and that was our first stop en-route back to the border. Aaron drove a little green Jeep which he liked to compare, favourably, to the Defender, we all knew that he wanted the Defender more than anything he had ever wanted his entire life and would gladly have swopped his beloved Marianne for it. Actually, Marianne, the beautiful, athletic and ravenously hungry daughter of a German mother and a Mexican father, meant everything to Aaron and though he acted cool, we all knew that he loved her with every fibre of his skinny surfer body. When sitting together chatting and Marianne entered the room Aaron would, without acknowledging Marianne, end a completely unrelated sentence with "and that is why Marianne is the most beautiful woman in the world. Oh, I did not see you there Marianne". Their little home was rustic and comfortable and we chatted about travel as we prepared a braai in front of the house. Marianne wanted to travel and Aaron wanted a happy wife, so we thrashed out a few ideas for them to be able to continue to work as marine biologists and to be able to see the world. Sailing was a good start for them, if they could sail around the Caribbean (where speaking Spanish was a huge advantage) they could find part-time work in the fishing industry. Australia would be another great option for them as they could earn a great salary, buy a boat and sail back across the Pacific islands to their beloved Baja.

In the morning, we left with hugs and a promise to return, we were going to cross back into the USA at the Tijuana border, the busiest land border in North America. Tijuana itself is a run-down, ramshackle little city which we would never visit at night for obvious reasons. It was in this city that drug dealers hung each other from bridges and where nefarious trade in people and drugs infiltrates deep into society and the government. We took a few wrong turns but eventually found ourselves in a tin can queue, jostling for position for entry into the wealthiest country on the planet. Beside the road stood rows of kiosks selling the most commonly expected Mexican curios, sombreros, ponchos, statues and gaudy knick-knacks which any decent

Mexican would not be caught dead owning. A small grey woman in a dented, rusted, old sedan played chicken with us as the lanes merged. She was trying to muscle into our lane and I was having none of it, to show weakness is to find yourself at the back of the queue, as every other motorist takes advantage of your lack of courage. She edged in front of me and I moved forward, millimetres apart until eventually, we made contact, her old Ford meeting the solid metal of my Defenders skull adorned bull bar. Luisa freaked out, but the old lady kept on moving forward, this was most likely her border car, scarred from many previous slow-motion battles, sacrificial and with a bad engine but excellent cooling system, it was hot out there in the blaring sun. The old lady won the battle and slid in front of us then chose to take on the black SUV in the faster lane beside us. She probably owns a beautiful Mustang in the US and only drives the border car when she must return to Mexico, an old Ford can be bought for less than $100. The US border official greeted us with a look of disdain, tourists like us always take so much longer to process than legal Mexicans and Americans. We were asked to turn off the engine and if we had any narcotics, of course, we did not and after explaining our itinerary and handing over our passports, we were given new tourist cards and dismissed.

14

Back in the USA

It took us a few days to drive from the border and San Diego back to Phoenix and then up to Flagstaff, Arizona. It felt like déjà vu, camping at the same KOA and meeting the same people we had met the year before. We had not made too much of a fuss about the conditions at the Snoverland Expo the year before and were happy to find that we had been given a prime spot on the expo campground, on the corner where we would meet the most foot traffic. I had been allotted a table in the authors' tent and was going to be rubbing shoulders with authors such as Jupiter's Travels author Ted Simon, Sam Manicom and Alison de Lapp. Luisa and the kids would man the Landy while I worked the sales at the authors' tent. I had a talk to myself before the event and I was determined to be in bed, sober, by at least 11 every night, I would be the first in the authors' tent in the morning and I would be the last to leave the tent at night. I would stand and greet people as they entered the tent and I would sell at least thirty books a day, we needed to get the word out! We had another challenge/opportunity as the BBC had recently interviewed us about our journey and there was a lot of interest from radio and television shows around the world. An ABC Australian breakfast show had contacted us and asked if we were able to do a live morning interview. Yes, of course, we can! The problem we had was finding a decent WIFI connection and a quiet place where we could do the interview which was scheduled for 10 am US time. The Overland Expo staff did not have those facilities, but our friend Jon offered to let us use his WIFI in his Fuso camper dubbed, Robinson Fuso. At

9.30, Jon and Emily handed the camper over to us and plugged our computer into his solar system, the Sony charger then chose that exact moment to commit suicide in a puff of smoke. Shit. Jon did not have a computer we could use, but we found that we could connect with the Australians via our Samsung tablet. With Luisa, the kids and I huddled around the kitchenette we were interviewed by a couple of beautiful people, trying to be relaxed and engaging, hoping that the WIFI connection would not cut out or the phone run out of battery. The interview went much better than expected and, relieved, we gave the camper back to Jon and Emily (that morning my friend Vernon in Perth happened to tune into the breakfast show and film our interview. I think we did just fine though I wish the kids had had more airtime). Back at the authors' tent, I resumed my mission as the wind whipped up and blew tents away. By the end of the day, our witty American friends had renamed the event Blow-verland (Bloverland) Expo. I really felt sympathy for the organisers, two years in a row they had had to put up with inclement weather, but everyone agreed that gale-force wind is much better than sleet and snow. We enjoyed the show, it is always a pleasure to be surrounded by the tribe and it was great to hang out with all our new old friends and Christophe, Scott Brady, blonde superman Chris and the rest of the Overland International crew.

The week before the show, I received a surprise request to do a presentation on the Sunday afternoon at 2 pm as the booked speaker had cancelled. We would be the last presentation on the last day and there had not been time for the organisers to change the printed schedule. I was only nervous that I would be speaking to a room full of chairs. I was trained to do presentations in an earlier life and I had had an experience which cured any fear of public speaking I might have once harboured. It had happened back in 2000, I was working as a marketing executive for a Johannesburg based company which was focussed on adult education initiatives. The new South African government had passed a law which made large corporations responsible for the basic education of adult employees. Luisa, baby Keelan and I lived in a plain house on a farm in an area called Lanseria. The Crocodile River which ran past the farm also ran through a township called Alexandria, a slum which over a million-impoverished people called home. The government had not been able to keep up with the expansion of the slum and did not provide sufficient running water, toilets and sanitation, the locals had no choice but to treat the river as an open toilet.

By the time the river passed our farm, the human waste was diluted, and we would spend the weekends hanging out by the river, gleefully unaware that we were essentially swimming in a toilet. After one weekend, I developed a painful and disgusting skin condition called impetigo, a condition which is caused by the surface of one's skin becoming populated by bad bacteria. There are also good bacteria, but those little guys do not cause your body to become covered in huge, swollen, pussy boils. After a few days, my body was covered with eighteen boils which volcanoes out of my thighs, arms, buttocks and face. There were boils on my forehead, my eyes, my lips, in my nose and on my cheeks. I was a bloody mess but continued to work hard promoting an event at the company's corporate headquarters where I was to be the keynote speaker and had confirmed close to four hundred attendees which included Human Resources directors from the largest industries in South Africa. The day before the presentation, I went to see my boss and asked him if he could do the presentation; I had not slept in days and was covered in pus-filled bleeding boils. The old, fat bastard said no and insisted that I do the presentation as planned. I can't remember ever hating anyone quite as much as I did that horrible narcissist. With the presentation scheduled to start at 9.00 am sharp, I found myself at the doctor's office being drained of blood and puss shortly after sunrise. The doctor did the best he could to cover my wounds, but there was not much he could do to stem the weeping, and soon a pink fluid made its way through the bandages, staining the legs and seat of my trousers and blotting my crisp grey shirt. My left eye was swollen shut and covered with a large plaster as were the boils on my cheeks. I again pleaded with my boss to relieve me, a presentation presented by a leper would do the company no good at all. Again, I was told, "no, get out there and do an excellent job". This is how a corporation will crush your spirit when you are at your lowest low, they will try to squeeze the last drop of profit out of you. I greeted shocked guests as they arrived at the venue, shaking hands was awkward. I stood at the podium, weeping inside and from my wounds, trying to make light of my ghastly appearance. I followed my training and spoke clearly and projected my voice, I paused often, engaged the audience, focussed on my posture and message and did the best I could to convey that message. That was one of the most difficult days of my life, but I know that I will never again have to do a presentation, under those circumstances, I could now address 10 000 people confidently.

The Overland Expo presentation went very well and despite not being listed on the schedule, we had an excellent turnout, almost all the chairs were full and we received enthusiastic applause at the end of the presentation. Two of the audience was an elderly South African couple who we have had the pleasure of spending some time with and who we respect immensely. Jan and Leonie Vorster are Land Rover enthusiasts who have been overlanding the planet since the early '70s. They have been to places others can only dream of or have never even heard of and managed to raise a family while travelling extensively and running a business back home. Jan is an incredibly knowledgeable man and there are few subjects of which he does not have an encyclopaedic knowledge. We chose to spend as much time with them as possible, we could have been hanging out with the who's who of the American overlanding scene but made a choice to spend as much time as we could with the couple, who have forgotten more than many could learn in a lifetime. Leonie invited us to dinner in their beautiful Forward Control Landy and for a while we were back home in South Africa, speaking Afrikaans and discussing subjects only other South Africans could understand. Leonie fussed over us, while we discussed our plans and by the end of the evening we felt like a weight had been lifted from our shoulders, we had a clearer vision of the future and had enjoyed the short "trip" back home.

Leaving the Expo, we planned to return to the KOA in Flagstaff and then make tracks towards Death Valley. Opposite our campsite at the KOA sat a silver

LA LUCHA

Airstream caravan with two chairs outside. The one chair faced forward, and the other chair was turned to face it. For some reason, I thought, "these people are in love". When we met the occupants that feeling was confirmed. Larry and Maggie were deeply in love and incredibly warm and funny people. Larry had movie-star good looks and incredibly warm and humble nature and Maggie was a beautiful farm girl with a sweet voice and gentle demeanour. We became instant friends and after spending most of the day chatting, we said goodbye and promised to visit them when we passed through San Diego.

First, we had to tackle Death Valley. "Death Valley National Park is a national park in the United States. Straddling the border of California and Nevada, located east of the Sierra Nevada, it occupies an interface zone between the arid Great Basin and Mojave deserts in the United States. The park protects the northwest corner of the Mojave Desert and contains a diverse desert environment of salt-flats, sand dunes, badlands, valleys, canyons, and mountains. It is the largest national park in the lower 48 states and has been declared an International Biosphere Reserve. Approximately 91% of the park is a designated wilderness area. It is the hottest, driest and lowest of the national parks in the United States. The second-lowest point in the Western Hemisphere is in Badwater Basin, which is 282 feet (86 m) below sea level. The park is home to many species of plants and animals that have adapted to this harsh desert environment. Some examples include creosote bush, bighorn sheep, coyote, and the Death Valley pupfish, a survivor from much wetter times". Thank you, Wikipedia. The plan was to drive down to Death Valley, do some exploring and off-road trails and then head to Las Vegas for a few days. I tried to talk Luisa out of going to Vegas, but she has always had a "thing" about the place and it is one of those iconic cities you simply must visit at least once in your life. I hate gambling, I only gamble with important things, like my life, but never money. The drive to Death Valley was uneventful and we dropped down into the valley late in the afternoon. We passed motels and hotels and eventually found a campsite which wanted a ludicrous amount of money for a parking spot without amenities. Luisa did some hunting and found a state camp which had a large overflow camp area which was cheap, had a pool we could use and was semi-deserted. As the sunset, we opened our tent and started a fire. The night sky was brilliant without much light pollution to dull the stars. Luisa and I had a good night, planning the route ahead and discussing our next steps, financially.

The Kickstarter campaign for Travel the Planet Overland had come to an end the day before and the project was 400% funded, if you are reading this and you contributed, well - you rule! The book was almost finished and we had a couple months to work on the final book and send it out to backers, the images had been chosen and I had written most of the content. We planned to print an extra 500 books which we would then sell out of hand. As the printing of the books was paid for by the Kickstarter campaign, the income from the extra books would be almost pure profit and because the campaign had been such a success, we were able to invest heavily in the quality of the book. It is worth mentioning that the weeks spent sending press releases and marketing material to various industry players paid massive dividends, but it was the endorsement of the campaign by industry leaders like Scott Brady which really pushed the campaign into the stratosphere. We had built an excellent name for ourselves with our previous work, now we needed to prove that we worth the investment.

We had met a German man at the Overland Expo and Andreas was the owner of a company called Total Composites and they supplied composite panels for the manufacture of refrigerated trucks and expedition vehicles. The company was just getting started in the North American market and I had suggested to Andreas that we could work together on a project, the rebuild of our Landy into a live-in camper. Andreas seemed positive about the idea, and while Luisa and I sat by the fire in the valley, we drafted an email to Andreas. We loved our roof tent, but we had had such a successful Kickstarter campaign that we would have some profit which we could then invest in transforming the Landy. We had also heard rumour of a tyre company which was looking for brand ambassadors and we were quite desperate for a new set of tyres, our BF

LA LUCHA

Goodrich KM2's had already done close to 90 000 kilometres and I was expecting some dramatic tyre failure soon, possibly on the trails around Death Valley. The tread was still good, but it was my experience that it is the sidewalls which fail after so many kilometres. We had also been talking to Bearmach Land Rover parts about becoming brand ambassadors, having them in our corner meant we could carry fewer spares and have the confidence that if the wheels came off in some remote area, they would get us the parts we needed even if that meant hiring the local donkey rider to deliver. We had made the shift from serious overlanders to professional overlanders and we were determined to be able to work our way around the world and having the right vehicle and the right companies by our side would make the journey that much easier.

I needed to focus on writing articles and Luisa needed to improve her photography skills and we all needed to make more videos about our adventures and the journey. If we could make $2000 a month, we would be able to cover all of our expenses at home and on the road and if we could make $3000 a month, we could begin to save for the future. A Patreon campaign was planned for the Europe to Asia journey and we decided that we needed to focus more on associate marketing and merchandising. I know, we are terrible capitalists but rest assured, every cent we earn is squandered on overlanding costs.

In the morning we awoke to a young man dressed in Fjallraven outdoor clothing, taking photos of the Landy. His name was James and he is the second African American overlander we had ever met. The first was a cool dude called Bernard, who has a thing for Land Rovers and Central America. We chatted to James for a while, he bought a book, and we packed the Landy and set off to explore, but first, we spent an hour swimming in the crystal-clear camp pool, chatting to a young Dutch family who was exploring the US in a rented motorhome. To say that the valley is hot is an understatement, it was about 40 C by midday and we wrapped wet shemaghs around our necks, which is by far the best way to stay cool in a hot vehicle with pitiful air conditioning. We made our way down, further into the valley and were surrounded by mountains and fields of dry grass, sand dunes and rocky outcrops. Our goal was to get off the paved roads and to find some back-road adventures. Which is exactly what we did, we drove a few hundred kilometres in Death Valley alone!

Jon and Emily, who had let us use their camper and WIFI for the Australian TV interview, had suggested that we meet them in the Saline Valley where there was a small oasis. We drove up out of the national park and found the dirt road which headed down to Saline Valley. Despite the heat, the Landy was driving brilliantly and we enjoyed the rough roads. There was evidence of cattle ranching in the area and when we drove out on the salt pan, we found the remains of a cable car system which carried salt out of the valley. The poor buggers who had worked the salt mine had to be the toughest, craggiest and most miserable human beings. The roads surrounding the pans headed off in various directions and we drove for long periods along corrugated white grey roads, hardly ever encountering another human being. There were no signs on the roads and we used a tourist map to make our way towards the oasis. We eventually reached the end of the valley and Luisa guided us off the main track and down another track of soft sand. It had been a very long and hot day and we were eager to set up camp and have a cold beer with our friends. We took a few wrong turns but eventually came to a post covered in metal bats. In the distance, we spotted palm trees and began to drive in that direction until we drove up to the small oasis. John came out to greet us and guided us around the only green we had seen in the last few days. It did not take long for us to realise that this oasis was run by an old hippie and it was very much a "clothing optional" camp. Jessica was horrified and refused to leave our campsite, not that we would have been too happy about her wandering around strange, naked men. I know that nudists are perfectly normal people and we had nothing to worry about but as "clothing mandatory" kind of people, it was a weird situation to be in. Keelan did not mind the nudity at all and stripped down to his underpants and went and hung out (excuse the pun) with John and Emily on the lawn at the centre of the oasis. That night we made a fire and relaxed, enjoying the cool of the night, dreading the heat of the coming day. In the morning, Jessica and I explored the area around the camp and found stone mazes. As we were walking among the circles of stone we heard a droning coming from the east. A fighter jet dropped down from the sky and buzzed us with a deafening roar, he was followed by another two jets which also used us for target practice. Apparently, this activity was common and the fighter pilots were known to use vehicles and people for dry run target practice and had been doing so for years. I was amused, hippies on the ground, the military in the air, sharing the same space but diametrically opposed philosophies. Donkeys mulled around the oasis, the males displaying massive manhood which ridiculed even the most gifted nude man. With Jessica happily back in camp and Keelan again hanging out on the lawn with the well-tanned, Luisa and I donned our swimming costumes and made our way to the shower. Luisa had insisted that we were not going to be doing any nude activities and I always do what my wife tells me to do. The "shower" did not have a door or even a plastic curtain but was instead built in the middle of the oasis and offered no privacy at all, in fact, mirrors had been cemented to the rocks in front of the showering, ensuring that everyone could have a good look at you no matter the angle. To shower, you stepped into a small bathtub, turned on the overhead sprinkler and washed with thermally heated water, the same water which filled the thermal pools. As Luisa showered, still dressed in her bikini, a young woman, perhaps in her mid-twenties, joined us, sat her slightly plump naked bottom on a rock and slowly washed her feet. Luisa was not impressed by this pretty, naked woman joining us and briskly finished her shower. Now it was my turn. I stepped into the bathtub, hesitated, then removed my swimming shorts and handed them to Luisa who turned almost purple with rage. I could hear her thoughts – "We had a deal! How dare he remove his shorts in front of this girl, I am going to kill him!". What would you have done? I showered purposefully, discreetly and towelled dry, Luisa shooting daggers at me through eyes which promised a slow and painful death. If that girl had smiled at me, I think we would probably both be dead and buried beneath the salty soil of the pan. As soon as we returned to the Landy, Luisa chewed me out properly, I had a laugh, it is sometimes good to make the wife jealous.

After two nights "chilling" in the desert, it was time to head back out towards Vegas, our fridges were not coping with the heat and we had not yet invested in solar panels, Jessica was still freaked out by all the naked people and a group of rowdy youngsters had made camp next to ours. John and Emily were having a great time, so we said goodbye, packed up and headed up, out of the Saline Valley towards route 95 which was very close to Area 51 where the US Air Force was rumoured to be in possession of a crashed aircraft and the body of a dead alien. Some say that the technological boom we have experienced in the last 30 years, is due to Air Force scientists finally cracking the code of the alien technology. Luisa had seen enough UFO's in the Chilean desert and could not be convinced to head out to the famous site (where recently they shot the movie Paul), she wanted to go to Vegas to see the bright lights and soak up the glamour. The desert road was arrow straight, bright and bordered only by dying old towns and correctional facilities. "Run in your orange jumpsuit, we can spot you a mile away and can blow you to pieces from the sky. Run". It was too late in the afternoon for us to enter Vegas and Luisa found some BLM land and a ski resort on a mountain called, Mount Charleston, forty kilometres from the bright lights, I believe this is one of Nevada's best-kept secrets. We turned right off the route 95 and drove up, up, up until the desert scrub gave way to pine forest, the temperature dropped and we found ourselves driving the beautiful alpine scenery. We found a campsite full of families and no empty sites, but we were not there to hang out with people in blue tents, we were looking for the free BLM land and Luisa pointed us in the direction of an un-signposted dirt road which we had driven past a few times. There were a few people camped out in the forest and very few sites to choose from, we eventually had to head deep into the forest before finding a clearing near a cliff and a family of women, children and barking dogs. The temperature soon plummeted further, and we were soon wearing jackets, cooking a pasta dinner and looking forward to curling up under the down duvets in the roof tent. The kids had grown so much in the last few years that we were beginning to run out of space. It was time for a change, Luisa joked that we could buy whatever vehicle we wanted when we hit the jackpot in Vegas. I told Luisa to dream on; she could gamble fifty dollars, but any more than that and she would be walking. Back when we were young and stupid, Luisa had convinced me that she could take our last fifty Rands and turn it into real money at our local casino. I told her that, with a week left before payday, if she gambled that money and lost, she could never gamble again. Never. She lost the fifty Rands and we spent a hungry week waiting for a pay check, I still can't eat cold Vienna sausages and mayonnaise. That morning we packed and headed back down the hill.

15

Viva Las Veg... wait, wtf?

We were all excited to drive into Vegas, baby! Those incredible monuments to wealth and opulence, the lights, the glamour, the beautiful people, the celebrities, the action, the restaurants and the all you can eat buffets! Incredibly there are more than a few campsites in the city and Luisa had booked us a spot at the Circus Circus RV Park. The "strip' is surrounded by low grey buildings and we did not enter a city of wealth and opulence but instead discovered a city with a perpetual hangover and a sour gut, a city waiting for the beer and Quaaludes to kick in before darkness fell and it could switch to vodka, Red Bull and coke, the white type. Apparently, dress codes were bad for casino business and you can now waste your money while wearing a wife-beater and a pair of orange work shorts. The streets were teaming with people dressed for a low rent Florida cruise. The staff of the RV park had recently arrived from another planet and had zero clue how to book a vehicle in for a night. I was convinced that the woman was playing solitaire while pretending to look for our booking. We were told to go to the main casino hotel to confirm our booking. Circus Circus lives up to its name and we were greeted by a throng of clowns dressed as dejected human beings. We queued with a hundred other people, waiting to be attended to by a wall of check-in clerks. We eventually reached a clerk, high on nail polish fumes and sugar-free Red Bull, but she was unable to locate our booking from the depths of the circus server. We were then referred to Roz, that old horn-rimmed reading glass tortoise from Monsters Inc, who regarded us as slugs and refused to make eye contact and had over the years perfected the art of making a scripted welcome greeting, sound like an invitation to go have sex with yourself. I had to feel sympathy for the old goat, she had spent her life watching people come and go, playing a part in the myth sold to the planet, what happens in Vegas stays in Vegas, Viva Las Vegas, Vegas Baby, The Hangover. Casinos and hotels lobbies are places devoid of natural light, you have the feeling of perpetual night, there is no fresh air, deodorised disinfectant fills your lungs perpetually. The old clerk had seen thousands come and go and she had seen them all lose. Perhaps 1% of the 1% who win, walk away but never come back. She had watched them lose and she had lost her soul. At home she closes the heavy drapes, if her shift leaves her with sunshine, she has learned to despise. She sits on the couch and watches reruns and the shopping network. She smokes a joint, eats cake, drinks vodka and falls asleep on the couch, while her husband leaves for his shift cleaning the Bellagio's pools.

It was not difficult to convince Luisa not to gamble after we had spent only half an hour in the hotel lobby, she wanted out, she wanted fresh air, she wanted to have a conversation with a human with a soul intact, but she was still not convinced that we were in neon purgatory, that would take a day longer. We drove up and down the strip after sunset. Traffic was aggressive and we were underwhelmed by the experience. We parked in front of the smoggy Las Vegas neon sign, next to the airport, Luisa ran off to take disappointing photos and was convinced that she had seen that celebrity, you know, that guy from Slumdog Millionaire. "The young guy?". "No. The other guy". "What other guy?". "The other guy!". We returned to the RV park and made a braai in the parking lot, a braai is our celebration of freedom and we will braai anywhere which does not have a "Do Not Braai" sign, or where there is a risk of starting a wildfire.

We all had terrible dreams that night and awoke to a hot day parked on tar. We swam in the pool and did some work, I had writing to do and Luisa has her endless tasks, each of which requires our full attention, lest the wheels grind to a halt. Chris Cordes and his lovely ninja girlfriend came to visit us at the camp and we spent a while making fun of his Toyota. They had had the hotel and restaurant experience and I suspected that we might have had a different perspective of the strip if we had ventured past the facades and into the world designed to seduce and retain you. Perhaps if we had spent the night in a beautiful hotel room and dined in a fine restaurant and swam in an opulent pool and won a few million dollars, we would have a more favourable view of the glitzy shithole. Chris did not believe that we would. That night we had a buffet, Vegas-style, deep-fried everything, masses of shrimp and chicken and mashed potatoes, pasta, doughnuts, ice cream, Coca-Cola, chocolate cake, tepid coffee. Half an hour later, we were ill and hungry again. Only the Brazilians do a good buffet, in my experience. We left Vegas the next day, only $200 poorer and that included accommodation, food, and a tank full of gas. I was incredibly proud of that figure, how many people can say that they were not raped by Vegas?

Of all the movies made about Vegas, only Leaving Las Vegas is even close to accurate, it is the only movie that shows the seedy underbelly, the whores, strippers, drug addicts, gambling addicts, alcoholics and degenerates, people who believe in fairy tales, that they are lucky, that they are special. We were all happy to leave and to head towards California.

16

Leaving Las Vegas

Our path towards California took us through a desert so hot and dry that it is inconceivable that anyone could imagine making a life on its dry, baked sand, and they were not until the invention of air conditioning and the building of many controversial dams. Yes, air conditioning populated the western deserts of the USA. You awake in your huge, cool, airconditioned home, have a hot shower and eat a hot breakfast before stepping into the air-conditioned garage and start the engine of your huge, air-conditioned car, which you then drive to your huge, cool, air-conditioned office. Not many places are hotter than Lake Havasu, where we journeyed to hang out with our Canadian friends, Alain and MJ. Since we had last seen them, they had bought an incredible truck RV, a beast among beasts, this vehicle had as much power as a long-haul truck and pulled a third of the weight, the engine would purr along at 70 mph all day long and provide all the comfort of a luxurious home. We sat outside together and shared a beer. We should have sat inside, but we were eager to enjoy one or two of Alain's cheeseburgers. It was too hot to drink a beer, the liquid turning into bitter syrup in your throat, you could drink water all day long, litre after litre, and never urinate. Incredibly the banks of the lake are populated by holiday homes and RV parks. To access our temporary RV park home, we had to drive over the London Bridge, yes, the original London Bridge which had been dismantled brick by brick in the UK, transported to the desert and rebuilt over a canal. Take that your Royal Highness. Alain gave me the keys to the black Jeep he towed behind the truck and Luisa and I went for a drive together. We rarely lose sight of the children and it is sometimes good for us to just be adults for a while, not just parents and providers but also individuals, in a relationship which has its own, sometimes foul, language.

We left Havasu, promising to visit Alain and MJ in Canada soon, perhaps we would be able to rebuild the Land Rover there, it would be fantastic to experience a Canadian winter, learn to use a snowmobile, ski and skate and explore the wilds north of Quebec. Time would tell.

The next couple of weeks would be spent driving in circles around California, as we visited friends and made arrangements before heading back into Mexico. We stayed at the house of Hollie, a beautiful blonde who we had met when we travelled through California the first time down the West Coast. We swam in the pool, drank a few cold beers, had a braai and were treated to sundowners on the beach. As we were leaving Hollies home, we stopped to refresh the directions on our navigator and a man came walking towards us, he was wearing a cap which read Falken Tires on it. He was a local distributor for Falken and he suggested that we should contact them, perhaps they would be interested in our story. The next day we emailed Falken and within a week we were offered a sponsorship contract which included a sponsorship fee and tyres, as we needed them. We drove from Los Angeles back up to San Bernardino and fitted a brand-new set of all-terrain tyres, finally! The poor Landy had been running on the same set of BFG's for so long, that I was never able to relax completely while driving, always waiting for that inevitable blow out. Now we rolled smoothly on the less aggressive tread pattern, the road noise almost non-existent. Ironically, we had been negotiating with both Falken and BF Goodrich at the same time, but Falken swayed us, the BFG contract required that we wear BGF sponsor clothing at all time and be available when required and attend events when requested and their offer was one set of tyres and a relatively small once off fee. We had been driving on BFG's for many years, but I liked the Falken SUV tyres specifications, enjoyed the relationship with the marketing team and could not resist their offer which included having tyres deposited across the planet for us to collect as we moved across (I declined that offer as we prefer to be able to choose a route as we please and a depot route would be expensive and potentially wasteful).

With our new rubber, we drove down to San Diego and stayed with our new friends Maggie and Larry in their hilltop home. We never really had that many friends back home in South Africa. I had made a few good friends with the people I had worked with at a company called, Italtile and we missed the couples we would socialise with; Johan and Charlene, Paul and Cerne and Gus and Tima. We had so many friends in the USA, people who were just like us, people who worked hard and had crazy ideas and love to travel and explore and people who tried to live life to its fullest. Maggie and Larry were our kind of people and we were very similar, but I knew, and we all know that we have crossed a line, the line of normality. Our lives have become so very different from those of anyone we know, that we have become, in a sense, peculiar. The experiences we have had are almost impossible for most people to relate to, but we are, at the end of a long hot day on the road, still an ordinary family. We have our ups and downs, we do not think that the sun shines out of our butts, we struggle with our weight, we laugh and fight, we miss our friends and families and the normal mundane life which we fought so hard to escape. Friends like Maggie and Larry and all the other people who have opened their homes and lives to us have made us feel like we are at home, not only in the good old USA but also in the many countries we have travelled throughout the world. People are inherently good. And Maggie and Larry are the best, in all the friends we have made, rolled up in one adorable package. Larry let me use his workshop to service the Landy and he took Jessica for a ride on his 1200

GS BMW, she returned smitten, I must teach her how to ride, if she loves bikes, she shouldn't have to rely on someone else, especially some young, dumb dude. We then made pizzas and had a few beers and a few bottles of wine. The next day we repeated it all again, but this time we made peri-peri prawns and picanha and we all partied until the sun rose. We had to leave before we ruined them and it was, as always, with promises to return, that we left and headed towards Mexico. We ate our ritual In-N-Out Burger before crossing the border back into Baja.

17

Baja!

Entering Baja from the USA is always a shock, how a line in the sand can make such a difference is almost incomprehensible. Donald Trump was ramping up his rhetoric back north and we could see from the southern perspective, exactly why the USA is so attractive. But, there are many thousands of Americans who seek a better life in Mexico and, according to 2015 statistics, more Mexicans were returning to Mexico permanently than Mexicans were heading north. Down on the Baja beach, you will find entire communities of Americans who chose to live the simple life in peaceful communities. Drive at night in Baja and you are probably asking for trouble, but during the day the peninsula is peaceful, in our experience. We made our way back to Ensenada, yet another city with which we had become familiar and which gave us a feeling of "home". Our friends Aaron and Marianne were waiting for us at their home and within half an hour it felt as if we had never left, we made plans to drive together down to the Bahia de Los Angeles, they wanted to show us a piece of Baja which many do not see and which, they assured us, would be worth the journey. In the morning Luisa scoured the Costco for discount specials and we drove the road back to the ranch, hoping that Chavez had not done any damage for which we could be blamed. It was August and we had made a commitment to take care of the ranch until October, but it was with mixed feelings that we drove back up that side of the mountain.

Arriving at the farm road, we could see signs of change. Both Keelan and I had spent enough time alone, exploring the farm, that we had learned to read signs for activity. Animal and vehicle tracks, scat or oil stains, rolled rocks or broken branches were signs of activity and you could read activity by reading the signs. We could see that the road had been used often and that someone had had a mechanical problem; a large oil stain marked a section of rising road. Sections of the road had been repaired and there seemed to be fewer trees in some sections of the ranch. The ranch yard itself was dry and dusty, not one blade of grass grew around the house! The lawn I had been nurturing had been poisoned and removed. The vegetable garden was empty, all the fruit and vegetables we had planted for our own consumption had been eaten, except for a few watermelons, our firewood stocks were almost completely depleted and the ranch yard seemed bare, emptied. Chavez wore a grin and greeted us warmly. "What happened here, Chavez?". Chavez suddenly could not speak a word of intelligible Spanish, a month before we had had a good, long conversation and a beer together. I had no idea what Bruce and Penelope had asked him to do around the farm and their tone had soured since we had asked for the month's gap. The house was in good shape but did not seem to have been occupied, after giving the dogs some love, fresh water and food, we unpacked our groceries, tidied the house and had a braai before going to bed, tired but relieved. The Land Rover had done extremely well, despite the hard work and incredible temperatures she had been subjected to, we had closed the Falken contract, had sold quite a few books and had introduced many new friends to our Kickstarter campaign and we had explored many parts out the West Coast we had missed before. It would be good to rest for a day though, continue working on the book and plan the build of the Defender.

The rebuild of the Defender would take elements of the vehicles we had seen personally and on the internet, we wanted a pop-top roof, sleeping for four adults, a long bench which would become a double bed and a kitchen bank. The vehicle had to not exceed our Defenders current dimensions, within reason, she must be able to fit in a high capacity shipping container, must not exceed the vehicle's weight (GVM), must be open and airy and must be a head-turner. We would also need to be self-sufficient with solar power, a water filtration system and a good fridge. But, perhaps the most difficult requirement was that there had to be seats for the kids and open access from the rear "pod" to the front "cab". If the two "halves" were separate, then they could act independently of each other as the vehicle articulated but, with the open access from the front to the rear, the construction had to be done in a way which allowed flex but would be rigid enough not to rupture under strain. This was a headache, could you imagine doing all that work to transform the vehicle and it breaks at the first sign of a hump? We had to design a vehicle which could take on the roughest terrain without changing the drive characteristics of the vehicle. No pressure. People study for years to do this kind of thing and still get it wrong.

I spent hours staring at the Landy, visualising the final vehicle, imagining the pop-top and the overhang, the width and the interior space, the height, the window position and the rear door. I drew endless pencil and Windows Paint drawings and refined the design until I had final dimensions for the pod, I could then at least send the dimensions to Total Composites and they could get the panels cut and ready to be sent. Keelan did the final 3D rendering and we sent that and the dimensions off to Andreas, it would take him a couple months to get the panels together and have them sent over to the states. When not busy designing the build, I was writing and re-writing Travel the Planet Overland, doing the layout and graphic design with Luisa and taking care of the ranch. Keelan and Jessica were catching up on their schooling and would spend seven hours a day paying for all those times when they had something better to do than their home-schooling. The build was to be a huge home-schooling project for Keelan, he would learn with me and be part of every step of the build, he would then be responsible for processing all the footage we would take of the build into a kick-ass YouTube video. No, he would not get a certificate for all that he learned, but certificates are overrated, experience and performance are the true benchmarks of ability.

This camper project had consumed my spare time for months and I would go to sleep dreaming of the construction, the dimensions, the layout and the end result. I was sure that we could use this build, I had been studying the internet builds for months and I had seen some really complicated and some uncomplicated projects. We would need to learn how to weld and a host of new skills if we were going to do this right.

We were tiring quickly of ranch life, my dreams of having an off-grid, isolated home were starting to fade, perhaps if the ranch had a dam stocked with delicious fish and some bloody grass to cut. It was hot and dry and dusty, Chavez had really made a low maintenance mess of the place, some people just don't understand the atmosphere. Aaron and Marianne emailed a month after we had returned to the ranch, "Yo, amigos, let's go to the beach!". We made arrangements, prepared the ranch, packed the Landy and drove down to the coast to meet our wonderful friends. Luisa set a course for Bahia de Los Angeles and after stocking up on food, wood and supplies, we drove the 500km road south towards the bay. The Baja Peninsula has a rugged beauty, the unpaved towns are built on the verges of the paved road and are almost purely functional, here there are very few beautiful Latino squares where the community meets every night to eat, drink and talk about each other. Here you find dust, sand and very few natural green things. The road to the bay crosses from the Pacific coast, over the virtually uninhabited interior to the Sea of Cortez which lies between the peninsula and the Mexican mainland. We had read an incredible story of a Mexican fisherman who had gone out to sea with an inexperienced labourer when a storm hit them hard and pulled them out to sea when their engine cut out. The GPS malfunctioned, and, in a fit of rage, the angry fisherman threw his cell phone and all the fishing nets into Pacific where they now drifted. With no shelter on the boat, no food and no water after 15 days the poor labourer gave up and died, the fisherman could not bear to be alone, so he kept the body of the man on the boat for a week, talking to the corpse. It was only when he eventually threw the body into the ocean, did he realise the immensity of his predicament. For three months he drifted across the Pacific, living on a diet of turtles and seabirds until eventually, the boat drifted onto the beach of a small island which was inhabited by a white man and a local woman who farmed coconuts. The fisherman asked for a cigarette. The farmers alerted the authorities and the international press flew to get the scoop on this amazing story of survival. Today the fisherman lives in Mexico and the family of the labourer have sued him, claiming that he ate their son to survive.

Aaron told me after we had left the last town, 250 kilometres from the bay, that there was no gas station in the bay, he hoped I had enough. I did not. He is wicked that Aaron. We continued regardless, there would be a barrel of diesel somewhere around the bay, we would just have to find it and hand over a large pile of pesos for the thirty litres we would need to make the return journey, where there are motorised vehicles, there is fuel. The desert morphed from unloved grey stone and dirt, shrubs and litter into a pristine landscape of massive cacti and sandstone boulders, the most picturesque desert we had ever seen. American hippies had attempted to settle in the desert, building dome-shaped shelters and biospheres. I guarantee that after five years of living without water, drinking mezcal and tripping on peyote, they eventually realised that Coca-Cola, cheeseburgers and air conditioning may not be better for the soul, but they are a hell of a lot easier on the body than a dehydrated existence, burned brown skin, sallow cheeks and yellow teeth. Some people love the desert, some people are insane, give me green and blue any day.

Arriving in the bay, Aaron led us to our camp on the water's edge, where we found a palm-fronded shelter and a ring of rocks campfire. We had a swim, rested, made a fire, grilled some chicken and drank a few beers. The next morning there was no sign of Aaron or Marianne, they had planned to go spearfishing and had risen before the sun rose and drove out to a point where the fish waited. We explored the area, walking on the beach, amazed by the American "community" which had dug into the shore. This was the land of the recluse, the religious fundamentalist, the conspiracy theorist, the hippie, the alcoholic and the fisherman (the last two are often the same). Old airstream caravans still stand shoulder to shoulder with ramshackle homes, beautiful cottages, large compounds and fishing boats moored on the grey sand beach. Aaron and Marianne returned from their fishing expedition carrying three large fish which Aaron cleaned and gutted at a small, tall table built for that purpose.

Seagull and pelican jostled for prime position to receive the offcuts, the big pelican intimidating the seagulls, swallowing the heads whole. Marianne worked in our camp, chopping raw onion, peppers and tomato to which she added the chopped clean fish Aaron had just cleaned, adding the juice of a few large limes, coarse salt, paprika and crushed black pepper. Ceviche! Fresh and delicious, served with tortillas. Marianne invited us to eat and we each had a plateful from the large bowl, then returned for seconds. Marianne, slim and fit, continued to eat until the bowl was empty, our jaws hanging, watching her feast. Where the hell did she put it all? Aaron, who was friends with the camp owner, had a chat with a few locals and arranged a boat trip to go and swim with Tiburon, whale sharks. The beauty of having local friends is that you pay local prices and instead of paying $450 gringo dollars for a short boat ride, we paid 700 Mexican pesos, for all six of us. We climbed into the old boat from the beach as a salty old man watched on, he then steered the boat to hug the beach, looking for tell-tale signs of a feeding giant. After fifteen minutes he found a young whale shark feeding and decided to continue to look for a larger specimen, which he found ten minutes later. We turned on our GoPro cameras, pulled on our flippers and goggles and fell backwards into the clear, cool blue water. Even though the Tiburon eat only micro-organisms, their massive bulk and mouths are intimidating. The shark swam in circles dipping and rising to the surface swallowing a massive amount of water. I wondered how much of our plastic these majestic animals ingest in bays less pristine than the one we were floating in. I wondered what the future held for the oceans and the creatures which inhabit them, oceans which we treat as a dump for our toxic waste. I want to boycott China, the world's largest polluter, but I simply cannot, I won't be able to live any semblance of a normal life without being complicit in the destruction of our oceans. I felt guilty, swimming with that incredible creature, I felt ashamed of our species, a species which values convenience, luxury and wealth above all else. After swimming with the depressing shark for ten minutes, we climbed back into the boat and set off to find another, even larger beast to harass. We found him and I was the first in the water; unfortunately, I jumped in as the shark was rising directly beneath me, I was almost swallowed and properly crapped myself, almost levitating straight back up into the boat. Marianne said I squealed like a little girl, I believed her (but later review of the GoPro footage proved that there was not so much a squeal as a very brave, manly "wo ooops").

That evening we relaxed and watched the sunset, as we grilled the other two fish, Aaron and Marianne, had provided us. We spoke about America, Mexico, Trump, Germany, conspiracy theories, alcoholics, religious nuts and fishing, wetsuits, surfing, Cape Town, Australia, Hawaii, the Ring of Fire, marijuana, Narcos, Colombia and South America, how Central America sucks by comparison, sailboats, pirates, the Caribbean, who finished the wine, I need to sleep, goodnight.

Oh, in case you are wondering, there is not one, but two gas stations in Bahia de Los Angeles. Aaron had been trolling me, as the kids would say. I had been driving like a contestant in a fuel economy race all the way to the bay. Aaron, you funny guy. We filled up with diesel and left our beautiful friends who were going to spend a few more days emptying the bay of large edible fish. Only when we stopped 300 kilometres down the road, did I discover that the gas station attendant had not replaced the fuel cap, luckily, I had a spare cap in the fuel crate (Aaron retrieved the forgotten cap from the gas station and returned it to us a month later). It was a long dry, drive back to the ranch which, by now, we had begun to loathe, we loved the dogs, but the ranch was just too secluded and we all began to experience cabin fever, up there, alone for weeks at a time.

We had a few adventures on the ranch in those last few, hot months.

One Tuesday morning the dogs began to bark, a bark we knew signalled a visitor, wild cattle or coyote. Luisa stepped outside to have a look, "Graeme, there are a group of people at the fence". We walked out to greet the people, we had only ever met a couple of locals who arrived on foot, to see a group of seven young Americans was a surprise, to say the least. They had been driving their 2x4 vehicles over from Mikes Sky Ranch and had gotten the vehicles bogged in the river bed, which formed part of the road. They were asking if there was another route back to the main road, but we were not sure if the road was passable, having not driven that road yet. I spoke to Luisa in Afrikaans, we were not allowed to let vehicles pass through the property. A voice piped up from the back of the group, "Hey, praat julle Afrikaans?" Bloody South Africans are everywhere. Our compatriot's name was Keith and his family had moved to the USA back in the '90s. After discussing the options for a while, and accepting our offer of fresh water but declining lunch, the group headed back to their vehicles to try another route. It was nice to have company, but they were absolutely nuts to head into the Baja mountains without a 4x4. We had explored the roads between Mikes Sky Ranch and us and there were a section which was definitely 4x4 only, particularly on our section of the road and especially when there was a constant risk of storms and flash flooding.

That evening the dogs began to bark again, signalling the return of our American friends. They had walked for the last few hours to reach the farm and were hot and flushed. They had driven the two vehicles down a road but came to massive erosion holes in the road, which they could not pass, unable to turn the vehicles around they tried to reverse the vehicles, but neither was able to grip and the wheels just spun. With the sun setting, we offered to let them stay in the cottage but had to charge them for the night and meals and for the recovery, feeding seven extra mouths at least two meals would deplete our stocks, I would drive out diesel recovering the vehicles (if I could). We have never charged people to help with recovery, but this was not a normal situation. We cooked spaghetti bolognaise which was served with cold beers, red wine and a salad. The group were famished and seemed to enjoy the food, the only female in the group, Kat, was a chef with a beautiful smile and Palestinian heritage. They were from San Diego and often went on adventures together, skydiving mostly. The most charismatic of the group was a New Zealander with a black tattooed arm and a great sense of humour. He explained to me how the vehicles were stranded and we discussed their options, if I could not recover the vehicles. Getting an American, or even Mexican, company to recover the vehicles would cost them thousands of dollars, they might have to ditch the vehicles if we were unsuccessful. Duncan, his friend Matt, Luisa and I left in the Defender after a scrambled egg and bacon breakfast (I really enjoy cooking for groups for some reason), and after we had loaded the Landy with hoes, spades, recovery gear and picks. I drove down towards the river bed and the Landy impressed our new friends, where they had been stuck for an hour in the sand, the Landy rumbled over without breaking a sweat. We drove over the rocks and through the narrow alleys between river bamboo, past thorn bushed which scratched at the Land Rover, up steep angled embankment, through sandy washes and up out of the valley. We drove on past secluded, deserted pastures, past a semi-wild herd of skittish cattle and came to a stop at a junction. If we turned right we would eventually reach Mikes Sky Ranch, if we turned left we would reach Rancho Coyote (our nearest neighbour) and if we continued straight we would reach two stranded, embarrassed American 2x4 pickups. We continued straight and as the road began to drop into the valley, it was suggested that we leave the Land Rover at the top of the hill and hike down to the vehicles, our new friends worried that we would get the Landy stuck. "Worry not my friends, this is a Defender". We engaged low range second for engine braking and headed down the hill and past a few twists in the road and, about 700 metres from the summit found the two vehicles parked at precarious angles, the first a Toyota Tacoma, stranded diagonally across the road, her nose on the verge of a steep drop off. The second vehicle, the lead vehicle, a Ford, sat in a ditch, one wheel on each corner high in the air. Luisa and I assessed the situation, neither vehicle could reverse out and we would have to winch both up the road to where a tree stood opposite a sloped wall of loose rock. There we would turn the vehicles around in a 36-point turn and tow each vehicle up the hill. I drove the Landy down to the first vehicle, Luisa attached the winch and with Duncan behind the wheel, we began to haul the Toyota up to the turning area. Two characteristics of the track made the recovery precarious, the sharp drop off to the left of the path and a section of the path barely wide enough to allow a vehicle to pass, a huge ditch to the right, the drop off to the left. I would have to negotiate this narrow section twice to recover the vehicles. We winched the Toyota until it could gain traction, but the wheels would only spin when we tried to reverse her, using the winch cable as a tow rope I engaged low range reverse, diff lock and pulled the vehicle up to the narrow section but Duncan reversed into the ditch and slid in, the front left tire suspended in the air. Slowly we winched him up out of the hole and parked the Toyota, while I turned the Landy around by reversing her up the rock wall. I then reversed back down to the Toyota and Luisa attached a tow strap to the slippery Japanese. I towed it up to the turning point, disconnected her from the Landy and pushed and pulled her until the vehicle was eventually facing uphill. The Landy then towed the Toyota up the pass until we reached an area wide enough and flat enough to park the Toyota while we returned with the Landy to rescue the Ford. During this entire operation, Duncan and Matt watched the action, slack-jawed as the Defender proved why she, really is, the ultimate 4x4. They did not know that a commercial vehicle could have the power and agility which the Landy possessed, where their tough-looking vehicles could only spin and die, our Landy could not only handle the terrain but could do it with a dead vehicle attached to her bulbar or bumper. Rescuing the Ford was to be more difficult as it was stranded over a large ditch and the vehicle had no recovery points at all, not even a rear tow hook or ball. We were forced to attach the winch to the bumper mount, Matt was willing to lose the bumper. I engaged low range, diff lock reverse and winched the Ford up while reversing. The Ford was a dead weight, but we managed to slowly get her back up to where the Toyota had been stricken. I did not have a rope to wrap around the winch cable (to prevent a backlash and broken windscreen (or worse) should the steel winch cable snap. Instead, we wrapped my favourite black hoody (which I had bought in Chile in 2013) around the cable. In the excitement, Duncan and Luisa did not keep an eye on the hoody and it choked the winch. We secured the Ford and fought with the Ramsey winch as you would a playful Pitbull, to remove the hoody. It was in tatters. With the winch free, we reconnected the Ford and dragged her up to the narrow section, but Matt was extremely nervous and would not reverse past the obstacle, losing momentum as he lost nerve, forcing us to push and pull and tow the Ford up to the area where we could turn the pick up around. Again, I turned the Landy and we pushed and pulled the Ford around, then towed her up to the waiting Toyota. We saved both vehicles! It took almost three hours of sweating and cursing, but the Landy had done an excellent job and our new friends had nicknamed her the Tank. Together we drove back towards our ranch and before we reached the sandy section where they had gotten both vehicles stuck, I taught them how to drive through the sand by using moment and rocking the steering wheel when necessary. Using this technique, they were both able to negotiate the river bed without getting bogged and by three in the afternoon we returned victorious to the ranch. The rest of the group was relieved to be liberated and after an hour of packing and picking apples (which were sweet, delicious and abundant), we gave them the secret code to the exit gate and said our goodbyes. They paid us about $500 for the accommodation, meals and recovery, we did not feel great about accepting the money, but we knew, and they knew, that they had saved thousands on recovery fees or the loss if they had deserted the vehicles. They messaged us to thank us again when they returned to San Diego and within a month both Duncan and Matt had traded their two-wheeled liabilities for 4x4's, not Defenders though, they are way too expensive in America.

The local herd of wild cattle could not resist the apple or fruit trees and would wait until dark to invade the farm, climbing over or through the barb wire fence. Those poor beasts ate dirt all year and an apple or peach must have tasted like pure heaven to them, a mere fence would not hold them back. At first, they broke through the rope gate at the main entrance but could not push past the tractor which I then parked across the entrance. They began to search the fence for weakness and, I would later discover, had found an entry point in the north-east corner of the horse field, the field was about twice the size of a football field. They were in! Each morning I would survey the damage to the fruit trees and try to find the cattle, but they were elusive, eventually, after a few days of night-time manoeuvres, I set out one morning, armed with a black irrigation pipe (the kind they use to chase cattle in Namibia). I tracked the cattle and noticed that they had beaten a path to and from the horse field. I followed the tracks which led to a small hill and a cluster of trees. I walked up into the little forest, over large boulders and past cacti until I reached the fence and found a large, fresh cowpat. And then another. Moving south along the fence I saw more evidence of the cattle, they were hiding in the forest! I heard a branch snap and rounded a corner to find the herd, standing as quietly as they could, the bull dropped his head, fight or flight? "YA, MOVE!". I swung the pipe and hit a rock, the sound of my voice and the whack of the pipe, spooked the herd and they stampeded back, out of the forest and into the field. "YA, MOVE!". I had blocked the gate into the ranch compound and the herd ran south, towards the stream. "YA, MOVE". I chased them, they would have to exit the field where they had entered and I would find the weak point which I could then repair or barricade. I chased them around the field, but instead of climbing through the fence they tried to return to the relative safety of the small forest, I saw that coming and ran across the field and cut them off. Bad move. The bull had had enough of this creature chasing them, he turned and trotted directly towards me, head high then stopped a stand-off. I had two choices, the forest was twenty meters to my right and if I was sure I could reach the trees before he reached me. Or I could stand my ground. The bull charged, I stood my ground, raised my arms too make myself look larger and shouted as aggressively as I could. "YAA! MOVE!!". The bull changed his mind, veered to the left and made a beeline for the fence, the herd followed, the larger beasts jumping over the fence and the smaller, younger animals forced their way through. I had possibly risked my life to save some fruit trees, I was sure the owners would appreciate the effort. With my heart still pounding, I returned to the "store" to find wire and pliers and set about repairing the fence. I decided then that I would rake up any dropped fruit and deliver it upstream where the cattle could eat their fill and we could have restful evenings. A couple of cowboys, also known as gauchos or vaqueros, showed up on the farm one hot afternoon, to check on the herd. They camped and lived off the land and worked hard, as generations had done before them. I had respect for them and handed each man an ice-cold beer, which they savoured. I told them about the problems we had had with the cattle and they said that they had come to take the herd back down to their grazing land. These men knew that you cannot run from the bull, he will chase you forever. It is a metaphor for life I suppose, stand your ground, stare down the bull.

Summer storms began blowing in from the Pacific, we could see them approaching from the ocean and enjoyed a few large storms which swelled the stream and dug deep gouges into the farm road. Do you remember Good Guy Steve? He sent us an email saying he would like to visit and we provided him with the coordinates, suggesting that he drive up the mountain on the paved road, as we had no idea of the condition of parts of the road up from Mikes Sky Ranch. A week later a huge storm hit and our internet connection failed for most of the evening, we awoke to find an email from Good Guy Steve, sent late the day before, saying that he was going to drive up to us from the Sky Ranch. Shit! The gate was locked, and we knew that the dry river bed would have suffered flash flooding from the storm. A follow-up email read;
"Well, we had an epic night last night.
We made it to Mike Sky Ranch then tried to follow that road to you guys... It is gnarly, gnarly. 1st gear low range gnarled... Then it started to rain hard. We were about halfway to you from Mikes when we turned around... Barely made it back to mikes it was so sloppy!
Then we backtracked to the 3 and tried to cut across to the 1, but the road was completely flooded, after driving a few miles literally in a river...at midnight we gave up.

So, we retreated to San Felipe this morning and we are going to go south for warmer weather. I'm so bummed we didn't get to see you guys! So bummed.
But it did give us a hell of a Landy adventure, it always does when you try to meet Landy people".

LA LUCHA

A couple joined us up at the ranch for some overland training. Luisa and I had the idea that we could help people to get the most out of their overlanding dreams by sharing the knowledge we had learned over the years and many thousands of kilometres. We needed to first establish if we were any good at it and would we enjoy training. The couple, Sunny and Karin, were fresh from the South and were planning to drive to Argentina. They drove a cool Land Cruiser, kitted with all the 4x4 gear you could imagine, including a rooftop tent and a winch. We have learned that before you invest heavily in a vehicle, you need to have a good long think about what, exactly, you intend to do with the vehicle. If like us, you intend to drive dunes and beaches and long jungle roads, then you need a capable 4x4. After spending hours chatting with Sunny and Karin, we concluded that their vehicle did not fit the picture they were painting. They planned to spend a lot of time in cities and, both being vertically challenged ladies, the roof tent was a real chore for them to open. And they had a large, old dog. We advised them to return to the USA, sell the Land Cruiser and buy a Westphalia or a small camper which they could live inside. Particularly while in the cities. We then unpacked and repacked the entire vehicle (you don't need this, don't need this, definitely need this, and this, and this, don't need this…), taught them how to use an axe and a machete, gave them some lessons in 4x4 driving, poured over maps of Central and South America, advised them to stay away from cities, taught them how to make a fire and cook meat on the fire, drank a few beers, told stories and answered questions and together solved the world's problems.

Sunny was a defence attorney back South and she told us horrific stories, from personal experience, of how the penal system was designed to persecute and exploit. A typical scenario would be that a young man is arrested and would be incarcerated in a holding area, while awaiting trial, which could take up to three months, sometimes longer. Juveniles accused of serious crimes would be detained with adults in large halls, without sufficient ablutions, no activities and poor nutrition. Eventually, a court date would be set and the case brought before a judge where a defence attorney, who had hundreds of cases per month, would represent the accused. After more months in detention (innocent or guilty) the accused would, almost certainly, be sentenced to serve time in a privately owned and run correctional facility.

My own investigations revealed that the corporations who run these prisons have fulfilment clauses and can sue the state if they are not provided with enough inmates each year. The sentenced inmate must pay for his incarceration, clothing, soap, shampoo, etc., and will often leave the prison with debt to the corporation upwards of $5000 for a five-year sentence. While incarcerated, the inmate is made to work for other corporations, such as McDonald's, Nike, Microsoft, Whole Foods, for less than $1 an hour. Incidentally, the CoreCivic (the new name of the Corrections Corporation of America) share price skyrocketed 43% the day after Trump's election, in anticipation of lucrative immigration detention centre contracts. The argument that these prison labour programmes are to combat idleness and teach inmates marketable skills barely hold up, particularly when recidivism is extremely high. Using prison labour for simple manufacturing jobs is not only morally questionable but it also leads to unemployment in the manufacturing sector, as it is impossible for even an incredibly low minimum wage to compete with prison labour rates.

It is almost impossible to comprehend that such practices are legal, the Thirteenth Amendment to the Constitution prohibits slavery and indentured servitude, "except as a punishment for crime", and in 2017 the new Attorney General, Jeff Sessions, rolled back Obama era legislation which would have phased out prison labour.

LA LUCHA

The ranch was the most remote place Sunny and Karin had ever been, but I was impressed with their ability to learn new skills and embrace new concepts. They were strong-minded and independent women, brave enough to leave the relative safety of home, despite the warnings of friends and family, and to set off into the unknown. (They would eventually drive down to Panama and had an epic time along the way. They partied in many cities, camped on the beach, drove through jungles and had the time of their lives. I still believe that they would have been better off in a camper and would have saved a ton of money if they had followed my advice to stay out of cities, make fires, shower once a week, wild and free camp, sleep at gas stations and rough it as much as possible, they would have stretched their budget all the way down to Ushuaia but that was not the point of their journey. They set out to discover the world and themselves, to meet people from all walks of life, get down and dirty, get slim, beautiful and glittering and party the night away. They followed their own path. Who cannot respect that?).

October dawned and we were now ready to leave the ranch and drive across the USA to Canada, where we would stay with our friends in Quebec but just as we were preparing to leave the ranch we received a message from Alain saying that there had been some developments which made it difficult for us to do the rebuild there, the apartment which we were able to use had been taken by a family member and the workshop on his business premises were no longer available. We were disappointed but understood that shit happens, life does not always go to plan. We reached out to the Land Rover community and within days received an invitation from a couple, Ron and Cherie. They had a large home in Florida with a shipping container full of tools and a covered area where we could work. After a short discussion, Luisa and I accepted their offer, instead of a white Quebec winter we would be enjoying a hot Florida Christmas. We hugged the dogs, handed the ranch back to Bruce and Penelope and happily drove back to Ensenada to spend one last evening with Aaron and Marianne. We might have had a bit too much fun in Ensenada, trying to convince Aaron to take the leap and hit the road, or ocean. We left late, we did not want to leave our friends, not knowing when we would ever see them again, but eventually, we were on the road to Tecate and camped at the same campsite we had stayed at when we had first entered the Baja Peninsula, almost a year before. A lot had changed over those twelve months, we had managed to turn our finances around by signing the contract with Falken, successfully completing the Kickstarter campaign, selling We Will Be Free and publishing articles in online magazines. We had achieved what we had set out to do, had learned so much and been on the path to becoming professional, full-time overlanders, who can work and travel the planet. The dream!

Before leaving the ranch, we had to hand over to Bruce and Penelope. After hearing more about the wonder which is Bruce, I invited her and little limp Penelope to walk around the ranch, so that we could do a proper handover, but only Penelope took me up on the offer. I showed him every building and the grounds, the water system which we had repaired and the tool storage area. Chavez had taken every copper tube he could fit into his truck and had also helped himself to other surplus plumbing supplies. I showed Penelope the empty space where the plumbing supplies had been and complained that Chavez had destroyed the lawn and emptied the vegetable patch. "Mexicans", was all Penelope had to say. We paid them $100 we owed for internet usage, hugged and left. A few weeks later I read Bruce's blog, (she is convinced that she is simply amazing) and she claimed that we had ruined the garden when it was clearly explained to her (with photographic proof) that her employee had destroyed the garden! That is so frustrating, but I take solace from the fact that she feels every house sitter is incompetent and she is a horrible, lonely little troll.

18

Hey, USA, we love you

The next morning, we drove to the border crossing and joined the queue. Our goal was to be granted another six-month tourist card each, drive across the country to Florida, completely transform the Landy and ship her to the UK. We have come to accept that doing the extraordinary has become ordinary for us, but not necessarily easy. The first obstacle to our plans was the physical border we had to cross, we had no way of knowing whether the US immigration agents would even allow us back into the country! Donald Trump was ploughing forward in the polls and the customs and immigration union had thrown their support, almost unanimously, behind Donald's promises to lock down the borders. As we sat, stewing in the sun, edging our way ever closer to the immigration control, we noticed a couple of immigration agents pointing at the Landy and having a discussion, this is not usually a good thing. They then approached the vehicle. "Good morning sir, we would like to ask you if you would be willing to help us, we are training a young sniffer dog and will need to attach this package to your vehicle". In his hand, he held a square metal box, roughly 10cm x 10cm x 5cm and the box contained narcotics. "Um, sure, that is not a problem, is there?". "No sir, no problem, we will attach this box to your vehicle and test the dog to see if it detects the narcotics". So, I was being asked to let a customs agent plant narcotics on my vehicle. "Sure, go for it". I trusted US law enforcement agencies and had done no wrong. The agent then tried to attach the box to the side of the Landy, it fell off. "The Defender is aluminium (I had learned the American version of the word aluminium), the magnet won't stick". He tried to attach the box to every part of the Landy but found only lightweight alloy. In 1948, when the Wilkes brother designed the first Land Rover, the most common metal available was aluminium recycled from WW2 aircraft, the Landy was therefore built out of aluminium, do not rust (well, the body doesn't), are lightweight and flexible. Eventually, the agent attached the naughty box to the external gas can and they brought a playful black Labrador to the Landy and ran it around the vehicle, the pup made four loops but could not pick up the scent, perhaps if they had attached the box to the chassis. It was a fun diversion in the heat of the midday, the agents thanked us and continued to play with the dogs, I had been told that dogs become addicted to drugs, so they will sniff them out, but the truth is that the animals are rewarded with play and chew toys for successfully sniffing out the drug mules and their illicit luggage. Eventually, we reached the immigration agent who quickly set about processing our documents. We had a special request though; as we were shipping out of Florida in a few months, we needed to get not only a six-month entry but also a special customs form to show that we had entered the USA with the vehicle, without this document we could not ship the Landy. The immigration agent hooked a thumb back towards an inspection area, "Go back there and wait to be assisted". We thanked the man, who looked one day short of suicide, and proceeded to the inspection area and pulled up in a red square. A female agent approached the Land Rover, took a look at the sticker on Luisa's door and said, "Obama, huh? A few more months and he will be history". We were puzzled. The sticker, four years old, battered and faded, was an image of our great former president, Nelson Mandela but the graphic was designed to mimic the Obama "Change" graphic, under the image of a smiling Madiba (the affectionate South African nickname for Mandela) stood the words "Freedom". It was one of the few Mandela images I had liked when searching the internet five years earlier and the Obama connection was purely coincidental. The agent began to ask a million rapid-fire questions about where we had been and what we were carrying in the vehicle. We told her our story and had nothing to declare. After a while, she seemed satisfied and sent us inside to inquire about the temporary import forms for the Landy and the visas for us. Inside, the agents were kind and respectful and set about trying to help us. Luisa sent me outside to fetch a bag of documents she had forgotten and I found the female agent digging through the front of the vehicle, emptying Luisa's handbag onto the front seat. I asked her if everything was OK and she gave me the sweetest sour smile I had ever seen. I opened the back of the Land Rover and she came over to inspect.

"So, you are from South Africa?"
"Yes, ma'am".
"Where in South Africa?" Still smiling that horrible smile.
"Cape Town, ma'am".
"You have a lot of diamonds down there, don't you?"
"Yes, and gold, platinum, copper, coal, you name it".
"Where would I be able to get hold of some diamonds". I smelled a rat.
"I have no idea. I once had an estate agent try to sell me diamonds, but that was not legal, the international diamond trade is controlled by De Beers, did you know that diamonds are not rare? All diamond mines have to sell their diamonds to De Beers, who set the purchase price, and jewellers have to buy the diamonds from De Beers, who set the selling price".
"Uh-huh. What do you have back here?"
"Uh, camping stuff, clothing, tools, a few spare parts, a bit of food, do you want me to show you?"
"No, just leave it open".

I returned to Luisa and the kids with the documentation and explained to them in Afrikaans what was going on outside. I had just finished speaking, when the female agent entered the small office, holding in a gloved hand, a fish skull one of the kids had found somewhere in South America.

"What is this?"
"It is a fish skull, ma'am".
"From where?"
"I am not sure, probably Chile, or maybe Brazil, or it could be from Ecuador".
"You can't bring this into the USA. Do you have more animal products?"
"No, ma'am. Not that I know of".

The agent stood smiling that special smile, holding the fish skull like an accusation. She then left and continued searching the vehicle. The "indoor" agents were the opposite of our "outdoor" friend. Unfortunately, they did not have the document we needed, even though Luisa was able to provide them with the document number. The agent assisting us asked his supervisor what he should do while a friendly lady chatted to us and processed our six-month visas, my passport was flagged for some reason, but the supervisor quickly gave the green light, "$16.00 per person please". I was concerned by the flagging, maybe I had been watching too much weird crap on YouTube. We had our fingerprints and photos taken and paid for the visas. The other agent, a man of Asian descent who spoke with an accent, had an idea which could help us. He would write a note on the bottom of our copy of the vehicle registration papers, staple his contact card to the sheet and stamp the page with the wax customs seal if the customs agents in Florida needed to confirm the information they could call him. That would have to do. We shook hands and thanked the "indoor" agents who wished us a happy journey.

LA LUCHA

Three agents were standing near the Land Rover, talking loudly about Trump. Trump this and Trump that. "Everything will change when Trump is president". I could not believe that we were being intimidated by US border officials. As we were about to leave the female agent came to the window. "So, are you guys communists? No? Socialists then? No? Well, enjoy your visit to the USA, you will see some really good changes in the next few months. Trump is going to win and he will undo all the stuff Obama has done to ruin this country in the last eight years, you will see".

We were shocked but did not take the bait. "Thank you, ma'am". We left the border, struggling to understand what had just happened. If that agent had found something, she would have punished us severely not only for the infringement but also for our political views. That is an abuse of power. I understand that the border guards are forced to experience the worst of humanity daily, they are on the front in the war against the cartels, who make billions importing narcotics and human beings into the USA. They are the soldiers losing one of the longest wars in modern history and they are desperate for change. When Trump described the Mexicans as rapists and criminals and promised to build the wall, the immigration agents found a new champion, someone who promised real, aggressive change.

On the road through California earlier in the year, we had met a Motswana man, a pilot, who explained the future of America to me, as explained to him by a Native American. He said that the Native Americans were taking the USA back by migrating north. Most Mexicans are not descendants of the Spanish but are indeed descendants of the Native American tribes which populated North America long before the Gringo's arrived. The Native Americans have been migrating north for many years and, within the next fifty years, could outnumber white people to become the majority. The southern states of California, Arizona, New Mexico and Texas already have massive Hispanic populations, but the cold northern states along the Canadian border have very small Hispanic communities. People see the changes happening in America as it moves towards becoming a liberal, socialist, multi-cultural country and Make America Great Again mobilised the conservatives, who are desperate to hold onto the America of the Eighties. Back when we first returned to the US from Baja, Luisa mistakenly handed the US immigration officer our Mexican visas, the officer quickly handed the documents back with the comment "I don't want to touch anything Mexican". Could you imagine being Mexican and being greeted by that man as you tried to legally enter the country? Our Mexican friends were not huge fans of the USA. When I mentioned that America has a massive talent pool and that the USA is always on the cutting edge of technology and progress, I received a cool response. Apparently, the USA absorbs exceptional skills and talents from around the world, they will pay higher than anyone else and they lure professionals for the sole benefit of the USA, those technologies are then sold at a premium back to the world. I had no knowledge of this but had met many foreigners in Redmond, Washington; Indians, Koreans, Chinese professionals who were employed by the tech giants. Corporations are not generally racist and, with the public education system deteriorating perpetually, it stands to reason that companies will headhunt abroad. This importation of skills and exportation of production has significantly narrowed the opportunities for the White American Male (WAM), who built the country into what it is today. And while WAM tries to pay for the education of his children, the healthcare of his family, his taxes and his bills, he does not want to pay for education and healthcare of immigrants, particularly not illegal immigrants. The middle class has been marginalised by corporate America, who buy politicians through Washington lobbyists. Obama was not popular with the WAM, who resented the move towards socialism in the country. Bernie Sanders was the hero of the Social Justice Warrior (SJW), the liberal who wanted Universal Healthcare and the 30-hour workweek and transgender bathrooms and open borders. The SJW worshipped Michael Moore and Uncle Bernie, but could not bear to even look at Hillary Clinton, who was doing her best to tip the scales in her favour as she needed to kill old Uncle Bernie if she was to win the Democratic nomination and go head to head with Trump. Trump offered the last chance for conservative America, the alt-right, the Christian fundamentalists and the good old boys to retain what was left of Grand Old America, the land of the free and the home of the brave, the planets sole superpower and the land of opportunity. The WAM had grown to despise and distrust the government, Trump's advisors knew this and his chief strategist, Steve Bannon, was delivering America to Trump, who promised to "drain the swamp" in Washington and Make America Great Again, or as the liberals say Make America White Again. The greatest problem with the American political system is that it is, essentially, a two-party state. The Democrats and the Republicans play a game once every four years, roll out their best candidates, put on a grand show and then retreat to the secretive halls of Washington to continue walking hand and hand with the corporations who fund the charade. The greatest Democracy on Earth needs more options! She needs six political parties who represent the various interests of the nation and form coalition governments when neither can win a majority. I entered the USA a liberal and left a liberal-conservative. Same-sex marriage? Go for it! Immigration? Immigrants must apply before entering the country and must-have skills and or qualifications! Universal Healthcare? Absolutely, Big Pharma and the medical industry has made plenty money over the last few decades, you can still pay for private hospitals if you can afford the premium (people losing their homes because they are ill is criminal). Social welfare? The richest nation on earth could, at least temporarily, house and feed and educate every struggling American with a fraction of the annual military spend, help them to get back on their feet and become productive members of society. Invest in renewable resources, reduce the reliance on foreign oil, decriminalise drugs and use the taxes from revenue to help treat and rehabilitate addicts, get the hell out of the Middle East and enjoy many years of progress and peace, while giving all American children the best education money can buy, that includes college and or University (again you can still have your top-notch private schools). I am an outsider, but I could see that Americans love America and each other and would do whatever they could to help their neighbours. Give a man a fish and he eats for a day, teach a man how to fish and he can eat for a lifetime.

LA LUCHA

With that in mind, I now give you:

Twenty-Five Things We learnt Overlanding the USA.

1. American people say, "That's funny" when they are amused, which makes you doubt whether all the other funny crap you said, was not funny.
2. You can return any item bought, in any state of use, at any time and you will either receive full credit, your money back or a new item (OK, not always, but REI will happily take any returns).
3. In most states, you can turn right on a red light if there is no oncoming traffic and crossing a solid line is usually legal.
4. You can withdraw money at a drive-through ATM. There are also drive-through liquor stores, drive-through sex shops, drive through libraries and a drive-through wedding chapel.
5. Smoking cigarettes is social suicide. Only the poor smoke publicly. All smoke shops are owned by Asian Americans.
6. A foreigner can open a bank account with only 50 bucks and a passport.
7. Americans are politically correct, South Africans are not, we raised many eyebrows.
8. The cities are huge and low level, with skyscrapers only in the city centre. You absolutely must own a vehicle if you live anywhere but Manhattan.
9. Most Americans believe that they are inherently good, are incredibly generous and take care of their friends and families. Military veterans are highly respected and regarded as heroes, as are policemen and firefighters. Most Americans are polite and conservative and enjoy small talk. Elders should be addressed as "Sir" and "Ma'am", especially in rural areas and down south.

320

10. The South is prosperous, clean, beautiful and surprisingly "liberal". There is more perfectly trimmed green lawn in the South than in a thousand England's. Texas is not part of "The South", neither is Florida.

11. The Imperial system is incredibly annoying and is used by everyone except scientists and the military. What the hell is an eighth of an inch?

12. In many states, you can refill your drink as many times as you want at a fast food joint and the quality of the fast-food available, depends on the wealth of the neighbourhood, regardless of the brand. McDonald's, Taco Bell and Chipotle always suck. Wendy's can be OK. In-N-Out Burger rules.

13. You can buy delicious, healthy but expensive food or GMO, plastic, fatty, sugary dirt-cheap food. Buying bulk is much cheaper than buying individual products.

14. There are two types of BBQ – the quick and easy Brats and Burgers (Brats are hotdogs) and the day-long Southern BBQ. Both have their merits if done well, but Southern BBQ is probably some of the best meat you will ever taste.

15. Americans do not do small, Americans do massive as they have so much space to fill, the country is enormous; hence the cities are huge, the roads are huge, the vehicles are huge, and the houses are huge. Americans are consumers, partly, because they have these huge spaces to fill. One household owning six or seven cars is not uncommon.

16. America has a gigantic talent pool and the talented can make it big. Very, very BIG.

17. Healthcare is big business and extremely expensive. Many people self-medicate we did.

18. Mainland USA is known to Alaskans as "the lower 48".

19. There are thousands of brands of beer - many good, many not. Coors Lite is gross, Yuengling Lager made me happy and fat.

20. Mormonism is an American religion created by Americans for Americans and exported to the rest of the world via a persistent knock

on the door. Not all Mormons have multiple wives and Salt Lake City is a great city.

21. An NFL football game can take four hours to play and there is an advert break whenever there is a stoppage in play. Brats and Burgers are consumed while watching football.

22. Many, if not most, Americans are fit and healthy, the obese exist and they park in handicapped parking spaces.

23. Overnighting in a 24hr Walmart parking lot is legal and common, except in California where free stuff is illegal.

24. Art imitates life and to drive across America is to drive through your favourite movies. Frat houses have brown walls, are double story and have white trimming. The desert is red and crisscrossed by tumbleweed, Utah is heaven on Earth, New York has a unique atmosphere, Alaska is the great wilderness. Much of the country is sublime, almost incomprehensibly beautiful, except for Idaho. And huge swaths of Texas. And many of the states in the middle (but even they have their own charm).

25. There is no better way to spend a Saturday than working on your truck while listening to NPR (National Public Radio). Shows like Car Talk and Wait, Wait Don't Tell Me and All Things Considered represent the very best of America – humour, intelligence, community and curiosity (despite the often-vitriolic liberal agenda).

I hope you enjoyed that, America. While you may not agree with my pragmatic politics, at least I know that you, while not always agreeing we with me (or not at all!) will defend my right to be able to share my opinion, as a friend of the American people. We do love you, America.

19

Get your kicks on Route 66

Do you remember that I had promised Luisa that we would return to Los Angeles to do the tourist thing when we returned to the USA? Well, she did not forget. Unfortunately. We had another reason to return to LA, the South African consulate is situated in Beverly Hills and we needed to apply for new passports, ours were not yet full, but we knew that the South African administration, in many cases, needed almost a year to issue new passports. We rushed to get into LA before the consulate closed at 1 pm and spent an hour submitting our applications. The staff were very friendly and professional and assured us that we would have the passports within a few months. We were not going to hold our breath.

The Landy was very low on fuel as we set out to explore Beverly Hills while singing the Fresh Prince song. The houses were beautiful, the avenues wide and palm adorned. Luisa had a celebrity map and she drove us around to view the garden walls and gates which belonged to incredibly famous and good-looking people. I was underwhelmed but I am not too impressed by celebrity, I know, how boring. We drove up and down and around, surrounded by black Range Rovers and beautiful people and eventually found ourselves on the famous Rodeo Drive. I had been searching for gas stations but did not find any which dispensed diesel, we had been driving the last 70 kilometres in the red and I decided that now was the time to top up the tank with the ten litres we had in a jerry can. So, picture the scene, I am parked, hazards on, next to a fire hydrant on Rodeo Drive, the rich and famous of the world wondering what the hell we are doing with the exotic Land Rover, with foreign plates, outside Versace or Valentino, I can't remember which. I took the jerry can off the roof rack and the jiggler syphon from the storage area and began syphoning fuel into the tank. Luisa, our designated photographer, completely missed the opportunity to photograph this hilarious situation, she was too preoccupied trying to spot celebrities through tinted glass. I will never forgive her! I managed to empty most of the jerry can before the cops arrived and we set off to see some more sights.

The Landy was turning heads as we drove around Hollywood and people in Ferraris were giving us thumbs up. Luisa and Jessica made me find parking so that they could go and have a look at the stars on the walk of fame and after an hour of fawning and photo taking (now she decides to take pictures!) we headed towards the Scientology church. If you have not yet seen the documentary, Going Clear, I suggest you do. In brief, L. Ron. Hubbard, a science fiction writer, created this religion which teaches about a superior alien race and encourages devotees to undergo "Dianoetic auditing" and to "go clear", which essentially requires telling all your secrets to the church. The more you commit, the higher you can elevate yourself within the "church" and eventually, if you have been devoted and valuable enough to the "church", you get to go on a boat ride and could become a member of Sea Org, essentially becoming a servant of the church for low pay but first you have to sign a billion-year contract. It is all just too bloody ridiculous, and you will never be able to watch a Tom Cruise, John Travolta or Juliette Lewis movie again, once you fully understand the insanity which they believe in and actively defend. Scientology is another religion designed by an American, for worldwide export and it is fitting that the bright blue Scientology church is located on Sunset Boulevard.

You could not make this shit up. I parked the Landy in front of the blue church, shuddering at the thought of what went on behind those walls. While Luisa snapped some photos, a young man dressed in a black security uniform approached the Landy. "We are just taking a photo or two, we will move soon". "No problem, sir. What kind of vehicle is this, it is really cool". We had a conversation for a few minutes, other security personnel, drifting past occasionally. The security guard told us that we should park the Landy and head into the visitor's centre. Over. My. Dead. Body. Thanks, but no thanks. We left Hollywood and headed back to San Bernardino, where we had a date with Falken Tires.

After driving up to San Bernardino to do a video interview with the Falken Tires team, we headed back down to our friends Maggie and Larry who had very patiently accepted a thousand Amazon deliveries for our Kickstarter campaign. Luisa had samples of books and stickers sent from all over the world to the beautiful house on the hill in San Diego. Anyone who has ever hosted us will know two things – we like to cook for our hosts and we will take advantage of their address for the delivery of crap we really, really need. Poor Jim and Linda back in Mukilteo are still receiving our crap! It is one of the challenges of being houseless (homeless is not a glamorous word and should not ever be used by Vanlifers or Overlanders to describe their lifestyle), we need crap delivered and we need to post crap and the governments, banks and corporations of this world, need you to have an address they can bill, or locate you at, or to them you are less than crap. Poor Maggie and Larry, we forced them to eat large amounts of peri-peri prawns, grilled chicken and steak, filled them with booze and kept them up until dawn, again. Larry has this unique ability, he will pause himself, a smile on his face, as we sit around the fire, the sky turning blue. If asked a question he reanimates, answers the question intelligently then goes into limbo again, while I monologue about the troubles of this world and Luisa giggles and tries to conquer the last bottle of red.

LA LUCHA

Our plan was to drive across the USA following the famous Route 66, beginning in California, then branching off to Pittsburgh where our friend John would host us, while we sent out the Travel the Planet Overland books, which would be collected from a company in Tennessee. We set off from San Diego and made our way to Flagstaff Arizona, through the desert. By now we had driven circles and had been to many places many Americans themselves have not visited. After another visit to the KOA in Flagstaff, we drove down into New Mexico and the city of Albuquerque to visit a new old friend, who had invited us for a beer and a burger. Tim runs the design company Sackwear and he had designed an A2A Expedition shirt. The beer, burgers, conversation and shirts were excellent and after a few hours shooting the breeze, we headed out to find a local Casino where we could sleep in the parking lot. While we slept we received an email from Total Composites saying that they were having second thoughts, I am not sure what brought about the change of heart, but after a few emails, we managed to soothe Andreas' mind and get the rebuild back on track. I had just recently turned down a very intriguing offer for the Defender, because I had committed to Total Composites, and there was no way I was going to let this opportunity slip away. Though it was not legal to register the 2003 Defender in the USA, it was not illegal to use the vehicle for spare parts or on private property or even to trailer the unregistered vehicle to trails and off-road events. We could have realistically sold the Landy for around $60 000, that was enough money to return to South Africa, buy another 130, kit her out and drive her halfway around the world. Love. It makes no sense.

With the build back on track, we continued heading east and were soon crossing back into Texas. We were surprised to see thousands of wind turbines pumping away across the windy plains, I thought Texans were addicted to oil and hated the idea of anything which did not burn fossil fuel. Once again, generalisations are a waste of time. Luisa directed us to a cornfield where 50's era cars were planted, nose-first into the field. The cars lay at 45-degree angles to the earth and were thick and heavy with layers of spray paint, we found a few cans and added our names to the layers of graffiti. A sign stood at the entrance to the outdoor exhibition, called Cadillac Ranch, "No Graffiti!". The sign was covered in graffiti.

Just before we left Texas, we passed a rest area which would have made an African dictator a happy home, the entire structure was completely over the top, a statement, a symbol of wealth and opulence, a place to take a dump. We crossed into Oklahoma and were immediately greeted by an equally impressive service area, spires and sculptures and mosaics and artwork, green lawns and statues. Apparently, Texas and Oklahoma have money to burn on symbolic, competitive shit houses. Oklahoma had more rolling hills than Texas, almost as many burger joints and almost as many Hilary for President billboards. We saw less Trump for President billboards, which surprised me. We spent the night camped outside a Walmart, in a deserted town and the next day drove through a small town with a proud Irish heritage. So far, our experience of small-town America had not been Gilmore Girls or Dawson Creek experiences at all. Small Town America was apparently killed by the interstate and Walmart and Costco and Amazon, the young and bright leave the first chance they get and move to the cities where they have opportunities for education and wealth creation. Those left behind live a quiet existence, empty streets, abandoned cars, empty stores. A pretty girl at the gas station quizzed me about where we came from and she could not believe the answer. She had done a school project about South Africa, but she never, ever expected one of us to walk into her store and ask how much an extra-large coffee was (I needed to drink a gallon of coffee a day if I was going to stay awake on the long, dead straight roads). At first, the girl and her manager/aunt were a bit wary of me, this large, exotic stranger, with the cool 4x4, foreign accent and unbelievable story. But they warmed up as I told them our story and listened to theirs. People around the world want only a few things from a world traveller; that you love their country and think it is the best, that you do not think you are better than them and that you want to know about their lives. Time and again we have met people, all over the planet, who only want to tell us their story, it is a knee-jerk reaction – "what you do is great, but I also have a great story to tell". And usually people do have an incredible story to tell, almost everyone is fighting a battle and trying to achieve their dreams, everyone desires to love and respect and admiration. I used to be a loner, but I have learned to listen to people and I have learned to have empathy. I introduced Luisa to my new friends and they asked her a hundred questions before selling us our coffee and wishing us a happy journey. I felt sad leaving the town, I realised that Boulder Colorado was an anomaly, I had searched but had not found Gilmour Girls America, no matter how hard we searched, up and down the West Coast and now as we drove across the USA, perhaps it was hiding up north. Perhaps my expectations were completely unrealistic. Perhaps I had been watching too much bloody TV and had somehow come to expect that every little town in America had to have a charming square with perfect trees, adorned with fairy lights, a restaurant where everyone hung out and a barbershop next to the post office where Mary- Lou, the prettiest and kindest girl in town, could be found wrapping gifts for the elderly. Perhaps I was seeing a decline where in fact there was progress. Perhaps small-town America is rural and always has been, perhaps people like it quiet and send the best and brightest off to the cities so that they can return with education and wealth to help build the community. Perhaps I had bought into the narrative of America in decline because my expectations were impossible to fulfil.

After another night sleeping in a Walmart parking lot, we crossed into Arkansas and then, a day later, we drove into Tennessee where we would be collecting our books.

20

The South – Land of the Lawn

My God, we have never seen so much lawn, anywhere, ever. Green and trimmed to perfection, lawn stretched out across the hills, bordered the roads, surrounded the shopping centres and the perfect homesteads. We crossed a bridge into Memphis and had an argument because Luisa did not have the camera ready and waiting to capture the moment. I also expect Luisa to navigate across continents using an offline phone, I expect her to take amazing photos and I expect her to make me snacks six times a day while navigating and taking photos or making a video. Is that too much to ask? No, I did not think so. We drove around Memphis for a while but had to press on, we needed the books and we needed to send them out as soon as possible, people were waiting and we did not want to disappoint. The sky was grey and the land green as we headed north, towards Clarksville. Luisa had found us a scenic route while making me my seventh sandwich of the day, and we journeyed off the beaten track, on small back roads, over rolling hills and past incredible countryside. We stumbled into a small town called Brownsville and were amazed, the place was perfect! The town had a charming square with perfect trees, adorned with fairy lights, a restaurant where everyone hung out and a barbershop next to the post office where Mary- Lou, the prettiest and kindest girl in town, was to be found wrapping gifts for the elderly. There was an art installation which Luisa wanted us to have a look at and we parked in front of a furniture store to have a look at Billy Tripp's life work called, Mind Field. Inspired by the death of his parents and his own life story, Mr Tripp had spent his life welding and bolting together a colossal steel structure, deserving awe. We walked around the structure, which seemed so out of place in the middle of the town, and I felt envy. This man had put all his talents and efforts into a work of art which one could only describe as inspiring. I had always dreamed of being an artist of some sort and to see this incredible manifestation of genius, love, compassion and self-expression was to remind me of what is possible in life if you follow your heart and allow your dreams to come to life. We did not get to meet Mr Tripp, but I do believe that he was the wealthiest man in town, though he probably spent every cent he had telling his story, I suppose there might be some parallels between his life's work and our own, doing whatever it took to make our dream, of travelling the world and educating our children and ourselves, a reality. After a brilliant hour spent marvelling, we returned to our Land Rover and had a conversation with the furniture store clerks, a couple of African Americans. They were amazed that we were from South Africa, "you should go sometime", we said. "Hell no, here I have a six-bedroom house and a cool car, I aint gonna hunt for dinner!". That's funny. We told them that if they went to Cape Town, they could eat the finest food in the world at the same price as a McDonald's meal and they could do it while watching Ferrari and Harley Davidson's roll by. They were not convinced but wished us a happy journey. They were such warm and friendly guys, we could have spent the afternoon hanging out with them.

Where were the hillbillies and the pickup trucks and the rednecks and the rebel flags, the roadkill restaurants, the Klan? Every second lawn in Brownsville had a Hillary for President banner. We were truly confused. The TV is a liar. We continued our drive to Clarksville and were amazed by the beauty of the countryside, a crisp, rich green we had not seen before. Every house was perfect in every way, well, almost every house. Now and then we would spot a plot of land, derelict, unloved, a wreck of a house or an old RV disintegrating, surrounded by wrecked cars, an overgrown lawn and abandoned toys. Just outside of Clarksville we drove up a hill dotted with domestic perfection and I looked to the right to see an RV, surrounded by debris, a pure white, hairless man, naked except for a pair of stained boxer shorts, standing behind a ripped fly door, his arms at his side, an evil look on his face, jaw jutted forward, staring. He scared the hell out of me, but no sooner had he ruined my day, he was gone and again we were surrounded by the American Dream – not one blade of grass out of place, gardens of flowers, sparkling windows, double story, pillared perfection.

As we drove into Clarksville, rain began to fall and the temperature dropped, it was going to be a cold and wet night camping, but we had bigger things on our mind, we needed to find the printers and have a look at Travel the Planet Overland. We had not been able to have a look at a physical proof of the book before approving the print run, as we had been in Baja, Mexico and there was no courier on the planet who would deliver a copy to the ranch. Luisa had put the book together on her terrible, Frankenstein computer and had not slept for weeks, trying to get the final book uploaded via the hand-cranked internet connection. We were nervous, we had printed 1000 books and if the books were terrible we would be in a bind, the printers took no responsibility for the layout, whatsoever. We arrived at the company's massive factory and waited in a warm, comfortable waiting area for the representative to bring us a copy of Travel the Planet Overland. She approached us with a box on a trolley, we quickly made the obligatory small talk, then opened the box, removed the first layer of protective paper and removed a book. It was beautiful! We had invested heavily in the quality of the book and were not disappointed – the cover was wax treated and stain proof, the spine bore embossed lettering and a small campfire flickered on the back cover when the book was wiggled under a light. The pages were thick and matte and the highest quality, the photographs were perfect and the font was exactly the correct size. It was even more beautiful than we expected it to be! We were proud parents, we took two copies and left the building and returned to the town, we were not going to sleep in the tent that night, we were going to treat ourselves to a room in a hotel, $60 a night including breakfast, only the best for us!

While the kids took turns showering and fighting over the TV remote, Luisa and I took turns pawing our printed creation. We could proudly send this out into the world. We could sleep well, warm and happy, once Luisa had given the bedding a once over with a black light and called the staff to replace a few stained pillowcases. Ah, Luisa, she is unique and I really do not have any idea what we would do without her. She fusses and worries and stresses and cleans, barks orders and keeps the troops in line. She organises our lives, overstocks the fridge and cupboards, finds the best places to sleep and keeps an eagle eye on our finances. Every so often I will hear the words, "We need to talk when you have a moment". When I hear those words, I know she is going to have a million things which need to be "signed off", I need to make decisions about where, when and how and I need to remind her where the cash is going to come from to pay for all of this. We thrash out ideas and remind ourselves of the grand scheme, the great goal, and keep on pushing. Luisa overreacts to everything and it is impossible to gauge by her initial reaction whether the taxman just stole all our money or she forgot to email her Mom, the drama is equal. But, I would not change a thing about her, we have been together for over twenty years and have been side by side, working together for a decade. We have our strengths and weakness and we work towards our strengths.

That morning Keelan and I went to the breakfast area to feast on the buffet. There was no buffet, there was a large TV tuned to Fox News, sausage, brown bread, sweet yoghurt, a selection of sugar cereal and piss coffee. Now, sausage in the US is not what is known as sausage in the rest of the world, it is flat, like a burger patty and you are supposed to pour gravy all over it and a "biscuit", which we would call a scone. Keelan loved the stuff, but I am a bacon and eggs kinda guy, Luisa skipped breakfast and Jessica shoved as much sugar as she could down her throat, before being dragged away from the cereals. Our dilemma was trying to figure out how on earth we could get the books to Pittsburgh, I could have loaded them all into the Landy, if we threw out half of our stuff but, as the books weighed more than a metric ton, the Landy would be overloaded. We took a drive to U-Haul, but a truck rental was extremely expensive, as was trailer hire (because we would be taking the truck or trailer out of state) and the tow hitch on the Landy was South African, we would have to install a new hitch and electrical connections. Eventually, we decided to have the printer courier the books to Pittsburgh as they offered a great rate. The books would take a week to arrive up north which allowed us to do some slow travelling up through Kentucky and West Virginia. There are an incredible array of Civil War monuments and sights which dot Kentucky and West Virginia, Virginia and North Carolina which was essentially ground zero of the war, which claimed almost 800 000 lives. In terms of territory, the war was fought in a relatively small area of the country and we saw many memorials and museums as we crossed through Kentucky. We went looking for a civil rights museum in Kentucky but could not find it but what we did find was a wealthy and well-maintained state, the municipalities of the West Coast could learn a thing or two from their Southern cousins. Luisa directed us through Kentucky and into West Virginia, coal mining country, the Appalachians, Deliverance! We crossed into the state at night and pulled up at a gas station, four state troopers, dressed in green with flat-brimmed hat, stood inside the gas station store and had a conversation. We entered the store and began the usual coffee routine, strong, cream, a little sugar. One of the troopers came over to talk to me, to ask where we're from and where we were going, it was a normal conversation except that the trooper would not look up at me (have you ever wondered why police headgear is tall? It is to create the illusion that the policeman is tall, thus commanding more respect). The trooper was a head shorter than me, but the flat brim of his hat prevented him from lifting his eyes, he would have to lift his head, and he was not about to do that. As a result, we had a five-minute conversation with him staring at my chest. The other troopers stood quietly and listened, showing no emotion at all. When we left the store, a large man was waiting to ask the same questions, but he struggled to believe the answers, he simply could not believe how we lived, how we travelled, where we were from and where we had been. We showed him Travel the Planet Overland and he asked if he could buy a signed copy and then offered us a room in his house. I was tempted to accept the offer, but my instinct suggested that I should decline, I seriously doubt that the man would have posed any threat whatsoever to us, but I have learned to obey my instincts. We waved goodbye and kept on driving, the rain began to fall and Luisa found a Walmart where we could park the Landy and get a good night's rest. Again, we were surprised as we entered the Walmart, expecting the worst, we instead found healthy, normal, friendly people going about their business. TV lies! What the hell were we expecting - coal-blackened faces and a special child strumming a banjo? When we told people that Americans were far fitter and healthier than the media portrays them to be, they all told us, "Wait until you go to the South". Well, people, you were wrong, dead wrong. We probably saw more happy, friendly, healthy-looking families in a few days in Kentucky and West Virginia than in all of the Pacific North West combined. I. Shit. You. Not. (PNW friends, next time you go out to a supermarket have a look at how many kids between the ages of 4 and 18 you see, I guarantee you will not see many if any at all). The next morning, we headed back out towards the interstate but first had to top up the fuel tank. People came and went wearing the colours of the West Virginia Mountaineers, a university team. People continued to be friendly, genuine and curious, so much so that by the time we re-joined the interstate, Luisa was saying, "Forget California or Washington, if we ever live in the USA we will live in West Virginia!". That is a massive statement, we had seen more of America than many ever will and this place is the one which gets the wife's stamp of approval? The moral of the story? Hollywood sells a distorted view of Americana, Malibu is portrayed as heaven on earth and the South is portrayed as Hicksville, full of reprobates, inbreeders, racists and the unsophisticated. From what we experienced, this simply is not true, the South we encountered was modern, beautiful, politically moderate, a far cry from places like Idaho, eastern Oregon, northern Washington state and huge parts of California (not to say that those places are terrible). As we drove along the interstate, people waved and honked their horns, a party atmosphere as they headed to watch their team take on an arch-enemy, Texas. Or Kansas, I can't remember. A lot of Americans had also told us to avoid the entire centre of the country, saying there was nothing there but cornfields and more cornfields. I think, when we return to the USA, we should rent a camper and travel through the Bible belt, we might find that there is a lot more to Middle America than we are told.

Luisa took us to the Trans-Allegheny Lunatic Asylum which had also served as a civil war hospital. What a horrible place to visit. There are numerous stories of the building being haunted and deranged people pay good money to sleep in the asylum, especially over Halloween. Who in their right minds wants to be scared witless? Not me, I refused to go any further than the reception area, and that was in broad daylight. Nope, never. Perhaps in a past life, I was imprisoned, drowned at sea or insane, either way, I am not interested in reliving terror, real or imagined.

21

Pittsburgh, Pennsylvania, Pizza, Beer and Radio and Work

We entered Pennsylvania and immediately noticed a change; the motorway lawns were not manicured, the roads were not as well maintained as those in West Virginia, there were a lot of unkempt open spaces and the weather seemed cooler. It was as if we had crossed into another country altogether. Our friend John had given us instructions to meet him on an offramp, he wanted to take us to the brewery he had shares in and had to run some other errands. He came flying up behind the waiting Land Rover, driving a white Jetta like a bat out of hell. We had spoken to John many times, I would phone him often and shoot the breeze and he had prepared an itinerary for us if we ever chose to live in Pittsburgh, or at least spend a fair amount of time there. We drove through old European neighbourhoods and arrived at Helltown brewery thirsty, the beer was delicious, but we still had to drive, so I kept my consumption down, John filled a few growlers and we set off back to his red home on a hill. The comfortable and tastefully decorated double story house had views of the neighbourhood and a Land Rover memorabilia aplenty. We made ourselves at home, it was at this moment that John knew, he'd stuffed up. After 10 days of cross-country driving, we were stinky and tired and the Landy, -parked below, next to John's 109, was a mess. We unpacked almost everything we owned and sat down to dinner after a hot shower. Downstairs was to be our work area,

Luisa and I slept on a bed in the office upstairs and the kids crashed on comfortable couches. John and I had a lot in common, particularly our love for beer, Land Rovers, good music and a morning cup of tea. Keelan soon became John's tea slave and Keelan was happy to keep our host going with endless pots. By the first morning, we were settled in and working on the fulfilments for the Kickstarter pledges, I had to make 110 leather passport pouches, we had already sourced the leather and the leatherworking tools. John introduced me to a radio station called WYEP and I soon fell in love with my new temporary life, drinking tea, working the leather, listening to the best music in the world. I was in the zone and would probably still be there if Luisa had not made other plans.

With the heater on, the radio playing through excellent speakers, a cup of tea and the family busy elsewhere, I was able to focus completely on the leatherwork and my thoughts. I had been watching John Neeman Tools (re-branded Northmen since January 2017) videos on YouTube and found the videos immensely relaxing and simultaneously inspiring. The Birth Of A Tool - Part III, The Birth Of A Dugout Canoe and The Birth Of A Wooden House are intoxicating to watch, for me at least. The philosophy of our existence is self-sufficiency, our Land Rover is our home and we travel the planet, seeking knowledge, experience and wisdom, tools are incredibly important to our way of life and if you can make your own tools, you can build your own home, metaphorically, that is how we progress and succeed. A bank full of cash is a wonderful thing, the security of wealth has allowed artists, philosophers and scientists to elevate our species and change the world. We can learn from these masters of intellect, integrate and accept their knowledge as our own but, ultimately, every man has to build his own home in this world. The skills and knowledge of our ancestors are incredibly valuable, we are not superior to them because we have smartphones and the internet, they lived more fulfilling lives, I believe.

LA LUCHA

By now, dear reader, you may have surmised that I am mildly obsessed with Northern Europe. My maternal Grandmother was born and raised in Paderborn Germany, my Mom was born and partially raised in the United Kingdom and my maternal Grandfathers name was Norman Norkett (Norman, a Germanic name meaning "Northman" referring to a Viking, and Norkett, a surname which evolved from the words northern cottage). My father was adopted and raised in an English speaking, South African home but came from Afrikaner stock, the Afrikaners are of predominantly Dutch heritage. Even though I was born and raised as an English speaking, South African, my Northern European ancestry has always drawn me, I never truly felt at home in my skin back home in South Africa. Even as a child, I felt like something was missing, usually my father, but there was also a sense of dispossession, of being a stranger in a strange land. Is it possible that thousands of years of location-specific evolution can create in a person, memories without experience, a longing for sights, sounds and a culture you have never experienced? I believe so... When hippies and spiritualists and bored romantics speak of past lives, perhaps they are not too far from the mark, we evolved and are the flesh of our ancestors, we may not have lived before as an individual, but part of us lived in our forefathers. Returning to Europe would be a return to home, at least culturally. Tall people are tall for a reason, blonde people are blonde for a reason, black people are black for a reason and we all evolved according to our long-term geographic circumstances. To be proud of one's ancestry, does not mean you are racist unless you believe that your race is superior to others. It is like being congratulated for being tall, smart or good-looking, you really had nothing to do with it. I look at the Scandinavian countries and their collective reaction to 30's and 40's Nazism (which is not pronounced Nazi-ism, and the plural of fish is fish and there is no such thing as over-exaggeration, you either exaggerate, or you don't). Nazi doctrine asserted, with the aid of cherry-picked science, that the Aryan race was superior to all others. The blonde hair, blue-eyed majority of the Scandinavian countries north of

Germany, however, did not embrace this ideology, why should they? The Scandinavians were not weak in their identity and did not need to elevate themselves to the impossible heights of living gods. The Scandinavians resisted the Nazis before and during the war and Norway in particular, had active resistance units. Yes, some Scandinavians were seduced by Nazi rhetoric, but the majority had no time for Hitler's fantasies. I am not interested in supreme races, I have found that those who declare themselves superior, to be the weakest of their tribe. I am interested in Taiga forest and snow and the old ways, I want to find a place in this world that the nomad in me is intently searching for. I am being called back to somewhere and one day, perhaps, I will settle there and build a home. Perhaps the nomad in me will never be satisfied and I will die on the road, searching. These are the thoughts I meditated on while I worked on the leather pouches.

We had had a leather stamp made and it took me a while to cut, sew, treat, stamp and clip each pouch, each one was unique and by the time I finished the 110th, I was ready for a new project. We had used only high-quality materials to make the pouches and I was proud of the end result, they were simple in design but would last many years, even if used daily.

Our books arrived in Pittsburgh, 71 boxes containing 14 beautiful books each plus a few hundred copies of We Will Be Free. Luisa had me driving around Pittsburgh on a mission to buy packaging materials, tape, envelopes, labels and wine. We had to sign each book individually, including a copy of We Will Be Free for many backers. Packages were made, and individual books wrapped, we worked sixteen hours a day for a week and eventually, we were ready to call the post office to collect. There is a reason that America has the world's highest GDP; they know how to do business. Customer service is alive and well, innovation ensures that systems improve constantly and the economies of scale justify the effort. The United States Post Office takes no tax dollars to fund it's operation, even though employees are Federal employees. USPS is a business and it is run like a business; therefore, your post arrives when it should, prices are competitive and systems are in place to please large clients. Luisa printed the waybills online and the post office sent a truck to collect the packages, they scanned each parcel and we were emailed tracking numbers for the hundreds of parcels which we sent out. We were left with thirty boxes of books, we had printed many extra books to sell once the reviews came back favourable, so that those who had not backed the project could still buy Travel the Planet Overland, which is exactly what happened. Esteemed publications reviewed the book with descriptions such as - "There are quite a few books available proclaiming to be the ultimate edifier of all things overland. I've read only a few of them, skimmed over most—but enjoyed only one. That book is also the newest in the mix and gives hope for an otherwise dull literary genre". We had plenty to be proud of.

With the majority of the books and fulfillment packages sent out, my mind now turned to the build of the camper. Luisa had hired a car and we were set to leave John's beautiful home and drive down to Florida. John had been an incredible host, though he might have been disappointed that we worked night and day and hardly took the time to explore his beloved Pittsburgh. He also could not believe that one family could devour twenty bananas a day. Fortunately, we did make time for a guided drive around the city, John, and his girlfriend Monica, driving his 109 and us following in our clean and empty 130. We had pizza and met school friends and marvelled at all the beautiful university students and drank a few beers and had a party, John inviting friends we had not yet met; Harold, Mark and Dave. Harold had offered his workshop and expertise for the build and with hindsight, it might have been a better idea to have done the rebuild in Pittsburgh, but, Harold had a business to run and limited space available. And we had already made a commitment to head down to Florida. I personally believe Luisa only wanted to go down to Florida because, while I look forward to an Arctic winter, Luisa has Italian blood in her veins and loves the heat of a summer sun. Before we left, we joined Mark, Harold, John and Morgan for a taping of their podcast, Centre Steer. Land Rover people never cease to amaze me and we left beautiful Pittsburgh content and determined to return if only to hang out with John and his friends, his beer, his basement and WYEP.

We packed the rental car, a new, red Ford Focus with boxes of books, careful not to overload it. We estimated the combined weight of Keelan and I would be about twenty boxes of books, the girls were going to drive the luxurious Ford and the boys would drive the Landy. John was out of town on business, so we cleaned the house as best we could and left a thank you note on the dining table. The route we had chosen would take us back into West Virginia, Virginia, North Carolina, South Carolina, Georgia down into Florida, our hosts were in Homestead, far south at the entrance to the Florida Keyes. We had a 2,000-kilometre drive ahead of us, it is difficult to comprehend the sheer scale of the USA until you drive across her, what a beast!

The drive was uneventful. Luisa was bored out of her mind having to drive the fast Focus at Defender speeds, but she kept herself entertained playing with the radio and the SatNav and the electric leather seats and the heater and the electric windows. She forgot that we were driving up and over the Appalachian mountains, that I needed to speed the Landy up on downhills so that she could climb the uphills, she forgot that she had the cruise control on, she forgot that she had to overtake for two vehicles, she forgot the braking distance of the heavy Defender and she forgot how to use the walky-talky, every time I buzzed her to tell her to move her ass or slow down. When we stopped I would give her hell and she would say, "Ag. Sorry man, I was listening to NPR, there was a really interesting interview with…". She promised to drive better but within ten minutes of being back on the road, she forgot her promise, hung an arm out the window and relaaaaaaaxed. If I would try and overtake her she would speed up, then slow down again and relaaaaaaax. I was ready to murder her and the next time we stopped, I banished her to the back of the convoy. "Ag, jeez, whatever man, take a chill pill!". The upside to driving the fast Ford, slowly, was that she was using next to no fuel and cruised for almost two days on one tank of fuel. We slept in Walmart parking lots almost every night and on the fourth day arrived in Florida as the sunset. The air was thick and hot as we entered Florida. We were expecting Hawaii shirts and gators and girls in bikinis and a hundred thousand million palm trees, Don Johnson in a car, a cop can't afford and Gloria Estefan on the radio. Our first night was spent parked at a rest area, which was a noisy but uneventful experience, before hitting the road south to Homestead, a distance of almost 700 kilometres. Traffic flowed freely as we made our way south, Luisa guided us along the coastal road towards Cape Canaveral where we visited The Kennedy Space Centre. Taking the kids to museums is an integral part of their home-schooling experience and Keelan, in particular, enjoyed the tour. This was the second space centre we had visited, the first was a little more remote, in French Guyana.

22

Flo. Rida.

We arrived in Homestead late in the evening, in the rain. Our hosts Ron and Cherie lived on a smallholding in the agricultural area and we drove to the wrong house before being redirected to Ron's house. Ron had lived in Homestead all his life and he, along with my overland friend, James (Home on the Highway) and 90% of the population of Homestead had lost everything in 1992, when Hurricane Andrew huffed and puffed and blew everything down. Ron was not going to go through that again and when he built his home, he built a fortress. The entire structure was constructed of poured, reinforced concrete and the roof consisted of concrete slabs. It would take a direct hit from a bunker-buster missile or a massive asteroid to destroy the home. Within the fortress, they had built another reinforced "safe" room. We entered to a loud welcome of parrots, pooches and the indomitable Cherie. We were given a tour of the fortress and told to make ourselves at home. The next morning, we awoke and had a look around. The fortress stood facing the road and was surrounded by a tall fence, fields and greenhouses which grew bromeliads (also known as air plants). An early 90's RV stood on the one side of the house and a covered work area on the other. Our first task was to give the RV a tidy and a wash before moving our crap in. I am not sure Ron and Cherie knew what they had signed up for, but we were grateful that they had opened their home to us, we insisted that we would cook breakfast and dinner daily and the kids would do the dishes and the grocery bill would be split down the middle for shared meals, as a family we do not eat very large meals and we provided the labour, cooking and cleaning.

We had one last camping trip with the Landy before she was to be overhauled. Our friends James and Lauren were in Florida and James had no desire to return to Homestead so, together with Ron in his awesome little Defender 90 (TDI powered in case you were wondering), we drove up to the Ocala National Forest for a weekend of fires, braais, beers, James' dangerous cocktails and a whole lot of chin-wagging. We had now had a braai with James and Lauren in Argentina, Brazil, Mexico and the USA. I wonder when and where we will break bread again, I am hoping for Asia or Africa, it will not be the Middle East, James has boycotted the region due to their oppressive and ill-conceived alcohol prohibition.

On November 7th, we sat with Ron and Cherie and watched the Presidential election drama unfold on CNN. No-one believed that Trump had managed to get this far in the race, but we had an idea that he might win. Having just recently travelled across the country, we had seen the posters and the billboards and the bumper stickers and the lawn signs. One neighbourhood in Pittsburgh had a Trump-Pence sign on every single lawn and the Hillary Kaine signs were few and far between across the entire nation. It was unfathomable to me that Trump could become president of this incredible nation, the man has no political or military experience. It was not up to me to decide, we were merely "international observers". With the writing on the wall, I chose not to watch the election results. Instead, I went to sleep to dream of building the ultimate escape vehicle. We woke to the news that Donald Trump had become the 45th President of The United States. Forty former presidents rolled in their graves.

The panels had been delayed by a few weeks and Andreas asked us to help with the shipping costs, we had not budgeted $800 for the shipping, but we were between a rock and a hard place. After much to and fro and delay, we had no choice but to pay the shipping and the panels arrived a month late. Luisa had found flights to Europe for only $500 and, wary of losing a deal, had paid for the tickets and set a departure date of 27th February, we had to be finished with the camper build by February 14th. I had given myself three months to do the build, but with the late arrival of the panels (December 17th due to the shipping company going out of business) and Luisa's deadline, I was now under pressure to get the Landy rebuilt and running and ready to ship. No pressure. The delay had given me some extra time to plan and source materials, I was determined not to be idle and with a wife like Luisa, there is no such thing as downtime until beer o'clock or Sunday, but then she wants to have her special "talks". I prepared and tidied the work area, Ron had a Defender rebuild project in the work area but he kindly offered to put his project in a storage area while we needed the workspace. A Florida winter is baking hot and I arranged a large fan and borrowed Ron's excellent Yeti cooler box which we would fill with ice every day while we worked.

Keelan and I needed to learn how to weld and Ron had all the tools and experience we needed to get started. He had picked up some metal offcuts from the metal merchant in town and got us started with a brazing weld using a blow torch and a brazing rod. Keelan and I had watched a hundred welding videos on YouTube while we waited for the panels to arrive and we had all the theoretical knowledge we needed to get started. Ron explained how we needed to heat the two pieces of metal equally and consistently hand feed the brazing rod and left us to practice. It looks a hell of a lot easier on videos than it is in reality. Working on a large metal work table in Ron's huge greenhouse, we continued to practice for hours until we had a weld which was strong and consistent. Keelan, I took turns and taught each other as we learned, each evening we would return to the house with strange welded works of art which were given to Luisa to admire. We then moved on to Shielded Metal Arc Welding which is commonly known as Stick welding. Stick is a lot easier than brazing as you do not need to coordinate two components; equally, one hand is free to play cards or darts or, more logically, to support the other hand while the weld hand makes repetitive C or D movements. We soon discovered that left-handed Keelan needed to practice writing C's and D's in order to improve his fine motor skills. The advantage of having a lefty on the team was that he could do the left-hand welds, which essentially made us an ambidextrous welding team. Welding in a hot greenhouse while fully dressed in protective clothing is not fun and welding takes a lot more discipline, concentration, preparation and planning than is immediately obvious and we soon learned that we needed to have a lot more respect for professional welders. Ron would regularly inspect our work and would keep us practising until he was satisfied that we had achieved a good, consistent weld before presenting us with new information and challenges. It was while we were welding that we were introduced to the greenhouse workers and we made new friends, Jesus and his wife, Lupita. Jesus worked hard all day, every day and the work he did covered a huge range of responsibilities, but he always made to time to stop and give us some advice or to unlock the large tool shed for us. Jesus and Lupita had recently become American citizens and they are the kind of people which the US needs more of, hardworking, industrious, committed to family and their new country. We spoke Spanish with Jesus and told him stories about our travels across Latin America while explaining our plans for the future, he thought we were loco. After a week of instruction and practice, Ron moved us on to MIG (Gas Metal Arc Welding) which is probably the easiest way to weld, considering all factors. We needed to adjust the wire feed speed and amperage according to the thickness of the steel being used. We soon learned that any gust of wind would ruin the weld and that the tensioner on the MIG machine had a habit of slipping, which left us staring down the nozzle of the welding "gun". C's and D's all day long until we achieved a weld which penetrated deep, was solid and strong. We learned the importance of giving the metal a good clean before welding, using an angle grinder and wire wheel as well as a metal brush to remove all contaminants, rust and paint. We grew to enjoy welding so much that Keelan even began to talk about becoming a professional welder. Again, this entire process was part of his home-schooling experience. He had focussed on other subjects intently as our circumstances demanded it and now he was learning welding, carpentry, metalwork, technical drawing, 3D modelling, painting and anti-corrosion preparations, mechanical applications, electrical installation, sewing, glueing, bonding, binding and a million other skills.

One of Andreas' concerns was that we would not have enough time to do the build, particularly considering that we had never done an expedition truck build before, but we had resources we could use to help us along but most of all we had the belief that we could do it. We had achieved so much in the past and we had always thrown ourselves in the deep end. With each passing day waiting for the panels to be delivered, I felt the pressure mount but alleviated that pressure as much as possible by researching and improving my skills so that when the work began, I would be ready, my head full of information. We were not looking forward to taking the Landy apart and, I will admit, that I made the decision not to sell the parts of the Defender which we removed until we were sure that the build would be a success. It was a small insurance policy which gave me at least some peace of mind. (You can watch the entire rebuild process on YouTube, Luisa documented the build and Keelan was tasked with sorting through hundreds of hours of footage. The video had almost 180 000 views within the first few weeks online).

LA LUCHA

Eventually, the panels arrived on December the 17th and we immediately set about doing a mock-up of the camper box with the panels and extrusions provided, could you imagine if the panels had been cut too small or if the quantities of the various components we required were supplied in insufficient quantities? The factory had done their job well, the crate which contained the panels was made, with no costs spared, to ensure that the panels were not damaged in transit and they had not cut the panels to the exact sizes we needed (that is a service that the company provides), but this was a good thing as it allowed me to make changes to the design and dimensions. We now had to take apart our beautiful Defender, a vehicle which had safely transported our family hundreds of thousands of hard, heavy overlanding kilometres, a vehicle which turned heads wherever she went and a vehicle which was more than just our home and pride and joy, she was part of the family. We started off removing the rooftop tent, which had served us so well, and then we removed the rear, aluminium canopy (or topper as they call it in the USA). Next, we had to remove the rear seats, doors and roof before unbolting the rear load tub, which Ron lifted gently with a forklift. The rear seat box was then removed and we were down to bare chassis all the way up to the front seats! It took us one day to strip the Landy down and the only cuts which I had to make, were to the sills which lie below the door line on either side of the vehicle. Two cuts! Land Rover Defenders truly are a grown man's Lego. I have seen images and video of similar conversions done to other brands of vehicles and half of the vehicle had to be cut off, the beauty of the Defenders modular construction is that if we one day decide to restore her to a standard double cab 130, the only real headache will be removing the pod and paying for the replacement parts. With all the parts removed, we could now have a good look at the chassis, chances were very good that we might find some horrible rust spots and might have to do some chassis repairs. Almost every second month for the last five years, I had power washed and coated the entire chassis with WDF40 lubricating spray and had made extra effort to get the spray into the hard to reach areas. Now was the moment of truth, we backed the now lightweight Landy out of the work area and gave the chassis a good scrub. There was zero rust! Hardly even any surface rust. "Are you sure it is a Land Rover", asked Ron. The same was true for the body parts we had removed, zero rust. Only the bottom of the rear doors had some cancer, but that is to be expected in a vehicle of that age. Structurally she was solid as a rock.

Our next task was to prepare the Landy for the build. With the chassis scrubbed and given a few coats of Rustoleum I lifted the right rear corner as high as I could with a trolley jack. We were looking for flex in the chassis, the more flexible the frame, the more I would have to tweak my design to compensate for that flex, we did not want the pod breaking when the vehicle articulated in an off-road environment. The chassis, being a solid ladder frame, did not flex much at all, the Defender is designed to be rigid with the suspension allowing the wheels to articulate, it is a small truck on a strong truck frame. Ron, our hero, had an early Defender roof lying at the back of the greenhouse and he donated it to our rebuild efforts, it was soon trimmed to fit the front of the Landy, I would recycle my old load bars to make a roof rack which sat above the front of the cabin, we would respray the roof and add a liner inside with storage boxes to accommodate Luisa's odds and sods and my Nanocom, Brut deodorant and Playboy magazines.

Ron had a collection of Dewalt cordless power tools, which we kept charged up, Cherie allowed me to take a Bose radio outside to the work area and I had my old Waeco fridge plugged in and stocked with Yuengling beer. While we worked, we would drink cold water, full of ice from the Yeti, while the fan did it's best to keep us cool and the radio kept us entertained. Soon I fell into a routine. In the morning I would wake at 6.00 am, leave the RV, try and make friends with the dogs, make a pot of coffee and then drag the cart full of power tools from the patio outside Keelan's room, over the ancient, bleached coral which surrounded the work area. I would listen to

LA LUCHA

NPR radio, while the sun rose and I studied the Landy, planning our work for the day. Three or four days a week, I would take a long walk around the neighbourhood, Keelan would join me most mornings and yak my ears off about gaming and the gaming community, eventually we agreed that he could talk about that stuff as we walked away from the house and we would talk about the build, and the insanity of Queen Luisa, as we returned. The house woke up by 7.30 am and, by then, I would be cooking breakfast on the industrial-sized griddle in the kitchen. Breakfast would be yoghurt and fruit, fruit juice, toast, coffee, tea and a fry up of bacon, sausage, tomato, onion, eggs and halved fried bananas. And cereal for Jessica. After breakfast, Luisa would return to the RV with a list of materials I needed and she would source them while taking orders for Travel the Planet Overland and We Will Be Free, organising the postage and fighting all day with the people who aspire to make our lives difficult. By mid-morning, she would set up the cameras to film Keelan and I as we worked, we were determined to document the build well. Jessica would make us sandwiches for lunch and at 5.00 pm Keelan was allowed to leave work and return to his beloved gaming friends (he had friends all over the world through gaming, and, as long as he went to sleep before 11.00 pm, I encouraged him to go online). By 8.00 pm the sun would begin to set and I would run out of energy, the days were very long and hot. I would open a cold beer and study the work I had done that day, perhaps finish spray painting or cleaning a part I had been working on and would sit outside and enjoy one cold beer after another until Luisa called me to supper. By 9.30 pm, I would be fast asleep in the RV, dreaming of grinding, cutting, bolting, spraying, searching for the bloody screwdriver which I had just put down but now it had vanished, "Keelan!".

Searching YouTube one day, I came across the singer Sia and became hooked to her uplifting anthems, they became my motivation music I would listen to as I went to sleep and when I woke up. This build was a massive undertaking and I had to keep my mind positive and focussed. Luisa mocked me and Jessica gave me a hard time "You are in love, Pappa". I was, don't tell Luisa, OK? (Writing this book, I listened to Erik Satie's Gymnopedie No.3 almost exclusively).

The one aspect which made this camper build incredibly challenging, was the need for open access from the cabin to the pod, a space large enough that we could climb through in case of inclement weather and if we were ever in a situation where there was an immediate threat and we needed to escape, I could jump in the driver's seat and drive away. The kids had to be accommodated as well and there was no way we could not have a four-seater, four sleeper. I had been studying a German build and contacted the creator, Mario. He had created a bulkhead which facilitated the connection of the camper body to the front of the vehicle via the B pillars. His advice was priceless and I set about making a template, now that the new roof had been cut and was in place, I had the shape and the dimensions I needed. I started working on the template, using one of the chipboard panels which had made up the panel delivery crate. Tracing the shape of the cab onto the board, I slowly trimmed away excess material until I had the exterior moulded and then traced the interior dimensions with the board held in place. Keelan and I then trimmed the internal material, until we had the complete template. We measured the distance to the existing chassis brackets, calculated the height of the floor including the subframe, the subframe floor and the insulated panel floor. My head was bursting with calculations, but Keelan is a natural mathematician and he accepted the responsibility of supplying the final dimensions which, when we eventually bolted all the parts together, were found to be correct within a fraction of a millimetre. Once we had the final dimensions, we traced the outline of the template onto a piece of treated marine plywood and trimmed and sanded the final bulkhead until it fit perfectly into the curves of the B pillar. It took us a week just to do the bulkhead and while I was busy with obsessive-compulsive trimming and sanding, Keelan was restoring the load bars and doing all the heavy lifting. Luisa would take a few hours every day to help us and, slowly, but surely we began to make progress. Based on the advice from Mario, we added a couple of "wings" on the outer of each B pillar which gave the pod to camper join, more structural surface.

Before the Land Rover had been stripped, we had been invited by Australian, Shayne and his lovely wife to visit them for a meal at their home in Orlando. Shayne is one of the nicest guys you could hope to meet and he soon visited us in Homestead, bringing with him a huge amount of hardware which he "donated" to our cause. We were gobsmacked, he had brought us boxes of stainless steel nuts and bolts, screws, washers, tools, hinges, electrical equipment and a host of other goodies he used to build his own and customers Land Rovers. His red 130 was impeccably outfitted and was described by Outside Magazine as the "best-prepared Defender they had ever seen". Shayne knew what he was talking about and exhausted me with ideas and recommendations (such as re-using our old auxiliary fuel tank and installing it upfront, under the subframe). He was willing to camp in a field and help me with the build, I should have accepted but, remember, my primary school report often stated, "Graeme does not play nicely with others". Shayne had a vast amount of experience, which intelligent people paid good money to tap into, but I was determined to build the camper the way I had planned and I was determined to do it at my pace. "Give me a hammer", Shayne! Shayne also had a huge amount of local knowledge and he knew exactly where we could source all the difficult to source materials we were looking for. The materials he personally provided us saved us hundreds of dollars and a lot of time, running trips to the hardware store. Thank you, Shayne and Sandra, we can't wait to meet on the road and share a cold beer with you guys.

With the new roof cut and the bulkhead in place, we were now able to start the job I had been preparing for and dreading the most, the subframe weld. I had been advised to use 50mm x 50mm (2-inch x 2 inches) steel tubing, but my calculations indicated that we could safely use the thinner and substantially lighter 25mm x 50mm (1-inch x 2 inches) tube. The thinner material would be lighter and sufficiently flexible and we would reinforce the welds to make the entire frame. We planned to make a frame which mirrored the ladder construction of the chassis and would mount to the existing chassis mounts, "hard" bolted at the front, where the subframe met the cab, resting on suspension rubbers in the middle and bolted through the rear and "soft" mounted on four polyurethane suspension rubbers, the kind used for shock absorbers and suspension components. The subframe would have box sections fore and aft of the rear wheels, which would support the width of the camper. Together Keelan and I planned the layout of the subframe, calculated the lengths we required and Luisa ordered the steel which arrived within a couple days. Keelan and I then cut the steel into a section, numbered them, ground the contact areas to an angle to allow for greater penetration and cleaned all the protective black paint from the contact areas. At first, we tried to weld the subframe in the work area, but January in Florida can be windy and lying on concrete, welding is less than comfortable, we loaded the steel and welding equipment into Cherie's pickup and drove across to the greenhouse and the large metal table where we welded for two days. Halfway through the first welds, Ron popped in to have a look and corrected a few mistakes we were making. We were happy with the welds and cut and welded triangular gussets to reinforce the corners of the frame and then added a few extra crossbars to further strengthen the structure. The welds and entire frame were then scrubbed clean with an angle grinder and wire brush before being sprayed four times with white Rustoleum and four times with black Rustoleum. We could now make the floor using more treated marine plywood and were clever enough to cut an access hatch for the easy replacement of the fuel pump. The time had eventually come to cut the first GRP panel, the floor panel. Together, Luisa, Keelan and I, measured three times, then three times again, and cut the shape of the floor using a guide supplied by Ron's carpenter, Rocky. We were past the point of no return and I decided it was time to sell the parts we had removed from the Landy. Within hours of putting the parts online, they were sold, it was heart-breaking to watch the parts of our old girl leave but we knew that the majority of parts would end up attached to a rich man's truck and would continue to live a pampered life. We sold the Howling Moon tent separately to an overlander in Canada and were happy that a new family would explore the world and have adventures with that excellent piece of kit.

Rocky, the carpenter, took a while to warm up to me, as did my new best friend, Pepper the Pooch but, unlike Pepper, Rocky never bit me. As a man in his 70's, Rocky had seen the world come and go and had travelled far and wide with the Navy. He had a quick sense of humour and a slow walk, he declined the breakfast I offered him every day and often stole Keelan to hold doors up, while he mounted them. Rocky would arrive in the morning and leave before lunch and soon he would pop in every day and have a look at the work we were doing. He showed me how to use his router, which I used to shave millimetres off our obsessively crafted marine bulkhead. We treated Rocky with respect and Rocky appreciated that he had no time for fools. The guide he provided was a bit short for our needs, but it was what we had to work with and it worked perfectly well, once we got used to it. Rocky would poke fun at us for being too tall and shake a shaky finger at us, a smile on his face. He was convinced that we were insane, but he made sure to stop by daily and offer any help he could. Pepper learned to love us because we would make a braai twice a week and cook delicious meat full of tasty bones. I would feed the dogs, Pepper, Bo and Snuggles, rib bones and give them each a rub. Once Pepper decided that I was his buddy, he became dedicated to me and where I went, Pepper went. At night I would sit on a camping chair, sucking on a Yuengling beer, staring at the Landy, making mental lists and Pepper would sit behind me in the dark, protecting me.

Somehow the days had flown by and we were already on the dawn of The Last Month – February. Luisa had made me a countdown chart when there were only 30 days left and already we were 10 days down, 20 days to go. Luisa does not play well with others either and she chose to take on the massive task of manufacturing the roof which included the designing the roof, measuring, mounting of solar panels, designing installing the canvas for the pop-top, sourcing the materials including gas struts and seals, etc. It was a huge undertaking, but I had enough on my plate and welcomed the opportunity to spread the load. We sat together and thrashed out some ideas and left her to it. Luisa is an incredibly capable person, but this would be the ultimate challenge of her technical skills, a challenge which she embraced. There is nothing a man can do, within the constraints of physiology, that Luisa cannot do, but there are many things Luisa can do which many men cannot. She is the most fiercely capable woman I know, she is not a feminist, not a flower, nor any man's property, she demands equality and earns respect.

With the base and floor installed, we were able to move on to cutting and mounting the front wall of the pod, cutting and glueing the extrusions. The glue needed a few days to dry and it was then that we measured and cut the walls and installed the windows. Keelan and I, welded and prepared the internal frame which would not only give the kids a steel exoskeleton of security but would also be the frame of a bunk bed of sorts; a permanent bed for Jessica and the two benches below, which would become Keelan's bed when we stopped for the night. Originally, we planned to have Keelan sleep up top, but he had grown so much in the USA, that we thought it better to have him sleep below on the lower bunk. We could not figure out why he continued to put on weight, we tried to keep his intake of sugar and bread to a minimum, he went for walks with me almost every day and he did physical labour most of the day. I was drinking a six-pack every night, but he did not, it was a mystery and still is, with all that activity he should have been all muscle. He was incredibly strong at least and he could lift more than two normal men, a huge help when we had so much lifting and carrying to do. I am proud of my son and always will be, I know that he is an incredibly smart, caring and brave soul. Unfortunately, the world expects perfection while being wholly imperfect. Keelan and Luisa helped me lift and glue the walls into place and, once the adhesive set, we were able to shuffle in the bed/security frame and marvel at the wonder of our creation. Finally, it was all coming together, adding the walls gave the illusion of massive progress and we began creating the rear wall and door. A side door would have been perfect if there were only two of us, but we had to accommodate four. A large two-piece rear door would allow us to open the pod to allow maximum airflow and allow flow into and out of the vehicle. Again, my goal was not to create a dank little box but instead a spaceship with large portals through which we could watch the universe go by. The rear was to be a giant headache; I had to accommodate the rear door, build in a departure angle which meant cutting the panels and extrusions and if I made a mistake it was game over (not quite, but please indulge me), I had no extra materials. The wheel arches also needed to be fabricated, the gas tank hoses installed, etc, my list seemed to be growing, not shrinking! Days were slipping by and with only days left, Keelan and I crafted the rear section. The local steel/welding shop had a bending machine and we scoured their yard for a thick length of aluminium, which we could be shaped to form the support, internal and external of the rear angle. The bending machine was old school and we had to fabricate a guide to which the aluminium section could be shaped. Over a few days we cut and moulded and trimmed and hammered and filed, until eventually, we had an angled rear. I then made the drop-down tailpiece and the pull up rear door mated and hinged the two. I wanted the rear of the pod to retain a Defender identity and installed standard 130 rear lights and the refurbished original light guards. I even used my old set of Defender door hinges to mount the rear doors which weas a headache because those hinges are offset and we needed flat hinges. Shayne returned to marvel at the brilliance of our workmanship and to help to install the electrical system, which Luisa had designed. He worked until late into the night while Keelan sanded, clean and masked the front of the Defender, we had planned to spray paint the Landy, the front white and the rear a matte grey/blue, the blue as close as we could match to an original Series Land Rover colour. A map of our journey reveals that we love the ocean and large bodies of water. A military colour would be an obvious choice for this build, but we were not too keen on an olive green or khaki, instead we chose a naval colour, something which would reflect our love for all things maritime and, the beauty of paint, is that it is, just paint, we could easily change it. Jesus came over and helped me set up the compressor and taught me how to paint. I had been watching YouTube tutorials in my spare time and had practised the robotic motions, left to right. Jesus set up a few old pieces of chipboard and had me practice until he was satisfied, he then mixed a container of paint for me and strained it and filled the pot and supervised my work. Jesus, like Rocky, would also visit our work area twice a day and check on our progress, offering advice or tools or a helping hand. If I lived in Homestead, Jesus would have been my best friend, our families would spend weekends together and we would eventually convince, and help, him to restore the old camper in his yard, then take the family on trips, introducing them to camping and overlanding. During our stay in Homestead, Jesus had invited us to his home at least once every two weeks to join his family and friends as they celebrated a birthday or an anniversary or a graduation. They treated us like royalty and although there was a gap where I ran out of Spanish and Jesus ran out of English, we understood each other perfectly. Salud, amigo!

LA LUCHA

Luisa had booked a train ride from Florida to Washington D.C and the day before that we had to drop the Landy off at the shippers' warehouse. Luisa, being Luisa, had found a vehicle transporter which charged almost half of what the competitors charge. With time running out, we spray painted the front of the Defender and continued to work in the rear, fitting the fuel hoses, completing the wheel arches, helping Shayne with the electrical installation and finished fabricating the rear door. That last day was a mad rush, Luisa had been determined to try and get the interior done in the last few days and, though I begged her to forget about the interior and instead help me, she persisted and only gave up on the morning of the last day. It is as if she was just trying to cause me to have a heart attack, she would remove my tools and not replace them, use the workbenches and not charge the power tools she was using. Once the paint was dry, Keelan had to reassemble the front end of the Landy, replacing the bumper, winch, bulbar, lights protective chequer plate and spare wheel mounting, he then had to mount the load bars, the jerry can holder and the large Pelican case Shayne had donated to us. With minutes ticking by, Luisa packed the rear of the Landy, while I rushed to install the rear lock, latches for the bottom half of the rear door, reconnect the battery and a million other little jobs which had to be finalised. We had to leave at 3 o'clock if we were to make it to the warehouse, they were 100 kilometres away and closed at 5 o'clock exactly. Together Luisa, Keelan, Shayne, Ron and I carried the roof from the large patio area inside the house where Luisa had been working and slid it up on top of the pod. The roof still had a lot of work to be done and had no latches, I hastily cut and bent four pieces of galvanised metal strips and drill and pop-riveted them into the roof and extrusions, hoping that that would be enough to hold the roof down. Luisa, Keelan and Jessica, then loaded the rear of the Defender with boxes of our possessions, I was still busy with the rear door and Shayne was putting the final touches to the electrical system.

At 3.30 pm, I started the Land Rover and drove her out of the work area. She was fully loaded, had to drive 100 kilometres in an hour and a half and we had not yet taken her for a test drive. I was on edge. We all were. What if we had miscalculated completely, what if the cab to pod mating cracked at the first sign of a bump, what if the roof flew off at 60 kph, what if the subframe cracked under the weight, what if, what if, what if... I drove the Landy out as Shayne filmed with his phone, I shouted at Luisa to get in the Landy, Ron was ready and waiting in his truck to take us to the warehouse. We did not even have time for a bloody test drive! I will admit that we were also excited and as we drove out onto the road, I began to relax, a little. Luisa, on the other hand, was a complete nightmare, every creek and bump would send her into a small panic, "What was that!?". We drove out of Homestead along back roads. The Landy was driving excellently, it was going to take a while to get used to being able to see out of the back window and seeing only a square pod in the side mirrors, but otherwise, she drove perfectly with not too much body sway or wind resistance. A few motorists gave us the thumbs up as they drove by and eventually even Luisa began to relax, the roof was lifting a bit at 90 kph but not so much that we feared it would blow off. All was going well until we had to swing around and enter the freeway. Oh, my good Lord! She had just left the work area and here we were on an American highway, driving at highway speeds. We had to get to the warehouse and this was the only road there, we had no choice! I had visions of the roof blowing off and causing a sixty car pile-up. At five to five, we pulled off the highway, without killing anyone, drove into an industrial estate, did a few u-turns and eventually pulled up at the warehouse. "Sorry, we are closed". "Bullshit, open this door, now!". A grumpy German man reluctantly agreed to open up for us and instructed me to drive around to the back of the building where we would then drive the Landy into the warehouse. "Eh, this vehicle is longer than you told me, I will have to charge you more". "Bullshit". "Wait, I will measure". The German produced a measuring tape and handed one end to a lackey. He then walked the length of the Landy, allowing the tape to lie slack behind, him, almost touching the floor. "You are a funny man, Fritz". Luisa and I then measured the Landy which was, surprise, surprise, almost a metre shorter than his measurement. "Ok, sure, I will give that to you, but I have to add $50 for the extra length". That is exactly what we needed after what was, easily, one of the most nerve-wracking days of our existence. "Fine, have your pound of flesh, let's just get this done". When I was not arguing with our new friend, I was standing with my forehead rested on Ron's shoulder. "We made it Ron, the Landy made it Ron, I don't have to think about this again for another month. Thank you, Ron". Ron was bemused and relieved I suppose, we had taken over his house for over two months, but he would soon be able to get back to his normal life. With the paperwork signed and handed over, we gave the keys to Fritz and strict instructions to take care of the vehicle and ensure that the battery must be disconnected once the vehicle is placed in the container.

We hugged the Defender and gave her a kiss, Ron drove us back to Homestead while Luisa and I relaxed for the first time in months. We had succeeded! Yes, the interior was not complete, but we had her roadworthy and driving well, her first test had been a baptism by fire and she had risen a phoenix!

23

Moving On

We returned to the fortress in Homestead and Ron and I sat in the now-empty work area and had a beer. It had been a monumental challenge and I felt a massive weight lifted. I had not been able to work as slowly and meticulously as I would have liked but instead had to achieve excellence within a forced time frame, Luisa and I had nearly murdered each other, and we had spent a ton of cash on the project but we had succeeded. The real test of the build would be in the short-term off-roading and 4x4 driving and the vehicles ability to deal with long-term overlanding over a variety of terrain and through many different climates. For now, all I needed to worry about was whether the beer in my hand was cold or almost empty.

Ron and Cherie had been incredibly welcoming and patient and generous. We had spent Christmas together, and even though I am a Grinch and Cherie starts celebrating Christmas in June, we had a wonderful family Christmas which we had not had in years. Ron and Cherie had listened to our plans and had gifted us a beautiful, red three-seater kayak, with high-quality paddles. Unfortunately, the kayak was too long to fit inside the Landy and as a result, we could not ship it across the sea and had to leave it behind in Florida, a shame. We had shared so many meals together and had become a family, sometimes we had laughed until the tears rolled and there were times when we just could not see eye to eye, but that is family. My only regret is that we were so busy working, that we never had much time to just hang out and have fun, I know Cherie was disappointed by our constant labouring. Jessica particularly had a great time bonding with Cherie, they would watch movies together and eat popcorn and sing karaoke and watch funny YouTube videos and have endless discussions about a huge variety of subjects. We did not see it happening, but we realised as soon as we left that Jessica had become an American in those few months; she spoke with a slight American accent and was so fully immersed in the culture that we came to call her "our little American". Leaving was traumatic. We had grown so fond of our new Floridian family. Ron drove us to the train station before the sun rose, there were tears.

Rebuilding the Defender had been an investment in the future and it had not been a small investment at all. We still had to build the interior but compared to the engineering required to build the pod, the interior would be a simple matter, theoretically. The goal was to be able to live comfortably and work anywhere, if we were going to able to achieve our goal to overland the planet, we would need to continue the reinvention, become a brand and market ourselves, this is easier said than done but we knew that we had no choice, we would achieve our dreams, no matter what the world threw at us, and the world loved to throw massive rocks at us, while we trod the path to paradise.

Overlanding North America had been an incredibly enriching experience. We had all fallen in love with Canada and Mexico but our hearts were stolen by the USA, by her incomprehensible beauty and amazing people. Yes, the country is incredibly complex and is experiencing huge changes but, as our good friend Carl explained, the country is young and dynamic, other western countries had many centuries to define themselves and become the societies they are today. We had met many wonderful people and had been accepted as Americans, despite clearly being foreigners. America is a country built by immigrants and we felt welcome and embraced. Some new friends were convinced that we should stop travelling and settle in the USA, perhaps they recognised in us the American spirit of industry, daring and exploration. We know that we will return one day and we know that we will be welcomed with open arms.

Our goal, leaving the USA, was to drive the Land Rover from the United Kingdom to Asia, but we knew it was not going to be easy. Between us and Asia stood Europe, Pakistan and Iran and perhaps insurmountable bureaucratic obstacles we would have to overcome.

We have the will to find a way and we will never give up the fight to be free.

LA LUCHA

Excerpt from book four, as yet untitled

The Land Rover dipped forward, one wheel precariously close to the edge of the cliff. The recent rains had left the road muddy and slippery, but the Defender had seen worse, much worse, than this Pyrenees mountain road. Luisa, who has a debilitating fear of heights and the misfortune to always be on the cliffside of the vehicle, withdrew from the window and leaned towards me. "Don't worry, Goose, the track is wide enough". "Whatever, why are we driving this road again"? She knew the answer, we were trying to prove to ourselves and others that overlanding in Europe could be an adventure. Northern Spain was, without a doubt, one of the most beautiful regions we had ever travelled, a mix between Switzerland and Colombia, with excellent food, free camping, friendly people and a surprise around every corner. The other reason was that we needed to put the recently rebuilt Land Rover to the test and she was performing excellently, the pod did not strain under heavy articulation, corrugated roads did not trouble her in the least and mud and deep sand seemed only to encourage her. We had created a monster.

A few months earlier we had arrived in the United Kingdom, which was essentially a return home for us, the beautiful and prosperous little green island was where much of our ancestry originated and I felt like I had been there before. I had never been to Great Britain, my dreams as a young traveller had not been fulfilled, but I had grown up surrounded by British culture. My favourite comedian was Benny Hill, who taught me to be a dirty old rascal before I had achieved puberty. Driving through English villages, I was reminded of the English-speaking suburbs back home, the larger houses resembled a medium-size house back in South Africa and it soon became clear to me why so many Englishman had chosen to resettle in South Africa. They were encouraged by the UK government at the time, as English companies owned most of the mines and a larger English population would vote in the interest of Her Majesty's government. The Afrikaner government realised this but encouraged British immigration, as they needed a large white population.

It was now early 2017 and we had only a few months before we were due to set off for Asia, but the Land Rover had still not arrived from the USA, it seemed that we would not be able to get visas for Europe, the vehicle carnet to enter Iran and India was beyond our means and we were chewing through our precious cash faster than Luisa can slap my bald spot when a pretty young thing bounces my way.

To be continued....

About the Author

Graeme Bell is a full-time overlander and author. He was born in Johannesburg, South Africa. He is currently travelling the planet with his wife, Luisa and two children, Keelan and Jessica, in a Land Rover Defender 130, affectionately known as Mafuta.

Connect with us

Did you enjoy this book? If so, help others enjoy it too.

Please recommend to friends and leave a review if possible.
Stay up to date with the Bell Family by visiting our website

www.a2aexpedition.com

Alternatively, visit our Facebook page a2a.expedition

Made in the USA
Monee, IL
26 May 2020